MASSEY FERGUSON
7499

THE ILLUSTRATED ENCYCLOPEDIA OF

TRACTORS

Fordson
Fordson

THE ILLUSTRATED ENCYCLOPEDIA OF TRACTORS

A comprehensive history and directory of tractors around the world with full coverage of all the great marques, designers and manufacturers

JOHN CARROLL

HH

ACKNOWLEDGEMENTS

The publisher would like to thank the following picture libraries and photographers for the use of their pictures in the book.

KEY: t=top; b=bottom; l=left; r=right; m=middle.

Agripicture: 26bl (Peter Dean); 77tl (Peter Dean); 129tl; 144br; 152t (Peter Dean); 164t (Peter Dean). **Alpha Stock:** 15b, tl; 16tl, bl; 17bl; 28r; 80bl; 129r. **John Bolt:** 30bl; 31tr, ml, bl; 33bl; 35tr; 45tr, br; 47br; 50b; 56bl; 65br; 77mr; 84bl; 89tr, br; 90tr, mr; 91br, bl; 94tl; 95tl, tr; 97 (all); 100tr; 101tm, tr, br; 106br; 107tr, b; 111bl, br; 113tl, tr, br; 114t, tr, b; 119t; 126b; 130b, tr; 132m, br, bl; 138br; 141bl; 142t, bl, br; 145tr, br; 146mr, bl; 150b; 155bl; 160tl, tr; 161br, tr; 178m; 189t; 194t, m; 180bl; 196b; 197bl, br; 202tl; 208t, m, b; 217tl, tr, m, b; 224t, m, b; 225tl; 227tl, tr; 228t; 248br; 249tm, tr; 251bl. **John Carroll:** 14 all; 16tr; 29bl; 60tr, bl; 62; 66tl; 79mr; 85mr, br, bl; 87ml; 88br; 92bl; 95b; 106t, bl; 116tr; 117t; 119m, b; 124b; 128t, bl, br; 129bl; 130tr; 131bl; 132tr, 133tr; 145tl; 147tl; 150m, b; 154t, m; 161m; 162tl; 167b; 180br; 181t; 195t, m, b; 199bl; 202tr; 210t; 211tl, tr, b; 212t,; 213t, m, b; 228b; 229br; 231b; 234t, b; 235t, b; 237m; 238t; 243t; 248t. **CDC:** 24–5 (Orde Eliason); 46br (Orde Eliason); 57br (Judy Boyd); 58; 59tr (Orde Eliason), b (Orde Eliason); 88tr. **C.F.C.L.:** 133tl; 237b; 242t. **Ian Clegg:** 65mr; 131t, mr; 138bl; 140t; 141t, br; 144bl; 152b; 197t, m; 199t, bl; 229bl. **Image Bank:** 240bl (Guido A. Rossi). **Impact:** 29ml (Alain le Garsmeur,), t (Alain le Garsmeur), mr (Alain le Garsmeur); 75ml (Erol Houssein); 78br (Tony Page); 134m (Tony Page); 162tr (Julian Calder); 240tl (Alain le Garsmeur), ml (Mark Henley), br (Michael Good); 242b (Anne-Marie Purkiss). **Imperial War Museum:** 35b; 36tr, br; 37br; 55b; 72mr; 81tr; 86mr, ml. **Peter Love:** 117b; 120tl, bl, br; 121t, b; 125t; 127t, b; 133b; 135b; 153t, b; 163b; 165t; 187t; 193b; 204t; 221b; 223b; 249b. **Massey Ferguson:** 89bl. **Andrew Morland:** 1m; 2; 3m; 5m; 6; 7b; 10 all; 11 all; 12tr, r; 13br: 18bl; 19br, tl; 20br, tl; 21b, tl; 22tl, br; 23t, bl; 27br; 32all; 33mr; 34bl; 35ml, bl, tl; 35; 36tl, mr; 37ml, tl, mr, tr; 44bl; 46tl; 52bl; 53bl, tr; 54 bl, tr; 55t; 67tl; 81b; 82b, m; 83t, bl, br; 86tr, bl; 87bl, ml; 92tr, br; 93t, b; 98bl, tr, br; 99t, b; 102tl; 104bl, tr; 105tr, m, br; 108t, br; 109; 115t, m, b; 116bl, br; 122; 123b; 125b; 136t; 137br; 138t; 139tl; 144t; 146t, ml; 147tr, br; 148t, m, b; 149tl, tr, bl, br; 151tr; 155t, br; 157t, m, bl, br; 165b; 190t, m, b; 191t, b; 192t; 202br; 203m, b; 206t, b: 207m, b; 209t, b; 210b; 214t; 215t; 216t; 218t, m, b; 219t, b; 220; 221t, m; 222t, b; 223tr; 225tr, b; 231t; 232; 233bl, br; 236ml, bl, br; 238m, bl, br; 239t, b; 241t, bl, br; 243b; 244t, b; 246bl, br; 247t, b; 250t; 254mr. **Public Record Office Image Library:** 87tr. **Ann Ronan Picture Library:** 12bl; 13tl, tr, r; 14tr; 17br; 74tr. **Royal Geographical Society:** 137t. **Rural History Centre, University of Reading:** 48m. **Spectrum Colour Library:** 38–39; 49t; 73tr; 74bl; 75mr; 89tr; 118b (E Chalker), t; 124t; 126t; 135t; 143t; 151tl; 153m; 164b; 177t; 181b; 182t; 200t; 201b; 202bl; 203t; 212b; 229t; 251mr; 254tl, b; 255tl, tr. **Still Pictures:** 64b; 77ml; 79br (Pierre Gleizes), bl (Jeff Greenberg); 91tl (Mark Edwards); 178b (Allan Morgan); 198t (Paul Harrison); 199br (Chris Caldicott); 237t (Pierre Gleizes). **Tony Stone Images:** 8–9 (Peter Dean); 47t (Colin Raw); 50tl (Gary Moon); 68–9 (Mitch Kezar); 70b (Peter Dean); 71mr (Arnulf Husmo); 72tl (Bruce Forster) 1/4 pg; 73tl (Kevin Horan); 75br (Bruce Forster); 78bl (Wayne Eastep); 79mr (Jerry Gay); 96 (Art Wolfe); 123t (Billy Nustace); 143b (Bertrand Rieger); 150t; 162bl (John & Eliza Forder); 163tl; 183t; 245t (Arnulf Husmo); 251br (Andrew Sacks); 253b (Andy Sacks); 255b (Bruce Hands). **Gary Stuart:** 26tr; 27t; 28tr, bl; 33tr; 34tr; 40r, bl; 41tl, tr, br; 42tl, br; 43t, bl, br; 44tr; 45bl; 48bl, ml, br; 49br; 50tr; 51t; 64 tr, m; 65tl; 66 br; 67br; 70mr; 71br, tl, tr; 72br, bl; 73br, bl, mr; 75tl, tr; 76tr, mr, bl; 77tr, mr, b; 78mr, tr; 79tr; 82t; 84tr, br; 90bl; 100bl; 102m, b; 103t, b; 110b, t; 111t; 112tl, m, br, bl; 120tr; 134t, b; 135ml, mr; 136b; 137bl; 139b; 140b; 145bl; 151b; 156t, b; 158bl, br; 159t, ml, m, mr, b; 160bl, 1/4 pg; 161tl; 162m; 163tr, mr; 166b; 167t; 168t, m, b; 169t, m, b; 170t, ml, , mr, b; 171m, b; 172t, bl, br; 173t, m, b; 174t, m, b; 175t, m, b; 176tr, m, tl, b; 177b; 178t; 179t, m, b; 180t; 181m; 182m, b; 183bl, br; 184t, b; 185t, m, b; 186t; 187b; 192 b; 193t, m; 196t; 198m, b; 199m; 200b; 201t, ml, mr; 204m, b; 205b; 207t; 215b; 216b; 226t, m, b; 227b; 230; 245b; 246t; 248bl,; 250m, b; 251t; 252t, b; 253t, m; 255m. **Superstock:** 12tl; 18tr; 30tr; 56tr; 57tl; 70t; 74br; 147br; 158t; 161bl; 171t; 214b. **Tank Museum Collection:** 19tr; 52tr; 61; 63br; tl; 79tr; 80tr, mr; 81ml, mr; 85t.

This edition is published by Lorenz Books
an imprint of Anness Publishing Ltd
info@anness.com

www.lorenzbooks.com; www.annesspublishing.com

A CIP catalogue record for this book is available from the British Library.

Publisher Joanna Lorenz
Senior Editor Joanne Rippin
Designer Michael Morey
Picture Researcher John Bolt
Production Controller Ben Worley

PUBLISHER'S NOTE

Although the advice and information in this book are believed to be accurate and true at the time of going to press, neither the author nor the publisher can accept any legal responsibility or liability for any errors or omissions that may have been made nor for any inaccuracies nor for any loss, harm or injury that comes about from following instructions or advice in this book.

Contents

SECTION ONE

LANZ

SECTION ONE

THE WORLD OF TRACTORS

Tractors are an everyday sight and are taken for granted as an essential farming tool. However tractors were not always so ubiquitous and the complete mechanization of farming has only been achieved recently. In some cases the mechanization of farming did not take place until the years after World War II. The United States, with its huge prairies to cultivate, pioneered the tractor and subsequent developments such as the combine harvester, with other nations – such as Great Britain – close behind. This section charts the development and history of the tractor as we now know it and the history of a number of the men whose efforts speeded up the development of farming machinery.

■ OPPOSITE *A 1923 12hp Lanz. Through use of a simple and reliable design Lanz became the predominant tractor maker in Germany.*

■ LEFT *At the beginning of the 1900s Case diversified into the manufacture of gasoline tractors after the success of its threshing machines.*

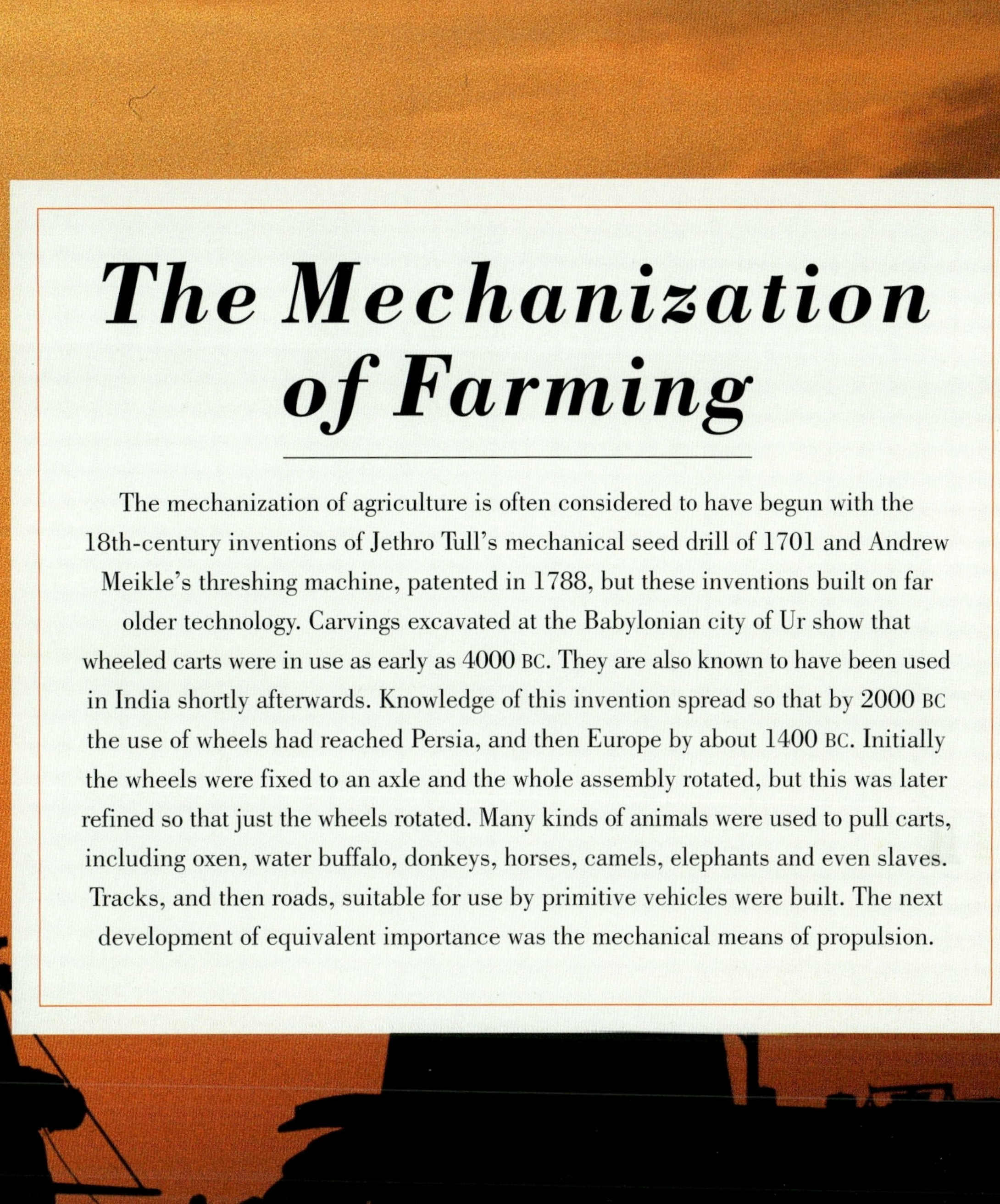

The Mechanization of Farming

The mechanization of agriculture is often considered to have begun with the 18th-century inventions of Jethro Tull's mechanical seed drill of 1701 and Andrew Meikle's threshing machine, patented in 1788, but these inventions built on far older technology. Carvings excavated at the Babylonian city of Ur show that wheeled carts were in use as early as 4000 BC. They are also known to have been used in India shortly afterwards. Knowledge of this invention spread so that by 2000 BC the use of wheels had reached Persia, and then Europe by about 1400 BC. Initially the wheels were fixed to an axle and the whole assembly rotated, but this was later refined so that just the wheels rotated. Many kinds of animals were used to pull carts, including oxen, water buffalo, donkeys, horses, camels, elephants and even slaves. Tracks, and then roads, suitable for use by primitive vehicles were built. The next development of equivalent importance was the mechanical means of propulsion.

THE AGE OF STEAM

Experimentation with steam power began as early as the first century AD, when Hero of Alexandria, a Greek mathematician and inventor, developed the aeolipile, a primitive form of steam engine. It consisted of a hollow sphere that was filled with water and heated so that the expulsion of a jet of steam through a nozzle produced thrust. This device was a major step towards self-propelled machines. In the 15th century Leonardo da Vinci worked on designs for mechanisms that would convert reciprocating movement into rotary movement, to enable a wheel to be driven. He also considered the workings of what is now known as a differential, by which two wheels on a common axle could describe curves of different radii at differing speeds.

In 1599 Simon Stevin (1548–1620) built a sail-rigged and tiller-steered cart and recorded some wind-powered journeys along flat Dutch beaches. At around the same time an Italian physicist, Giambattista della Porta (1535–1615) began experimentation with steam pressure. He constructed a steam pump that was capable of raising water and realized that there must be a way to harness this idea to

■ ABOVE *Once the technology of steam engines was proven it was developed rapidly for agricultural use. Buffalo-Pitts of New York made this 16hp machine in 1901.*

■ RIGHT *Early tractors, using engines other than steam for propulsion, adopted a steam engine configuration as shown by this 1903 10–22hp two-cylinder Ivel.*

■ ABOVE *Minneapolis Threshing Machine were among early manufacturers of steam traction engines and threshing machines dating back to 1874. This is a 45hp model of 1907.*

■ LEFT *This working machine is a Corn Maiden, a Ruston steam traction engine that was manufactured in Lincoln, England in 1918.*

■ RIGHT *Large steam traction engines were suited to the cultivation of the Midwest United States. This is a 25hp machine made by Reeves in 1906.*

■ FAR RIGHT *Case manufactured its first steam engine in 1876 and continued making them until the 1920s. This is a 110hp model manufactured in 1913.*

provide a means of propulsion. One of della Porta's pupils, Solomon de Caus, was intent on trying out the idea of steam propulsion in France but was incarcerated in an asylum at the instigation of members of the French clergy who disapproved of such experimentation. Another Italian, Giovanni Branca, combined della Porta's and de Caus's ideas and built a steam turbine. Steam from the boiler escaped through a nozzle into the perforated rim of a wheel and so turned it. Branca coupled this through a gear to a grinding machine and published an account of his experiments in 1629. Meanwhile another Jesuit, Jean de Hautefeuille (1647–1724), was experimenting with an internal combustion engine of sorts that used small amounts of gunpowder as the fuel.

A piston and cylinder were first employed in connection with steam by a French physicist, Denis Papin (1647–1712). In 1690 he designed a machine that used water vapour to move the piston inside the cylinder. The water within the cylinder was heated externally; as it vaporized it moved the piston upwards, then as it cooled the vapour condensed and the piston moved downwards through gravity. By 1707 the device was working well enough to power an engine in a boat. Unfortunately the local boatmen who had watched Papin testing his machine saw it as a threat to their livelihood and destroyed both the engine and the craft.

The first commercially successful atmospheric steam engine is acknowledged to have been the machine patented in 1698.

■ RIGHT *Case steam engine production peaked in 1912 as the company began to manufacture gasoline engined tractors. This is a 1916 65hp steam engine.*

■ LEFT *Horses were the primary source of power until widespread acceptance of the tractor. Many early adverts suggested that, unlike horses, tractors only "ate" when hungry.*

■ TOP RIGHT *The large machine such as this 1912 locomotive-style 18hp Avery would be superseded by smaller, more compact, machines in a decade.*

■ BOTTOM RIGHT *Nichols, Shepard and Co made this 20–70hp steam engine but later were one of the four companies that merged to form Oliver Farm Equipment in 1929.*

An English military engineer, Captain Thomas Savery (1650–1715), designed and built a pistonless mechanism for raising water, which became known as "The Miner's Friend".

Worthwhile experiments with steam power continued and led to the manufacture of workable engines. Amongst the early machines was the steam pump invented by Thomas Newcomen (1663–1729), that combined ideas from both Papin and Savery. Newcomen constructed a more efficient and less dangerous atmospheric steam engine and he formed a partnership with Savery, who possessed a general patent for such devices. The first practical engine was built in 1712. The pair refined the low-pressure atmospheric steam engine to the degree that most mines in Britain were using one by 1725. Across the Atlantic, the first low-pressure steam engine was installed in a copper mine in Belleville, New Jersey in 1753.

Meanwhile, Nicholas Cugnot (1725–1804), a French army engineer, built a steam-powered artillery carriage in 1769. This vehicle was the first machine designed especially for haulage and it could be said that this was when the era of mechanically propelled transport began. Cugnot's invention established Paris as the birthplace of the automobile in all its forms. His machine was a rudimentary three-wheeled vehicle, capable of speeds of up to 6.5kph/4mph. It was demonstrated on the streets of Paris, when it carried four people. The potential of Cugnot's invention was not perceived immediately and lack of support prevented its further development.

Technological advances specifically for agricultural purposes included Jethro Tull's seed drill and Andrew Meikle's invention of

■ BELOW *The mechanization of farming began with developments such as Jethro Tull's version of the plough (Figure 1) as well as rolling (Figure 7) and harrowing (Figure 6).*

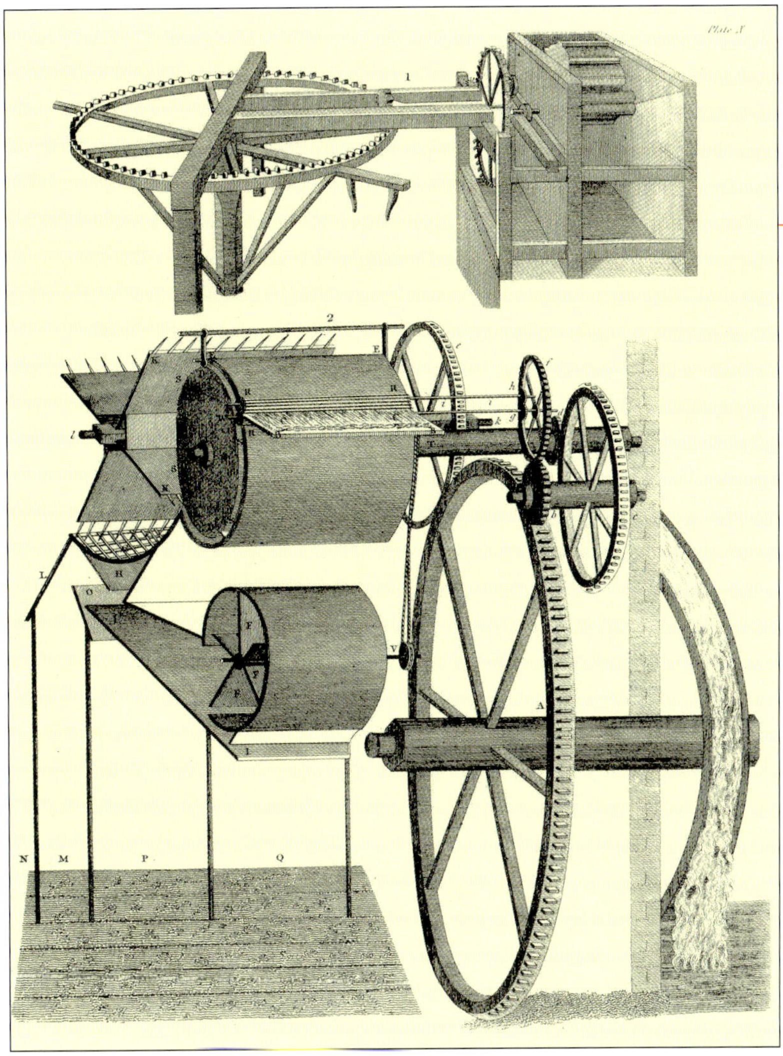

the mechanical thresher. Jethro Tull (1674–1741) devised a workable horse-drawn seed drill which dropped seed in rows. Andrew Meikle was a millwright from Dunbar in Scotland who, in the 1780s, developed a threshing machine for removing the husks from grain. Henceforward, after centuries in which farming techniques had changed little, the pace of development increased dramatically.

■ ABOVE RIGHT TOP *This illustration from 1756 shows the horse-drawn hoe-plough developed by Jethro Tull in the late 17th century.*

■ ABOVE RIGHT BOTTOM *Abbe Soumille's 18th-century seed drill which still relied on the power of human muscle.*

■ ABOVE *An 1811 engraving of Andrew Meikle's threshing machines. The top one is powered by a horse while the later one used a waterwheel.*

■ RIGHT *Threshers were further developed, as shown by this Oliver Red River Special of 1948 threshing in Illinois.*

Steam Power to Gasoline Engines

■ BELOW *From 1876 Case manufactured in excess of 35,000 steam engines before shifting its entire production to gasoline tractors during the 1920s.*

In Britain in the 1780s and '90s, William Murdock (1754–1839) and Richard Trevithick (1771–1833) experimented with steam-powered vehicles using steam at above atmospheric pressure. A Welsh inventor, Oliver Evans (1755–1819), who had emigrated to America and lived in Maryland, produced an elementary steam wagon in 1772. In 1787 he was granted the right to manufacture steam wagons in the State of Maryland. His wagons never went into production but he did build a steam-powered amphibious dredging machine in 1804, which he engineered to be driven under its own power from its place of manufacture to the River Schuylkill, where it was launched for its voyage to Delaware. In 1788 a vehicle of a similar configuration, known as The Fourness, had been assembled in Britain.

In America in 1793 Eli Whitney patented the steam-powered cotton gin, which mechanized the cleaning of cotton fibre. This made cotton a commercial commodity in the eastern states, assisted by the growing transport network – including transcontinental railroads – around the United

■ ABOVE *Steam engines worked in pairs and pulled a large plough backwards and forwards across a field by means of the cable on the drum under the boiler.*

■ LEFT *The angled lugs arranged at intervals around the circumference of the driven wheels were intended to aid traction in wet and heavy soils.*

■ ABOVE LEFT *By the late 19th century, threshers were portable and powered by a steam engine. This later one has pneumatic tyres.*

■ ABOVE RIGHT *A portable threshing machine from around 1895. It had wooden-spoked wheels and was belt-driven by the steam engine that towed it.*

■ BELOW *Despite such mechanization, threshing was still a complex and labour intensive process as this vintage thresher shows.*

States. Thomas Blanchard, from Springfield, Massachusetts produced a steam carriage in 1825 and a year later, in New Hampshire, Samuel Morey patented a two-stroke gasoline and vapour engine – this was America's first internal combustion engine.

Early farm implements were drawn by horses but in order to make them more productive it was clear that there was a need for an independent mechanical source of power. The advent of road travel and the railway locomotive again focused attention on the possibilities of steam-powered machinery that was independent of both roads and rails. Gradually the technology began to diversify: the steam traction engine became more refined and a practical proposition for farm use, while experiments proceeded with the gasoline-powered, internal combustion engine. American steam pioneers included Sylvester Roper of Roxbury, Massachusetts, John A. Reed from New York City, Frank Curtis from Massachusetts and the Canadian Henry Seth Taylor. Generally speaking at this time, the steam traction engine was reserved for providing power for driving equipment such as threshing machines.

New inventions took place throughout the 19th century, and these transformed farming practice. Cyrus McCormick's reaper of 1831

■ LEFT *The Princess Mary is an English Fowler ploughing engine of the sort designed to work in a pair. The cable is clearly evident on the drum.*

■ ABOVE RIGHT *Charles W. Hart and Charles H. Parr began pioneering work on gasoline tractors in the late 1800s in Wisconsin. They began the manufacture of machines such as this one in Iowa in 1900.*

was to revolutionize grain-harvesting. In 1837, John Deere developed a self-scouring steel plough especially suited to heavy prairie soils: farmers no longer had to stop constantly to clean their ploughs. In 1842, in Rochester, Wisconsin, Jerome Case perfected a machine that was both a thresher and a fanning mill. In 1859 oil was discovered in Pennsylvania and kerosene and gasoline were distilled from it. Kerosene was immediately a popular choice as a fuel oil because it was cheap.

In the closing years of the 19th century, vehicles powered by internal combustion engines started to make an appearance and names like Nikolaus Otto, Karl Benz, Gottlieb Daimler, Wilhelm Maybach, Albert De Dion, Clement Panhard and Armand Peugeot became prominent in Europe as a result of their efforts. Of these, it is the first who made the greatest mark as he patented the four-stroke gas-powered engine. When Otto's patents expired in 1890 the age of the internal combustion engine dawned. It was but a short step to the development of a practical agricultural tractor.

Companies specializing in agricultural equipment were active around the globe. In 1870 Braud was founded in France to manufacture threshing machines. In 1884 Giovanni Landini started a new company in Italy to manufacture agricultural implements, that went on to become a major tractor maker. In the United States in 1895 the New Holland Machine Company was founded in Pennsylvania and specialized in agricultural equipment. The J. I. Case Threshing Company had been formed in 1863 to build steam tractors. Its first experimental tractor appeared in 1892, powered by a balanced gas engine devised by an engineer called William Paterson. The machine was not as successful as its designers had hoped, however, and it never went into commercial production. Case continued to build large steam engines. John Charter built gas engines in Stirling, Illinois

■ BELOW *An English Fowler steam ploughing engine, no 15516, built in 1920 in Leeds, Yorkshire.*

■ BELOW *An illustration of an earlier Fowler ploughing engine from c1862. The flywheel for the steam engine is located on the side of the boiler and the governor towards the rear.*

and manufactured a tractor by fitting one of his engines to the chassis and wheels of a steam traction engine. The resultant hybrid machine was put to work on a wheat farm in South Dakota in 1889. It was a success and Charter is known to have built several more machines to a similar specification.

By 1892 a number of other fledgling manufacturers were starting to produce tractors powered by internal combustion engines. In Iowa, John Froëlich built a machine powered by a Van Duzen single-cylinder engine, and formed the Waterloo Gasoline Traction Engine Company. The company later dropped the word "Traction" from its name and manufactured only stationary engines until it introduced another tractor in 1916, the Waterloo Boy, the first successful gasoline tractor.

The Huber Company of Marion, Ohio had some early success: it purchased the Van Duzen Engine Company and built 30 tractors. Two other companies, Deering and McCormick, were building self-propelled mowers at this time; they were later to unite to become International Harvester. It was clear that the speed of mechanization of American farming was increasing. The name "tractor" was coined in 1906 by Hart-Parr, which had made its first gasoline tractor in Charles City, Iowa in 1902, and merged with Oliver in 1929.

■ ABOVE RIGHT *Before ploughing engines worked in pairs the concept of drawing the plough backwards and forwards relied on an anchor and pulley wheel.*

■ BELOW LEFT *A Fowler ploughing engine demonstrating drawing a five furrow anti-balance plough across the field.*

■ BELOW RIGHT *A mid-19th century illustration of a Garret and Sons steam engine ploughing across a field in England.*

The Beginnings of Mass Production

The contrasting economic conditions facing farming on either side of the Atlantic prior to World War I meant that America was where the majority of tractor production took place. Because of the differing sizes of farms on the two continents, designs that were specific to American prairie cultivation began to emerge and machines designed for drawbar towing of implements, especially ploughs, were experimented with.

■ ABOVE *The increasing mechanization in farming inevitably led to mass production as demand for machines grew. This is a 1930 Case corn planter.*

The International Harvester Corporation was formed in 1902 through the merger of McCormick and Deering. Along with other companies, such as Avery, Russell, Buffalo-Pitts and Case, they built experimental machines at the beginning of the 20th century. Case built one in 1911 and by 1913 the company was offering a viable gasoline-powered tractor. Another early tractor was manufactured by two engineers, Charles Hart and Charles Parr. Although this first model was heavy and ungainly, they quickly went on to produce more practical machines, including the 12-27 Oil King. By 1905 the company was running the first factory in the United States dedicated solely to the manufacture of tractors. Many early tractors were massive machines styled after steam engines, because their

■ LEFT *International Harvester was among the first makers of gasoline tractors and made more than 600 of these Type A Mogul tractors between 1907 and 1911. This is a 1908 model.*

makers assumed that the new gasoline-powered machines would simply replace steam engines as a source of power and perhaps did not envisage the much wider role that tractors would come to play in farming. The trend to smaller tractors started in the second decade of the 20th century. Among the pioneers who made small tractors were the Bull Tractor Company with a three-wheeled machine, Farmer Boy, Steel King, Happy Farmer, Allis-Chalmers and Case. The latter manufactured the 10-20 in 1915.

As early as 1912, the Heer Engine Company of Portsmouth, Ohio produced a four-wheel-drive tractor. The Wallis Tractor Company produced a frameless model known as the Cub in 1913 while, six years earlier, the Ford Motor Company had built the prototype of what was intended to become the world's first mass-produced agricultural machine. The company did not actually start mass production of its first tractor, the Fordson Model F, until 1917. The frameless design, light weight and automobile-style method of production meant that the Ford Motor Company was soon among the industry leaders in tractor manufacture.

Many early tractors were built with two-cylinder engines as their source of power but even this allowed for a variety of configurations, including horizontally opposed cylinders, vertical and horizontal twins and the design of crankshafts, which varied as engineers sought to make engines as powerful and reliable as possible. John Deere's two-cylinder machines earned their "Johnny Popper" nickname from

■ ABOVE LEFT ***Huber Manufacturing of Marion, Ohio started by manufacturing steam engines but moved into gasoline tractor manufacture in 1911. By 1925 its Super Four model was rated at 18–36hp.***

■ ABOVE RIGHT ***Henry Ford designed the Fordson tractor in an attempt to do for farmers what the mass-produced Model T car had done for motorists in general.***

■ RIGHT ***Case continued to produce threshing machines alongside tractors after its first prototype gasoline model was completed in 1892.***

■ LEFT *Henry Ford was unable to call his tractors Fords because the name was coined by a rival manufacturer. His 1917 Fordson was, however, far more successful than its rival.*

the distinctive exhaust note created by a crankshaft on which the con rods were offset by 180 degrees. The theory behind the offset crankshaft was that it would eliminate much of the engine's vibration. J. I. Case favoured the horizontally opposed twin in an attempt to minimize vibrations.

The popularity of tractors soared and, while a handful of only six tractor makers were recorded in the United States in 1905, there were in excess of 160 operating by 1920. Many of these companies were not realistic long-term propositions and others were bankrupted by the Wall Street Crash, while a number of companies all but disappeared in mergers.

In Britain, Hornsby of Lincoln was building tractors by the 1890s. Its first model, the Hornsby-Akroyd Patent Safety Oil Traction Engine, was completed in 1896. It weighed 8.5 tons and was powered by an oil-burning Stuart and Binney engine that was noted for its reliability. The engine was started by means of a blowlamp that created a hot spot in the cylinder head and so allowed the single-cylinder engine to fire up without the need for an electric starting mechanism. Hornsby used a 20hp engine with a horizontal cylinder for its tractor and constructed four of these machines. One of them was exhibited at the Royal Show in 1897 and was awarded the Silver Medal of the Royal Agricultural Society of England. In September of that year a landowner called Mr Locke-King bought one of the tractors: this was the first recorded sale of a tractor in Britain. The Hornsby Company supplied various machines to the British War Office with a view to military contracts, and experimented extensively with crawler tracks. The patents that it took out for these tracks were later sold to the Holt concern in the United States.

Petter's of Yeovil and Albone and Saunderson of Bedford both built tractor-type machines. Dan Albone was a bicycle manufacturer with

■ BELOW *The Hart-Parr 28–50 was a four-cylinder tractor of a basic design that endured in two- and four-cylinder types until Hart-Parr merged into the Oliver Farm Equipment company.*

■ ABOVE *In 1917 the 8–16 Junior was introduced by International Harvester in response to the demand for smaller and cheaper tractors, and asserted IH's position as a tractor maker.*

no experience of the steam propulsion industry, so he approached the idea of the tractor from a different viewpoint. He combined ideas from the automobile industry with those of agriculture and built a tractor named after the River Ivel.

Albone's machine was a compact three-wheeled design, which was practical and suited to a variety of farm tasks. It was a success and went into production; some machines were exported and the company would no doubt have become a major force in the industry had it not been for Albone's death in 1906. The company ceased production in 1916.

Herbert Saunderson was a blacksmith who went to Canada where he became involved with farm machinery and the Massey-Harris Company. He returned to Britain as that company's agent and imported its products. Later he branched out into tractor manufacture on his own account. Initially Saunderson built a three-wheeled machine because Albone's Ivel was attracting considerable attention at the time. Later, in 1908, a four-wheeled machine was constructed and the company grew to be the largest manufacturer and exporter of tractors outside the United States. A later model was the Saunderson Universal Model G. When World War I started, Saunderson was the only company in Britain large enough to meet the increasing demand for tractors. In the mid-1920s Saunderson sold his business to Crossley.

■ RIGHT *Avery manufactured gasoline tractors in Peoria, Illinois after switching from steam. Its largest machine was the four cylinder 40–80, one of a range of five models in 1919.*

■ LEFT *The Waterloo Boy Model N was the first tractor tested by the University of Nebraska in what became the noted Nebraska tractor tests. The company was later acquired by John Deere and helped to establish that company as a tractor maker.*

Other manufacturers were also developing tractors at this time, including Ransome's of Ipswich. Petter produced its Patent Agricultural Tractor in 1903. Marshall and Daimler built machines and looked for export sales. To this end a Marshall tractor was exhibited in Winnipeg, Canada in 1908.

In 1910 Werkhuizen Leon Claeys, founded in 1906, built its factory in Zedelgem, Belgium, to manufacture harvesting machinery. There were other, similar, tentative steps being made in numerous European countries. However, because labour was more plentiful and cheaper in Europe than in the United States, technological innovation was slower as it was not such an economic necessity. In Germany, Adolf Altona built a tractor powered by a single-cylinder engine that featured chain drive to the wheels. This machine was not wholly successful but considerable progress was made in Europe as a result of Rudolph Diesel's experiments with engines.

Diesel (1858–1913), sponsored by Krupp in Berlin, created a low-cost reliable engine that ultimately bore his name; it operated by compression-ignition and ran on heavy oil. Diesel experimented in France, England and Germany and found widespread acceptance of his engines throughout the world. He disappeared off a British cross-channel steamer during the night of 29 September 1913 and is believed to have committed suicide.

Deutz introduced a tractor and motor plough of what was considered to be an advanced design in 1907. Deutsche Kraftplug, Hanomag, Pohl and Lanz were four other German companies involved in the manufacture of tractors and powered agricultural machinery.

In France, De Souza and Gougis were two of the manufacturers that entered tractors in a tractor trial held at the National Agricultural College at Grignon, near Paris, where tractors undertook a variety of voluntary and

■ BELOW *While a number of tractor makers relied on an in-line four-cylinder engine configuration for their tractors Case persevered with Crossmotor models such as this 15–27 model of 1921.*

■ RIGHT *The merger of McCormick and Deering in 1902 led to the production of Mogul and Titan tractors for respective dealers of each make. This is a 1919 22hp Titan.*

compulsory tests. Elsewhere in Europe, progress was also being made. Munktell in Sweden made a tractor in 1913 and in Italy Pavesi made the Tipo B. In 1910, Giovanni Landini manufactured the first tractor with a fixed-mounted "hot-bulb" engine. In Russia an engineering company produced three designs prior to World War I.

Experimentation with tractors, crawler tracks and agricultural machinery continued until the outbreak of World War I. Farming had been depressed during this time, but the war demanded a huge jump in productivity. The British wartime government instituted policies

■ RIGHT *Advance-Rumely of LaPorte, Indiana was founded in 1915 and was one of the early tractor makers that was later absorbed into the Allis-Chalmers Company.*

to encourage increased domestic food production, including speeding up the rate of mechanization in an attempt to increase productivity and reduce the labour needed. A number of tractor producers had gone over to war-related work – Ruston Hornsby of Lincoln was involved with tank experimentation – but Saunderson tractors were in production and Weeks-Dungey entered the market in 1915.

Importing tractors from the United States was seen as a quick way to increase their numbers on British farms. The International Harvester Corporation marketed the models from its range that it considered to be most suited to British farming conditions: the Titan 10-20 and the Mogul 8-16. The Big Bull was marketed as the Whiting-Bull and a Parret model was renamed the Clydesdale. Another import was the Waterloo Boy, sold in Britain as the Overtime by the Overtime Farm Tractor Company. The Austin Motor Company offered a Peoria model and marketed it in Britain as the Model 1 Culti-Tractor. The war was to have far-reaching effects on both the economics of farming and on the production of tractors.

McCORMICK-DEERING

The Evolution of the Tractor

By the end of World War I, the tractor was generally accepted as being a practical agricultural machine: Britain and the United States were exporting machines around the globe to countries as distant as Russia, South America and Australia. Henry Ford's mass-produced Fordson tractors, launched in 1917, established themselves commercially; they were initially manufactured in the United States for sale in Britain and beyond. The end of the war brought irreversible socio-economic changes and this meant that agriculture became increasingly mechanized as the 20th century progressed.

The Post-War Boom in Tractor Production

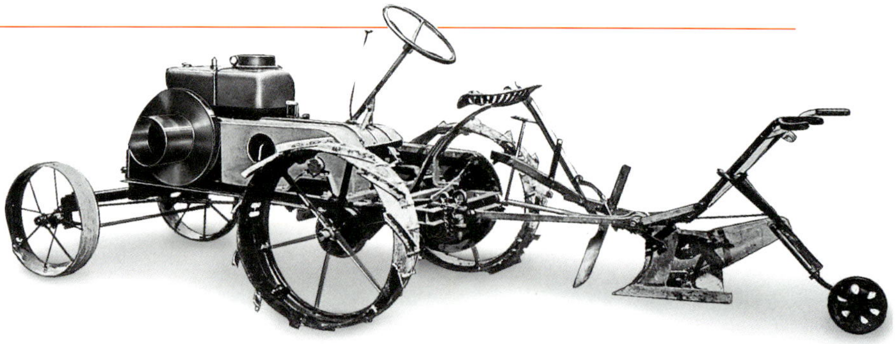

A period of prosperity followed World War I and in this boom the number of tractor manufacturers around the world quickly increased, while the tractor market shifted significantly. Acceptance of the fact that smaller tractors were practical changed the emphasis of the industry and threatened some of the established companies. Many of the new concerns were small companies with limited chances of success, especially when mass-produced machines, such as the Fordson, were gaining sales everywhere. Ford's tractor sold in vast numbers, achieving 75 per cent of total tractor sales in America. It was cheap to produce, so a greater number of farmers could afford it. Many small manufacturers struggled against this, producing insignificant numbers of various machines. They experimented and innovated but their products were never realistic long-term propositions.

By 1921 there were an estimated 186 tractor companies in business in the United States and production totalled 70,000 machines. There were also tractor producers in most European countries by the 1920s, including Breda, Pavesi, Fiat, Bubba and Landini in Italy, Steyr in Austria, Hofherr and Schrantz (HSCS) in Hungary, Hurliman and Burer in Switzerland and Kommunar in the USSR. Tractor makers in Australia included Ronaldson and Tippet. In the United States some of the small new companies included Bates, Ebert-Duryea,

■ ABOVE *Diesel engines became popular in European tractors after World War I. This 1930 Fendt Dieselross has a 1000cc Deutz single cylinder diesel engine.*

■ LEFT *Taken in 1993 this photograph shows Jessica Godwin at 101 years of age, reunited with Fordson tractor number one made in 1917 when she was 25.*

■ ABOVE *This 1928 Deutz tractor is fitted with a side mower, powered by a single cylinder engine of 800cc/50cu in displacement. It runs on benzine fuel.*

Fagiol, Kardell, Lang, Michigan and Utility. A representative European product of the period was the Glasgow tractor, named after the city in which it was built between 1919 and 1924. It was produced by the DL Company, that had taken over the lease of a former munitions factory after the Armistice. The Glasgow was a three-wheeled machine, arranged with two wheels at the front and a single driven wheel at the rear to eliminate the need for a differential. The design was typical of a number of budget tractors built by small companies in both the United States and Europe.

Despite the influx of new manufacturers, the American tractor market soon developed into a competition for sales between Fordson, International Harvester, Case and John Deere. Fordson cut its prices to keep sales up, and in order to compete with the International Harvester Corporation offered a free plough with each tractor it sold. Having cleared all its outstanding stock with this marketing ploy, the

■ RIGHT *Large machines such as the Advance-Rumely Oil Pull 16–30 Model H became outdated during the 1920s, and were superseded by lighter, more compact tractors.*

■ RIGHT *John Deere's Model D debuted in 1924 and production lasted until 1953, during which time more than 160,000 were manufactured. The GP was developed alongside the Model D intended for specific row crop cultivation.*

company was able to introduce its 15-30 and 10-20 models in 1921 and 1923 respectively, following these with the first proper row crop tractor in 1924. Called the Farmall, it was designed to be suitable for cultivation as it could be driven safely along rows of cotton, corn and other growing crops.

From then on the rival manufacturers used innovation as a way of staying ahead of the competition. Allis-Chalmers, Case, International Harvester, John Deere, Massey-Harris and Minneapolis-Moline all sought to offer more advanced tractors to their customers in order to win sales. For example, following Ford and International Harvester, Case introduced a cast frame tractor and although the engine ran across the frame, the model proved popular. Not to be outdone, John Deere offered its own interpretation of the cast frame tractor with the Model D of 1924. It was powered by a two-cylinder kerosene engine and had two forward gears and one reverse.

In Britain, the car maker Austin manufactured a tractor powered by one of its car engines. It sold well despite competition from the Fordson and stayed in production for several years. Ruston of Lincoln and Vickers from Newcastle-upon-Tyne manufactured tractors and Clayton made a crawler tractor

■ ABOVE *Steam engines such as this Fowler ploughing engine of 1920 were gradually replaced by tractors that towed ploughs from the rear drawbar.*

■ LEFT *As well as towing farm implements the tractor was eminently suited to the belt driving of machinery, as this John Deere illustrates. Tractors were rated with both drawbar and belt hp.*

■ RIGHT *In communist and Eastern Bloc countries tractor production was carried out under the auspices of the State, as seen here in the Polish Ursus tractor factory.*

■ RIGHT *As a result of the pioneering work by Henry Ford, tractor production was soon carried out on assembly lines. This method of production spread to all manufacturers, including Ursus.*

■ FAR RIGHT *Centralized production and farming were among the cornerstones of Soviet policy and reached Poland in the aftermath of World War II.*

■ ABOVE *The German manufacturer, Lanz introduced the Bulldog tractor in 1921.*

but, as in America, the other manufacturers were continually competing against the volume, price and quality of the Fordson tractor. The 1929 transfer of all Ford tractor manufacturing to Cork in Ireland showed that there was, by now, much in common between the tractor industries on each side of the Atlantic. Five years earlier the low-priced Fordson Model F tractor had gone on sale in Germany, meaning that German manufacturers also had to compete with Ford. Despite the similarities in worldwide tractor manufacturing there were still differences: one was in the different types of fuel employed by Ford and the Germans. German manufacturers such as Stock and Hanomag publicly compared the Fordson's fuel consumption unfavourably with that of their own machines that used diesel fuel. Lanz introduced its Feldank tractor, that was capable of running on low-grade fuel through use of a semi-diesel engine. The Lanz company later introduced the Bulldog which the company became noted for. The first Bulldog models were basic and in many ways not as advanced as the Fordson. The Lanz HL model had no reverse gear, and power came from a single horizontal cylinder, two-stroke, semi-diesel engine that produced 12hp.

THE NEBRASKA TRACTOR TESTS

■ BELOW *The purpose of the Nebraska tractor tests was to give an independent evaluation of the abilities and power outputs of tractors such as this Allis-Chalmers.*

The purpose of tractor trials was to evaluate tractor performance and allow realistic comparisons to be made between the various models and makes. The Canadian Winnipeg Trials of 1908 were a success and became a regular event, continuing until 1912. A small tractor trial was held in Britain in 1910 while in the United States trials were held in Nebraska. The Nebraska Tractor Tests became established as a yardstick for determining the relative capabilities of tractors, preventing their manufacturers from claiming unlikely abilities and inflated levels of performance.

The tests were instituted as a result of a member of the Nebraska State Legislature acquiring both Ford and Bull tractors. Ford tractors were made by a Minneapolis company which had formed the Ford Tractor Company using the name of one of their engineers, and had nothing to do with the famous Henry Ford. The tractor did not amount to much and the eminent Nebraskan customer, Wilmot F. Crozier of Polk County, was less than satisfied with it, as he was with the Bull tractor that he had also purchased. Consequently, he sponsored a bill to make tractor testing mandatory in the state.

■ BELOW *A 1948 John Deere Model, a version of the model introduced in 1934 which achieved 18.72 drawbar and 24.71 belt hp.*

Starting in 1920 a series of tests was undertaken to examine horsepower, fuel consumption, and engine efficiency. There were also practical tests that gauged the tractor's abilities with implements on a drawbar. The tests were carried out at the State University in Lincoln, Nebraska. The law decreed that manufacturers must print all or none of the test results in their publicity material, ensuring that no one could publish the praise and delete the criticism. The Nebraska tests were noted for their fairness and authority and this led to their general acceptance far beyond the boundaries of the state.

The results of Nebraska Test Number 266 serve as an example to show the quality of the data supplied. A Massey-Harris Pacemaker made by Massey-Harris Company of Racine,

■ RIGHT *The Minneapolis-Moline U Models such as this 1942 UTS were introduced in 1938 and were rated at 30.86 drawbar and 38.12 belt hp in Nebraska tests.*

Wisconsin was tested between 10–19 August 1936. The tractor's equipment included a four-cylinder I-head Massey-Harris engine run at 1200rpm, with 9.84cm/3.875in bore and 13.3cm/5.25in stroke. It had an American Bosch U4 magneto, Kingston carburettor and a Handy governor. The tractor weighed 1837kg/4050lb. The Test H Data was as follows: in gear two a speed of 2.28kph/3.67mph was achieved, as was a load of 750kg/1658lb.

■ LEFT *The belt drive pulley is seen here adjacent to the steering wheel on this International Harvester Corporation 8–16 Junior Model.*

■ BELOW *The horsepower rating was 8 drawbar hp and 16hp at the belt, hence the 8–16 designation.*

The rated load was 16.21 drawbar hp and fuel economy equated to 6.65hp hours per gallon of distillate fuel. A maximum drawbar pull was achieved at 2.4mph in low gear with 1305kg/2878lb load. Fuel economy at the Test C maximum load of 27.52 belt hp was 10.39hp hours per gallon and the Test D rated load of 26.69 belt hp yielded 10.27hp hours per gallon. The standardized data meant that the results for each tractor were directly comparable.

Tractor trials were instituted at Rocquencourt, France in the spring of 1920. These tested both domestic and imported models as part of a government drive to mechanize farming in France. In the autumn of the same year further trials were held at Chartres and 116 tractors were entered, coming from 46 manufacturers from around the world. In Britain, tractor trials were inaugurated at Benson, Oxfordshire in 1930.

The first running of the event attracted a variety of interest from English and American tractor manufacturers, including Ford, whose Fordson tractors were at this time being made in Ireland. The British manufacturers who submitted machines included AEC Limited, Marshalls, Vickers, McClaren and Roadless. Tractors came from further afield too: an HSCS tractor manufactured in Hungary competed in the Benson trials.

The Advent of Pneumatic Tyres

One of the first men to experiment with pneumatic tyres was Charles Goodyear, a resident of Woburn, Massachusetts. In 1839 he purchased the patent rights to a sulphur treatment process that helped him in his development of vulcanization, which made rubber both elastic and non-sticking, thus rendering it suitable for use in pneumatic tyres. Goodyear died in 1860, leaving a rich legacy to the auto industry, but also thousands of dollars of debt incurred in the widespread promotion of his product. The first car built by Alexander Winton in 1896 ran on pneumatic tyres made by Benjamin Franklin Goodrich. These were the first pneumatic tyres manufactured in the United States. Eight years earlier, in Ireland, the pneumatic tyre had been rediscovered by John B. Dunlop. The pneumatic agricultural tyre was the next major advance in improved tractor technology. The lack of practical pneumatic tyres had, until the early 1930s, hampered the universal use of tractors: while those with lugged metal wheels suitable for ploughing could not be used on surfaced public roads, solid tyres suitable for road use were inadequate in wet fields. Solid lugged wheels were also unsuitable for cultivation purposes, as they caused too much

■ ABOVE *This Farmall F-12 of the mid-1930s still has the old steel rimmed wheels that were in use before the advent of pneumatic tyres for tractors.*

■ LEFT *Pneumatic tyres were initially made available as an option in place of steel wheels, but soon became ubiquitous. They are fitted to this 1934 Farmall F-20.*

■ RIGHT *Like everything else connected with farming pneumatic tyres have become sophisticated, and various types and sizes are in use on this Massey Ferguson 6160 tractor and 139 baler.*

■ RIGHT *While Allis-Chalmers was the first to promote pneumatic tyres for tractors, other manufacturers quickly followed. Shown here is the Case 1938 Model R.*

damage to the roots of crops. In the United States, Goodrich experimented with a zero-pressure tyre while Firestone explored the use of modified aircraft tyres. These had moulded, angled lugs and were inflated to around 15psi, giving them enough flexibility to cope with uneven surfaces. In 1932 Allis-Chalmers Model U tractors fitted with aircraft-type tyres inflated to 15psi were successfully tested on a dairy farm in Waukesha, Wisconsin. The company used the new tyres on a tractor with a four-speed transmission capable of working at ploughing speeds and also achieved 24kph/15mph on the road. It advertised this achievement widely in the farming press, but also hired racing drivers to display its new tractors with pneumatic tyres at speed, and unveiled a "hot rod" tractor at the Milwaukee State Fair of 1933. The tractor was shown working with a plough then a local racing driver, Frank Brisco, took it to 57kph/35.4mph on a race track. This created a sensation and Allis-Chalmers capitalized on the success by starting a tractor racing team. Valuable publicity was generated and by 1937 around 50 per cent of new tractors sold in the United States were fitted with pneumatic tyres.

Scientific tests on tractors fitted with pneumatic tyres showed that fuel economy improved. University of Iowa tests showed that although rubber tyres added around $200 to the price of a tractor it took as little as 500 hours' work to recover this additional outlay. Rubber tyres enhanced a tractor's versatility, making it more suited to road use, and before long manufacturers offered higher top gear ratios to allow faster highway travel.

■ BELOW *The advent of four-wheel drive and high-speed tractors has placed greater emphasis on the performance of pneumatic tyres, both in the field and on the road.*

The Slide into Depression and World War II

The Wall Street Crash of 1929 and the economics of production and competition meant that the 1930s started on a different note to the previous decade. Gone was the optimism, and with it the numerous small tractor manufacturers with only a partially proven product. Only a few large companies remained producing fully workable tractors, whose new models reflected the increasing use of engineering technology. These included simple refinements such as the oil bath air filter, that gave engines a longer life when used in dusty conditions. Alongside these developments were improvements in vehicle lighting and fuel-refining techniques that enabled improvements in the efficiency and workability of tractors to be achieved. The Depression only slowed innovation rather than eliminating it, and it did not entirely deter new manufacturers from entering the market. In some countries the tractor-making companies had to take their chances in a competitive capitalist market, while in others there was less competition. In the USSR, created as a result of the Russian Revolution of 1917, tractor production continued under the auspices of the State.

■ ABOVE *As the tractor became more accepted and affordable it was not uncommon to see it being used with horses, as with this John Deere during harvesting.*

■ BELOW *The Depression reached its depths in 1932 but tractors were still being produced, as evidenced by this 1932 McCormick-Deering 10–20.*

Charles Deere Wiman, a great-grandson of John Deere, had taken over direction of the John Deere Company in 1928. Through the Great Depression, despite losses in the first three years of that decade, the company made a decision to support its debtor farmers as long as was necessary. The John Deere Company was fortunate that it had sufficient capital to be able to do this and was no doubt aware that it needed farmers to buy tractors as much as farmers depended on the machines.

During the worst of the Depression the total tractor production for 1932 was in the region of 20,000 and by 1933 only nine principal American manufacturers remained in the tractor business. These were Allis-Chalmers, Case, Caterpillar, Cleveland Tractor, International Harvester, John Deere, Massey, Minneapolis-Moline and Oliver. The Depression affected Europe equally badly but the major companies survived. In the years to come after World War II the tractor market would be divided between these makes, although mergers and amalgamations within the industry meant that numerous small tractor

■ LEFT *Despite worsening economic conditions International Harvester produced the 10–20 model while McCormick-Deering developed the similarly powered Farmall.*

■ RIGHT *The World War would necessitate intensified production of tractors in order to increase agricultural production.*

■ LEFT *Changing economic conditions caused Henry Ford to abandon tractor production in the United States in 1929 and transfer to Ireland, then England.*

■ RIGHT *Lanz tractors such as this 1923 12hp model, were basic and lacked reverse gears – the engine was simply run backwards to change direction.*

■ LEFT *The English Rushton tractor of the 1930s was closely modelled on the Fordson. This is a 14–20 four-cylinder model.*

makers, as well as makers of agricultural implements and specialized equipment, would eventually become constituent parts of the handful of global corporations manufacturing agricultural machinery. The tractor industry has, throughout its history, been characterized by takeovers and mergers of both fledgling and established companies in the race for sales and technological advances.

Around the globe, in the shorter term, technological progress was made. In 1940 New Holland changed owners and, following

■ BELOW *In the late 1920s Caterpillar introduced a series of smaller crawler machines aimed at farmers. This one is haymaking in England in the 1930s.*

■ LEFT *The Lanz Bulldog concept proved popular in Europe to the extent that it was manufactured by numerous other companies.*

■ BELOW *During World War II British women took over men's jobs. These women are using a Fordson tractor and reaper for haymaking.*

a company reorganization, began production of the first successful automatic pick-up hay baler. A year earlier Harry Ferguson and Henry Ford had made an agreement to produce tractors together and the result was the Model 9N. The 9N was virtually a new design although it had some similarities with the Fergusons of the mid-1930s manufactured by David Brown.

When World War II broke out in Europe on 3 September 1939, there were three major tractor producers in business in Britain: Fordson, Marshall and David Brown. It was immediately clear that once again a larger number of tractors would be required if farmers were to be able to feed the nation through the oncoming war. It was also apparent that tractors (like much other war material) would have to be imported from the United States, initially as ordinary purchases and later by means of the lend-lease scheme. This meant that the major American tractor manufacturers would be supplying their products in considerable numbers. Allis-Chalmers, Case, John Deere, Caterpillar, Minneapolis-Moline, Massey-Harris, Oliver, International Harvester and Ford machines were all imported. Ford also continued production at its British factory and the machines were redesigned to use less metal, and painted to make them less obvious in fields. Two years later, in December 1941, America entered the war, with the Japanese airstrike on Pearl Harbor in Hawaii. The might of American industry was now dedicated to winning the war, but the wartime exports had popularized American tractor brands far beyond their place of manufacture.

■ RIGHT *Hanomag was one of the German tractor-making companies that thrived during the 1930s with the production of both wheeled and tracked diesel engined machines.*

■ BELOW *Tractors found a wartime role on airfields. Here, a Fordson is seen towing a bomb trolley for the RAF Lancaster bomber seen behind its returning crew.*

■ LEFT *A 1934 MTZ 320 Deutz diesel tractor. Deutz, like Hanomag, specialized in diesel and semi-diesel engined tractor manufacture, as these engine types were favoured in parts of Europe.*

■ RIGHT *In the aftermath of World War I few tractor manufacturers existed in France although the likes of Latil, Renault and Austin did produce tractors there.*

■ LEFT *An earlier example of the Deutz diesel engined tractor which found favour in Europe prior to the outbreak of World War II. Steel wheels are indicative of the basic design.*

■ RIGHT *Before World War II, tractors were more stylishly advanced in America where, by 1934, the Model A was in production.*

Shortages caused by the war led to the modification of designs. The numerous Japanese conquests in the Far East resulted in a rubber shortage, for example, which meant that steel wheels came back into use. Pre-war designs became standardized and remained in production throughout the war period, with only minor and necessary changes being made. The changes could wait but the war years allowed the manufacturers to assist the war effort and plan for the post-war decades. John Deere's factories, for example, produced a wide range of war-related products, ranging from tank transmissions to mobile laundry units, but throughout this period, John Deere nonetheless maintained its emphasis on product design, and developed a strong position for the post-war market through the efforts of Charles Wiman and the wartime president, Burton Peek.

International Harvester and White manufactured half-tracks that were to provide the basis for a variety of special vehicles, including armoured personnel carriers, mortar carriers, self-propelled gun mounts and anti-aircraft gun platforms. Vast numbers were supplied under the lend-lease scheme to Britain, Canada and Russia, and many of the machines produced by International Harvester went abroad in this manner. Massey-Harris made approximately 2,500 tanks for the US army. Case made 15,000 tractors specifically for the military out of a total of 75,000 made for the war effort. Case employees assisted the war effort in another way: volunteers from the factory formed the 518th Ordnance Company Heavy Maintenance US Army.

■ BELOW *Although this is an early Fordson, steel wheels became common again during World War II due to rubber shortages caused by Japanese conquests.*

690
MASSEY FERGUSON
MF

The Innovators

The development of the tractor and other farming machinery was given additional impetus as a result of the efforts of numerous individuals in different countries. John Deere developed a steel plough suited for prairie use; later Henry Ford brought the capabilities of mass production to tractor manufacture; Messrs Holt and Best developed successful crawler technology; Jerome Case developed a workable thresher, and Cyrus McCormick a reaper. Adolphe Kégresse developed light crawlers with rubber tracks and later Harry Ferguson developed the three-point linkage for attaching implements to tractors. The sum of these men's efforts has led to the production of the technologically advanced tractors of today.

JOHN DEERE (1804–1886)

The story of John Deere, who developed the world's first commercially successful, self-scouring steel plough, closely parallels the settlement and development of the midwestern United States, an area that the homesteaders of the 19th century considered the golden land of promise.

John Deere was born in Rutland, Vermont on 7 February 1804. He spent his boyhood and young adulthood in Middlebury, Vermont where he received a common school education and served a four-year apprenticeship learning the blacksmith's trade. In 1825, he began his career as a journeyman blacksmith and soon became noted for his careful workmanship and ingenuity. His highly polished hay forks and shovels, especially, were in great demand throughout western Vermont, but business conditions in the state became depressed in the mid-1830s, and the future looked gloomy for the ambitious young blacksmith. Many natives of Vermont emigrated to the West, and the tales of golden opportunity that filtered back to Vermont so stirred John Deere's enthusiasm that he decided to dispose of his business and join the pioneers. He left his wife and family,

■ ABOVE *John Deere the blacksmith from Vermont, United States whose company is now the only tractor-making one to still have its founder's full name as its brand name.*

■ LEFT *John Deere developed the self-scouring plough and his successors developed tractors such as the GP models of the 1920s, seen here being used in the construction of a haystack.*

■ ABOVE LEFT *John Deere became a "full-line" agricultural product manufacturer, making ploughs as well as harvesting machinery. Recently the company has considerably diversified.*

■ ABOVE RIGHT *Row crop tricycle tractors, high crop clearance models and other specialist machines have long been produced by John Deere, enabling the company to stay at the forefront of agriculture.*

who were to join him later, and set out with a bundle of tools and a small amount of cash. After travelling many weeks by canal boat, lake boat and stagecoach, he reached the village of Grand Detour, Illinois, a place named after a river meander, that had been settled by pioneers from his native Vermont. The need for a blacksmith was so great that within a short time of his arrival in 1836 he had built a forge and was busy serving the community. There was a lot of general blacksmithing work to be done shoeing horses, and repairing ploughs and other equipment for the pioneer farmers. From them he learned of the serious problem they encountered in trying to farm the fertile but heavy soil of the Midwest. The cast-iron ploughs they had brought with them were designed for the light, sandy New England soil. The rich midwestern soil clung to the plough bottoms and every few steps it was necessary to scrape the soil from the plough. This made ploughing a slow and laborious task. Many pioneers were discouraged and were considering moving on, or heading back east.

John Deere studied the problem and became convinced that a plough with a highly polished and properly shaped mouldboard and share ought to scour itself as it turned the furrow

■ RIGHT *John Deere became involved in the tractor-making business after acquiring the Waterloo Boy company in 1918. It then had to catch up with established makers such as Ford.*

■ LEFT *A photo that illustrates how far John Deere harvesting technology has come in the course of a century, from binder to combine harvester: a Sidehill 6600 model.*

slice. In an attempt to provide a practical solution to the problem he fabricated a plough incorporating these new ideas in 1837, using the steel from a broken saw blade.

The new plough was successfully tested on the farm of Lewis Crandall near Grand Detour. Deere's steel plough proved to be exactly what the pioneer farmers needed for successful farming in what was then termed "the West", though his contribution to the growth of American agriculture would in due course far exceed the development of a successful design for a steel plough.

As a result of economic constraints, including those of labour and manufacturing costs, it was the practice of the day for blacksmiths to make tools to order for customers. John Deere's bold initiative was to manufacture his ploughs before he had orders for them. He would produce a stock of ploughs and then take them into the country areas to be sold. This was a wholly new approach to manufacturing and selling in the pioneer days, and one that quickly spread the word of John Deere's self-polishing ploughs.

Despite this innovative approach, there were many problems involved in attempting to operate a manufacturing business on the frontier including a lack of banks, a poor transport network and, worst of all, a scarcity of steel.

■ BELOW *A pneumatic tyred John Deere seed drill behind a row crop tricycle tractor. It is planting four rows at once.*

As a result, John Deere's first ploughs had to be produced with whatever pieces of steel he could locate. In 1843, he arranged for a shipment of special rolled steel from England. It had to be shipped across the Atlantic by steamship, up the Mississippi and Illinois Rivers by packet boat, and overland by wagon 65km/40 miles to Deere's infant factory in Grand Detour. In 1846, the first slab of cast plough steel ever rolled in the United States was made for John Deere and shipped from Pittsburgh to Moline, Illinois, where it was ready for use in the factory Deere opened there in 1848, to take advantage of the water power and easy transport offered by the

■ RIGHT *More than 150 years after John Deere developed the self-scouring plough that helped make cultivation of the prairies possible, his name is still prominent on the sides of tractors such as this.*

Mississippi River. Within ten years of developing his prototype, John Deere was producing 1,000 ploughs a year. In the early years of his business, Deere laid down several precepts that have been followed faithfully ever since by the company he founded. Among them was an insistence on high standards of quality. John Deere vowed, "I will never put my name on a plough that does not have in it the best that is in me." In 1868, Deere's business was incorporated under the name Deere & Company. The following year John Deere's son, Charles, who was later to succeed him as president, was elected vice-president and treasurer. One of his early partners chided him for constantly making changes in design, saying it was unnecessary because the farmers had to take whatever they produced. Deere's viewpoint was more far-sighted: if he did not improve and refine products, somebody else would. As a result the John Deere Company has continued to place a strong emphasis on product improvement, and consistently devotes a higher share of its income to research and development than many competitors. Its role as a significant force in the tractor industry began when it purchased the Waterloo Gasoline Engine Company in 1918, and produced its Model D in 1924.

■ RIGHT *Charles Deere, the son of John Deere, became vice-president and Treasurer of the company and later succeeded his father as president of the company.*

■ FAR RIGHT *One of the innovations successfully employed by John Deere's successors was that of styling tractors. Henry Dreyfuss styled the range in the 1930s and this design continued into the 1950s.*

Jerome Increase Case (1819–1891)

Jerome Increase Case founded the J. I. Case Company in Racine, Wisconsin in 1842 and soon gained recognition as the first builder of a steam engine for agricultural use. During his tenure as president of the company, it manufactured more threshing machines and steam engines than any other company in history. In addition to his innate talents as an inventor and manufacturer, Case also took an interest in politics and finance. He was made mayor of Racine, serving for three terms, and he was also returned as state senator for the Racine area for two terms. He was the incorporator and president of the Manufacturer's National Bank of Racine and founder of the First National Bank of Burlington (Wisconsin). Case also founded the Wisconsin Academy of Science, Arts and Letters, was president of the Racine County Agricultural Society and president of the Wisconsin Agricultural Society. He was often referred to in manufacturing and agricultural circles as the "Threshing Machine King". Case received a different kind of recognition as the owner of "Jay-Eye-See" (the phonetic rendering of his initials) – a black gelding racehorse acknowledged as the world's all-time champion trotter-pacer.

■ ABOVE *The company founded by J. I. Case became noted for the manufacture of threshing machines and later steam traction engines. Mass tractor manufacture was not started until 1911.*

■ LEFT *The company found itself in the doldrums in the mid-1930s and the sales people believed they could only sell the CC models, such as this, if IH dealers had sold all their F-12 models.*

At an early age, Jerome Case is said to have been inspired by an article in an agricultural newspaper about a new machine that would thresh wheat. For the farmer of the early 19th century, little had changed since biblical times: he cut wheat with a scythe, threshed it by hand with a flail and winnowed the grain from the chaff by tossing it in the air. It was back-breaking and time-consuming work. Each worker could thresh only six or seven bushels a day, thereby creating a bottleneck that prevented farmers from expanding the size and productivity of their holdings. Manpower in this period in the United States was relatively scarce. In 1820, the year after Case's birth, the population was about 5.5 million, although this figure did not include slaves. The further west one travelled the fewer people there were, so that farmers on the frontiers could count on little more than their own families as their workforce, which was one reason why farm families tended to be large. Case was born and lived during a pivotal period for Americans, when the technological achievements of the Industrial Revolution were underpinning the expansion of the United States. He was to become a part of this process, along with other innovators such as Cyrus McCormick and Eli Whitney whose inventions transformed American agriculture. By applying ingenuity and technology to farming, these men so raised production levels that North America would become the breadbasket of the world.

■ ABOVE *The Case LA was a redesigned version of the Model L tractor. Its more rounded lines reflected the increasing emphasis on the appearance of tractors.*

Case began his business by refining a crude threshing machine in Rochester, Wisconsin; soon afterwards he moved to Racine to take advantage of the area's plentiful supply of water to power his machines. By 1847 he had constructed the three-storey premises which

■ LEFT *Case introduced the row crop Model CC tractor in 1930. The machines were painted grey, and had a distinctive side steering arm which was variously nicknamed the "chicken perch" and the "fence cutter".*

■ RIGHT *Case introduced a bright new hue for its tractors in 1939 with the R-series of tractors. The new colour was called Flambeau Red and was one of a number of refinements to the range.*

In 1863 Jerome Case formed a partnership, J. I. Case and Company, with Massena Erskine, Robert Baker and Stephen Bull. Two years later the firm adopted Old Abe as its mascot. Old Abe was a bald eagle that had been the mascot of Company C of the 8th Wisconsin Regiment during the American Civil War. In this year the Eclipse thresher was introduced. This was a further improved version of the earlier models, designed to provide a cleaner separation of grain and straw and cope with larger capacities of wheat.

became the centre of his agricultural machinery business. At this time a horse-driven J. I. Case threshing machine retailed at between $290 and $350.

Case's business prospered to the extent that by 1848 it became, and remains, the largest employer in Racine. As the business grew, Case continued to develop his threshing machines. In 1852 he wrote to his wife after demonstrating one of them to a group of farmers, "All were united in saying that if the machine could thrash 200 bushels in a day it could not be equalled by any in the country." In the afternoon of the demonstration he hitched up the horses and, in half a day, "thrashed and cleaned 177 bushels of wheat".

By 1862 Case's threshers were much improved and a system known as the "Mounted Woodbury" was employed to power them. Horses were hitched in pairs to long levers that looked like huge spokes on a horizontally positioned wheel. The driver stood on a central platform to drive the horses and the power they generated was carried through a set of gears to long rods that drove the gears of the thresher. One machine so equipped was the Sweepstakes thresher – the first of Cases's named threshers – a machine capable of threshing up to 300 bushels a day.

■ ABOVE *The VA series of tractors, still in Flambeau Red, were introduced by Case in 1942 with the intention of increasing profitability by manufacturing more parts in-house.*

■ BELOW *Although J. I. Case built his business on threshers it is unlikely that he envisaged that machines such as this, seen here harvesting maize in Zambia, would bear his name.*

Steam power was the next major innovation to be embraced by J. I. Case and Company. The first Case steam engine was constructed in 1869 and was the first of approximately 36,000 to be built. The early models were stationary engines, mounted on a chassis and pulled by horses. The engine was used simply to provide power for belt-driven implements such as threshers. By 1876 the company was building self-propelled steam traction engines, one of which won a Gold Medal for Excellence at the Centennial Exposition in Philadelphia. In this year the company sold 75 steam engines and in the following year increased this figure to 109.

In 1878 steam engine sales more than doubled and in that year Case's first export sale was made at the Paris Exposition.

In 1880 the J. I. Case and Company partnership was dissolved and the J. I. Case Threshing Machine Company was incorporated in its place. Refinements to the line of threshers were being made continually and in 1880 the much refined Agitator thresher was introduced, using an improved method of horse propulsion, namely the "Dingee Sweep" horse power. The company diversified into the manufacture of steam engines to power sawmills.

A story from 1884 gives an indication of Jerome Case's character. The company had sold a thresher to a Minnesota farmer and it was in need of repairs which the local dealer and a mechanic were unable to carry out. Jerome Case himself travelled to the farm to inspect the disabled thresher. A crowd, surprised by his visit and the distance he had travelled, watched as he attempted to repair the machine. He was unable to remedy the fault and was so concerned that a defective machine had left his factory that he burned the thresher to the ground. The following day a brand new Case thresher was delivered to the farm.

■ ABOVE *A Case tractor collecting mown grass for silage on an English farm. Case acquired the noted English tractor maker David Brown during 1972.*

■ BELOW *The Case DEX was especially manufactured for the British tractor market. As with the LA the final drive was by means of enclosed chains instead of gears.*

In 1885 Case, by now the largest steam engine maker in the world, looked towards the growing South American market and appointed a distributor for its west coast. This was followed by the opening of a Buenos Aires office in 1890. Jerome Case died in 1891 and his brother-in-law, Stephen Bull, became the company's president. In his lifetime Jerome Case had made an invaluable contribution to the mechanizing of agriculture and a line of farm machinery – Case IH – still bears his name to this day.

Cyrus Hall McCormick (1809–1884)

The International Harvester Corporation was formed in 1902 through the merger of the McCormick and Deering companies. However, Cyrus McCormick's involvement with agriculture had begun in Rockbridge County, Virginia in 1831, when he demonstrated his grain reaper which was an improvement on ideas tried earlier by his father, Robert McCormick. Cyrus McCormick had patented his reaper by 1834 and sold one by 1840. It was a major step in the mechanization of the grain-harvesting process. The mechanical reaper obviated the need for endless hours of scything and trebled the output of even the best farm labourer with a scythe. The new machines meant that productivity could be increased massively.

Having proven the reaper in Virginia, Cyrus McCormick moved west because, like Jerome Case and John Deere, he was aware of the potentially massive agricultural market on the

■ LEFT *Cyrus Hall McCormick, whose involvement with agricultural machinery went back to 1831, when he demonstrated his improved grain reaper in Virginia.*

■ FAR LEFT *By the time the merger between McCormick's and Deering's companies was being worked out in 1902, the gasoline tractor was already a practical machine.*

■ ABOVE *The simple design of drawbar allowed the draft of numerous implements, especially ploughs and harvesting tools.*

■ BELOW *Pneumatic tyres and row crop machines were still to be developed at the time of the merger, but the company would survive against Henry Ford's price cutting.*

■ ABOVE *From early in its distinguished history the McCormick-Deering IH company relied on overseas sales and manufacture. These tractors and implements are awaiting sale in France.*

prairies. McCormick established a plant to manufacture reapers in Chicago, Illinois in 1847. Production was soon under way and McCormick's brothers, Leander and William, joined him in the blossoming business. The demand for reapers ensured that the company flourished and the brothers prospered.

William died in 1865 and in 1871 the company's plant was burned down. The firm struggled as a result of this catastrophe but, despite a financial loss, built a new factory on a larger site. In 1879 the company was incorporated as the McCormick Harvesting Machine Company. Cyrus was the second brother to die, in 1884. Six years later Nancy McCormick, his widow, and his son Cyrus Jr, bought the shares held by Leander McCormick. Cyrus Jr went on to head the McCormick Harvesting Machine Company successfully for several years.

■ RIGHT *Tractor design generally follows trends: having become more rounded in the post-war years, it again became more angular during the 1960s and 1970s.*

■ RIGHT *A classic F-Series Farmall tractor at a vintage tractor rally in the United States. It has the front wheels positioned close together in the standard tricycle row crop configuration.*

■ BELOW *A farmer seated on his International Harvester tractor against the blue sky of Nebraska.*

The company had a policy of buying patents that appeared to have potential, as well as making developments of its own, and so held its own against rival companies. The biggest rival faced by the McCormick concern was the Deering Harvester Company. As recently as 1870 William Deering, a successful businessman from Maine, had invested in the company which made the Marsh Harvester, a forerunner of the corn binder, patented by the brothers Charles and William Marsh in Illinois in 1858. The company prospered and by 1880 William Deering had become the owner of what was now known as the Deering Harvester

■ BELOW *The names McCormick, Deering, International Harvester and Farmall all appear on this tractor. IH owned McCormick-Deering, and Farmall was the name of the series of tractors.*

Company. As the years went by the two companies became embroiled in a sales war. Deering tried to sell his company to McCormick in 1897 but no agreement could be reached. Five years later a merger plan was worked out that combined the assets of both McCormick and Deering as well as some smaller companies. The new company was to be known as International Harvester and was massive by the standards of the day, being estimated to be worth approximately $120 million.

The new corporation set out to expand and did so considerably by exporting to much of the British Empire and beyond. A new factory was constructed in Hamilton, Ontario and other companies were purchased, including the Osborne Company, Weber Wagon Company, Aultman-Miller and the Keystone Company. This increased both the size of the operation and the number of product lines offered. As early as 1905 the company made inroads into Europe, building a plant in Norrkopping, Sweden and followed this with plants in Germany and Russia. Not for nothing had it prefixed its name with "International".

■ ABOVE *The Farmall Model M was one of three new models that made its debut in 1939 having been comprehensively styled by the noted industrial designer Raymond Loewy.*

■ BELOW *Tractor cabs were an innovation that were slow in coming despite Minneapolis-Moline's experimentation. Modern tractor cabs are now soundproofed and dustproofed.*

DANIEL BEST

Daniel Best was born in Ohio on 28 March 1838, the ninth child of 16 from his father's two marriages. As a youngster he lived for a time in Missouri, where his father ran a sawmill, before the family moved to Vincennes, Iowa to farm 400 acres. An older brother had already made the move to the West and encouraged Daniel to do the same. In 1859 he did so, working as a guard on a wagon train, and for the next ten years he earned a living in a variety of ways, mostly connected with the mining and timber industries.

During a spell working with his brothers, who produced corn in California, he designed and built a transportable machine for cleaning grain. The brothers operated the machine during the 1870 harvest season, and were able to clean up to 60 tons of grain per day. Best patented his machine in 1871 and entered a partnership with L. D. Brown; in the same year "Brown and Best's unrivalled seed separator" won first prize at the California State Fair. Best went on to patent a seed-coating machine and then a clothes-washing machine. He continued to dabble in the corn separator market, especially when Oregon mandated that grain be cleaned before sale or transport. He went into partnership with Nathaniel Slate in Albany, Oregon and they opened a branch of their business in Oakland, California, choosing the location because it was a shipping port for grain and wheat as well as being a broker's market. Best then moved with his family to Washington to pursue more mining and timber interests.

■ ABOVE *Daniel Best's patents left him in a position to charge a licence fee to other crawler manufacturers.*

■ BELOW *The Best 60 crawler was among the first machines to take crawler technology into the fields.*

The demand for Best's inventions continued to grow and he manufactured a variety of machines aimed at increasing productivity as well as mechanizing farming. Because of the growth in his business Best felt obliged to acquire larger premises. He sold some of his other interests in Washington and Oregon and bought the San Leandro Plow Company from Jacob Price. Renaming the concern the Daniel Best Agricultural Works, he moved production to San Leandro from both Albany and Oakland. At this time he also patented a combined header and thresher and a fan blast governor that allowed the machine to work at a constant speed regardless of variations in the speed at which it moved across the field. This innovation was acknowledged as a major step

■ RIGHT *Following the merger of Holt and Best, the new company's tractors became known as caterpillars. This is a 1929 model 30.*

towards quality control in grain harvesting and cleaning, as well as combining the two functions into a single machine. Over the next few years Best's company sold 150 of the machines to farmers in the states of Oregon, California and Washington.

■ BELOW *The 1939 caterpillar R2 is powered by a 25–31hp gasoline engine.*

The difference between Californian farms and those of the Midwest was their size. Most Californian wheat farms were much bigger and harvesting was a major labour-intensive task: some farms required the services of 150 horses. Best was of the opinion that the technology existed to mechanize the harvesting in order to save both man- and horsepower. That technology was steam power, which was already extant in two forms for agricultural use: the horse-drawn steam engine as a source of power and the self-propelled steam traction engine.

Best bought the rights to manufacture the Remington "Rough and Ready", a patented steam traction engine proven in both agricultural and logging applications. He went a step further than the blacksmith Remington had done, and contrived to make it both tow his combine harvester and power its auxiliary engine. He was successful and patented the machinery in 1889.

Charles Henry Holt

Charles Henry Holt was born in Loudon, New Hampshire. He went to school in Boston, where he subsequently studied accountancy. After periods working in his family's business, and then in the accounts department of a New York shipping company, he embarked on a ship in 1865 and sailed to San Francisco. He gained employment teaching and book-keeping some distance north of the city. Within two years he had amassed $700 and returned to San Francisco with ambition.

His family was in the timber business back in Concord, New Hampshire. They specialized in the supply of hardwoods used in the construction of wheels and wagons, so Charles Holt established himself, as C. H. Holt & Co, by buying timber from his father and selling it to Californian wagon and boat builders. There was considerable demand for this service because of the scale of developments then taking place in California. One of his brothers, Frank, also moved out to California and established a branch of the business to produce wheels and their respective components. This was not entirely successful as the wheels made in the wetter atmosphere of the east were not suitable for the much drier western summers

■ ABOVE *The Caterpillar D2 diesel was manufactured between 1938 and 1947 with only minor upgrades to the design.*

■ ABOVE *The Caterpillar diesel 40 is powered by a 55hp 3-cylinder diesel engine. It is seen here in highway yellow, the trademark colour adopted by the company to replace the previously used grey.*

■ LEFT *A 1935 Caterpillar 28. It produced 37hp at the belt pulley when tested at Nebraska.*

■ RIGHT *A Caterpillar 2 ton. On the early models such as this the Caterpillar brand name is arranged to resemble a caterpillar insect.*

and frequently failed. To try to overcome this problem, wood was shipped to California and seasoned before being made into wheels, but this, too, was not wholly successful and the brothers looked for a place where the climate was more suited to their particular needs. They settled on Stockton, 150km/90 miles inland from San Francisco and formed the Stockton Wheel company. After around 60 years of successful manufacture of steam engines, and some of the first viable crawlers, the Holt and Best companies merged to form the Caterpillar Tractor Company in 1925.

In 1931 the first Diesel Sixty Tractor rolled off the new assembly line in East Peoria, Illinois, with a new efficient source of power for track-type tractors. By 1940 the Caterpillar product line included motor graders, blade graders, elevating graders, terracers and electrical generator sets.

■ BELOW *A Caterpillar tractor exported to England to assist with the war effort.*

HENRY FORD (1863–1947)

Henry Ford was born on his father's farm near Dearborn, Michigan in 1863. He grew up with the drudgery of farm work and horse-drawn implements and it was this experience that fuelled his interest in things mechanical. By 1893 Ford was an engineer and an employee of the Edison Illuminating Company in Detroit, Michigan. In his spare time he experimented with internal combustion engines and their potential for vehicles. Henry Ford completed his first four-wheeled vehicle, a twin-cylinder, four-stroke engined, gasoline-fuelled quadricycle, on 4 June 1896. It had two forward gears and was capable of 16kph/10mph in low and 32kph/20mph in high. The ex-farmer and skilled mechanic went on to build another car while still in Thomas Edison's employ – this was the "autobuggy", a tiller-steered two-cylinder car with planetary gear transmission and chain drive.

In 1899 he left the Edison Illuminating Company and founded the Detroit Auto Company, that was initially heavily involved in car racing. It metamorphosed into the Henry Ford Company, which Ford later left after a disagreement about the direction that the company should take: he wanted to build

■ ABOVE *Henry Ford sitting in one of his experimental automobiles constructed while he was still in the employ of the Edison Illuminating Company.*

■ LEFT *The Fordson E27N was a tractor manufactured at a Ford plant in Dagenham, England. It was a development of the World War II era when Fordson had contributed to Britain's war effort.*

■ LEFT *It is hard to overestimate Henry Ford's contribution to the development of the transport industry. As well as tractors he also progressed the methods of mass production and the success of the automobile.*

low-cost, affordable machines while his colleagues wanted to build luxury motorcars. After his departure, the company was re-formed as the Cadillac Company.

In 1902, Ford built an experimental people's car and in June 1903 he and 12 other men raised capital of $100,000 and set up the Ford Motor Company. Ford's Model A was staked as the equivalent of $25,000 and in the next few months 1708 of them were sold at $850 each. In 1905 the Society of Automobile (later Automotive) Engineers was formed and Henry Ford was elected as one of the vice-presidents. This was at a time when the proponents of steam and electric cars were falling by the wayside and the internal combustion engine was becoming dominant. In the 1906–7 sales year Ford became the world's largest car maker with the manufacture of 8423 four-cylinder 15hp Model N cars, retailing at $550 each. Ford owned 51 per cent of the company's stock and the company made a profit of $1 million. Henry Ford's reputation was assured.

In the same year Ford turned his attention to the possibility of making tractors and assembled a prototype with a view to building the world's first mass-produced agricultural tractor. It was based around the engine and transmission from a 1903 Model B car. Experimentation continued until 1915, when Henry Ford announced that his first tractor would be a light two-plough tractor that would sell for $200. His aim was to do for farmers with an affordable tractor what his affordable

■ RIGHT *These tractors are harvesting in the Rusitu Valley, Zimbabwe. Ford tractors were later given a distinctive blue livery which made them recognizable all over the world.*

■ ABOVE *Mass production of tractors by companies including Ford has led to the mechanization of farming in most countries around the world, regardless of the crop type.*

cars had done for motoring in general.

While development of the tractors was under way Henry Ford did not neglect car production or his workforce. In January 1914 he guaranteed that wages of not less than $5 per day would be paid to non-salaried employees and that there would be a profit-sharing scheme. In August he announced to the motoring public that if the company sold more than 300,000 Model T Fords in the next twelve months he would rebate up to $60 on the price paid. As a result, production soared to three times that of his competitors. The company had a dividend of $12.2 million in the next year and the employees divided up a $10 million bonus. In 1915, as he had promised, he refunded $50 to the purchasers of Model T Fords, having exceeded the 300,000 figure. The company made its millionth car in this year, with the Model T retailing at $440. The Model T was by this time so ubiquitous that a number of companies, such as the Pulford Company of Quincy, Illinois, offered axle conversions to enable the car to be used as a tractor to pull ploughs and harrows. Another similar conversion was offered by Eros.

In 1917 Ford was preparing to assemble his new tractors in Britain, but the pressures of the war meant that production had to be transferred to the United States instead. Within four months the Fordson Model F was being produced. The design appeared unconventional in an era of large tractors and three-wheeled machines. It was powered by an in-line, four-cylinder, gasoline engine and used the magneto ignition system of the Model T Ford car. However, the reputation of Ford's automobiles ensured that the new tractor would be taken seriously. Sales achieved a total in excess of 34,000 in 1918 and increased exponentially.

Ford produced tractors that were reliable and incorporated refinements gradually as technology advanced. As early as 1918 the Fordson had a high tension magneto, a water pump and an electric starter. Ford continued to make the Fordson Model F during the 1920s and sold the model in numbers commensurate with the recession. This period saw Fordson engaged in a sales war with the International Harvester Corporation. Cutting prices was one tactic and moving production was another. Production of tractors by Fordson in the United States ended in 1928 but it continued elsewhere, including Ireland and England.

The next step was to introduce even more innovative but affordable tractor technology.

■ RIGHT *A Ford tractor with the distinctive blue oval logo at work on a coffee plantation in Zambia. The driver is wearing protective clothing.*

■ BELOW *A Ford tractor being used in conjunction with the development of arable crop cultivation in Luanshya, Zambia.*

Henry Ford made a deal with Harry Ferguson, which was sealed with only a handshake. Ferguson had invented the three-point hitch and Ford agreed to put it on his new Ford 9N tractor. This innovative technology endeared Ford's tractors, and in particular the Model 9N, to his farming customers. This was one of Ford's last major achievements in agricultural technology. He died on 7 April 1947 and his grandson, Henry Ford II, assumed charge of the company. It is impossible to quantify the impact Henry Ford had, not just on the tractor industry with the 1.5 million tractors made by his company in his lifetime, but on industry as a whole with his pioneering of mass production and assembly line techniques.

ADOLPHE KÉGRESSE

Half-track crawler technology was conceived as a way of keeping vehicles mobile away from surfaced roads, where more conventional wheeled vehicles soon became bogged down. Its history extends as far back as the early decades of the 20th century. In the United States and Europe manufacturers sought to produce useful half-tracks, mainly for agricultural work. Holt, Nash and Delahaye were three such companies but their machines tended to be slow and cumbersome.

The breakthrough was achieved in France during the early 1920s as a result of the efforts of Adolphe Kégresse. Kégresse, a Frenchman, worked for the Russian royal family as technical manager of the imperial garages. Around 1910, the Tsar wanted to follow a winter hunt in one of his motorcars and would not accept Kégresse's argument that the idea was impractical. Kégresse drove one of the cars into the snow, embedded it in a snowdrift and produced photographs of the stranded car for the Tsar. To overcome the problem, Kégresse began to work on a system of continuous rubber tracks running on light bogies that would give a car mobility in snow. His system was a success and he converted the Packard and Rolls Royce cars belonging to Tsar Nicholas II to improve their performance in the snow. Subsequently, Austin armoured cars were also converted.

■ ABOVE *One of the Citroën Kégresse machines built specially for the successful 1922-3 crossing of the Sahara desert.*

■ BELOW *Adolphe Kégresse developed his half-track system in the Russian snow for Tsar Nicholas II.*

Following the Russian Revolution of 1917, Kégresse fled home to France via Finland. He left behind him about a dozen almost-completed converted cars, which were seized by the Bolsheviks and employed in military actions against the Polish. The Polish army captured one and despatched it to Paris, where it was examined by the French army.

In Paris, the industrialists André Citroën and M. Hinstin became interested in Kégresse's system. In 1921 the first "Autochenille" was manufactured based around a Citroën 10 CV Model B2 car. The Kégresse-Hinstin bogies pivoted on the driven rear axle to which they were fitted in place of wheels. An important difference between Kégresse crawler tracks and those used on tanks at the time was that the former were made from rubber and canvas. The advantage of this was lightness of weight and considerable flexibility, which ensured that the tracks followed every contour of the ground. The tracks were fitted with rubber teeth on the inside to engage with the pulleys. Experimentation had proved that steel teeth were prone to collecting snow, which was packed into the joints by movement until the tracks stretched beyond breaking point. The snow did not adhere to the rubber teeth.

Tests of the new vehicle were carried out in the snow of the French Alps and the innovative development was greeted with acclaim. Adolphe Kégresse went to work for André Citroën, who was fascinated by the potential of this development. The Swiss post office was one of Citroën's customers for the Autochenille, and its vehicles were equipped with skis at the front.

Citroën was of the opinion that if the machines were effective in snow they would work equally well in sand and loose stones. In the winter of 1921–2 trials took place in the deserts of North Africa and a few improvements were made as a result of this testing. The developed half-tracks earned a formidable reputation and widespread publicity when the first motor vehicle crossing of the Sahara Desert was carried out by a team driving five Kégresse machines. They were equipped with additional radiators and used aluminium in their construction to minimize weight. Power came from 1452cc/88.5cu in engines with a bore and stroke of 68 x 100mm/2.68 x 3.94in driving through a three-speed transmission. The back axle was a two-speed unit, thereby increasing the range of the three-speed transmission, and enabling the machines to deal with varied terrain. The Autochenilles

■ RIGHT *Adolphe Kégresse demonstrating the cross-country prowess of one of his converted Citroën machines with a general-purpose trailer.*

■ LEFT *As well as in the sand the Citroën half-track system excelled in snow, as here in the Alps.*

were capable of a maximum speed of 45kph/28mph. The 3,600km/2,250 mile trip took place between December 1922 and January 1923 and was led by Georges Marie Haardt, Citroën's managing director, and Louis Audouin Dubreuil, a man with considerable experience of the Sahara. Nine other men, including five Citroën mechanics, and a dog, Flossie, accompanied the vehicles. With relatively few problems the team made the crossing to Timbuktu. Haardt and Dubreuil together also led a Central Africa Expedition, the Croisiäre Noire, from Algeria to the Cape between November 1924 and July 1925.

The British experimented with the Kégresse system and installed bogies on Crossley lorry chassis, of both 1270kg/25cwt and 1524kg/30cwt capability. In Italy, Alfa Romeo built an experimental Kégresse crawler tractor that could be driven in either direction as it was equipped with two steering wheels and two driver's seats. The Kégresse system of endless rubber band tracks was a success from the start and soon there was demand for a heavier duty version of the system. Adolphe Kégresse redesigned the components, refining his idea considerably, and produced the new version with a completely new style of bogie. It differed from the original in that the driven axle was now at the front of the track and was fitted with sprockets rather than relying on friction. Citroën, Panhard, Somua and Unic all used the new design on vehicles throughout the 1930s. Somua built the MCL and MCG half-track tractors with four-cylinder petrol engines that produced 60bhp at 2000rpm. The company also produced the S-35 cavalry tank and the AMR Gedron-Somua armoured car. Unic built

■ ABOVE *The advantages of Kégresse's rubber tracks were immediately apparent in heavy soil conditions such as those experienced here.*

the Model P107 artillery tractor. In Poland, Polski-Fiat built their Model 621L with Kégresse bogies while in Britain Burford-Kégresse produced the MA 3 ton machine and in Belgium FN manufactured Kégresse-equipped machines. Most of these were used primarily as gun tractors. A third Kégresse-borne expedition in 1931 took French crews in seven half-tracks from Beirut to French Indochina (now Vietnam) between April 1931 and March 1932. A Kégresse P17 half-track was shipped from France to the United States for testing and evaluation in May 1931. Cunningham, Son and Company of Rochester, New York built their version, the T1, and in 1933 the Rock Island Arsenal built 30 of an upgraded model, the T1E1. This in turn led to the International Harvester half-track by the end of the 1930s. Although he was not as directly involved with agriculture as some of the other innovators, Adolphe Kégresse made a substantial contribution to the development of crawler track technology around the world. It is noteworthy that the most modern agricultural crawler tractors use rubber tracks like those pioneered by Kégresse.

■ RIGHT *A Kégresse converted machine being used to power a binder during an English harvest in the 1920s.*

HARRY FERGUSON (1884–1960)

Harry Ferguson was the son of an Irish farmer. He was still a young man when he showed a flair for mechanics and engineering. During his early twenties, he worked for his brother as a mechanic and a race pilot. Later, he designed and built several aeroplanes which he piloted. He became the Belfast agent for Overtime tractors (Waterloo Boy models renamed for the British market) and this first experience with tractors, together with a spell working for the Irish Board of Agriculture, started him thinking of better ways of attaching implements. After researching agriculture and, in particular, tractors and ploughs, he devised a two-bottom plough to be directly attached to a Model T Ford car. It was raised and lowered by a lever and, unlike other similar conversions available at the time, was simple to operate and did not

■ ABOVE *An enamelled lapel badge made to promote the Ferguson System used on Ferguson tractors in the aftermath of Harry Ferguson's split with Henry Ford.*

■ LEFT *Harry Ferguson, the Irish engineer who developed the acclaimed three-point hitch, which changed the face of farming and led to the manufacture of an eponymous range of tractors.*

■ BELOW *A Massey-Ferguson tractor in use in the village of Baaseli in the Rajasthan State of India.*

require wheels or a drawbar. Ferguson later developed a plough suitable for use with the Fordson Model F tractor. His first system was devised from a series of springs and levers. In 1925, with Eber and George Sherman in the United States, he founded Ferguson-Sherman Inc which produced a plough with the "Duplex" hitch system compatible with Fordson line tractors. He made his first Ferguson hydraulic system for his prototype tractor, for which the British David Brown Company had made the differential gear and transmission. In 1933, in partnership with David Brown, Harry Ferguson founded the Ferguson-Brown Company. The result was 1,250 Ferguson-Brown Model A tractors. All of these were equipped with the Ferguson hydraulic system. After this, Ferguson and Brown went separate ways as they had different ideas about the direction the development of tractors should take.

In 1938, Harry Ferguson met Henry Ford and as a result of their so-called "handshake agreement" Ford was able to produce Ferguson System tractors. Both parties brought different assets to the agreement: Henry Ford's reputation and manufacturing capacity were involved as well as an important part of his financial resources. Harry Ferguson brought the patents for the innovative ploughing system which offered Ford an advantage in his ongoing sales war with International Harvester.

Called the Ferguson System, the three-point hitch was put together using a combination of linkages, three different linkage points – two on the bottom and another one on the top – and hydraulics. Hooking up an implement to a tractor had previously been a complicated affair. Farmers used hoists, helpers, jacks and all kinds of imaginative ways to get heavy implements hooked up. With the Ferguson System they needed only to back up to the implement, hook it up, raise it on the linkage and drive off. The Ferguson System was used on Ford's 9N and

■ ABOVE *Following the split with the Ford company Harry Ferguson began manufacture of the TE20, seen here, ploughing, in England.*

■ RIGHT *The TE20 was similar in design to the Ford 9N but differed in that it had a four-speed transmission and an overhead valve engine.*

■ BELOW *In the UK mass production of the TE20 was carried out by the Standard Motor Company, and production frequently exceeded 500 tractors per week.*

■ LEFT *In Britain the TE20 became affectionately known as the "Grey Fergy". The number produced and reputation for reliability has ensured that many, including these two, have been preserved.*

2N Models. At the same time, through Harry Ferguson Inc, Ferguson continued to sell tractors, parts and equipment, including several machines produced by Ferguson-Sherman Inc. Towards the end of 1946, Henry Ford's grandson, Henry Ford II, advised Harry Ferguson that his agreement with Ford would be ending on 30 June 1947. Ford then introduced a new model, the Fordson 8N, that had similarities with the Ford-Ferguson 2N.

When the Ford Motor Company started to sell its new model, Harry Ferguson took two courses of action. First, he commenced litigation, pursuing the Ford Motor Company and its associates for millions of dollars. Second, he negotiated with the Standard Motors Company in Britain for it to produce his own tractor, the Model TE20 (TE was an acronym for "Tractor England"). This was similar to the Ford Models 9N and 2N. Nonetheless, it differed from the 9N in having a four-speed gearbox, an overhead valve engine, two foot-operated brake pedals on the left side and a one-piece bonnet (hood). Ferguson drove his first Model TO20 ("Tractor Overseas"), built in Detroit, in 1948.

The Models TO20 and TE20 were identical except for their electrical systems and transmission cases. The TO20 had a Delco electrical system and a cast-iron transmission case, whereas the TE20 had a Lucas electrical system and an aluminium transmission case.

The litigation with Ford dragged on for four years until in April 1952, Harry Ferguson settled out of court for $9.25 million. As by this time some of Ferguson's patents had expired, Ford had to make few changes to its designs in

■ LEFT *An unusual use to which the TE20 tractor was put was in support of the expedition to the South Pole led by Sir Edmund Hillary. The Ferguson tractors were fitted with special tracks and cabs, but were otherwise almost standard in specification.*

■ ABOVE *Harry Ferguson sold his company to Massey-Harris, of Canada, in 1953. The resultant company became known as Massey-Ferguson and later made machines such as this Model 180.*

order to continue building tractors with hydraulically controlled three-point hitches. The following year, Ferguson merged with Massey-Harris and Harry Ferguson turned his attention to developing a four-wheel drive system for high performance sports cars and racing cars. He died in 1960.

A particularly unusual task to which some of Ferguson's tractors were put was as vehicles for the Antarctic expedition led by Sir Edmund Hillary. The various accounts of the expedition contain numerous references to the tractors used during the course of the Commonwealth Trans-Antarctic Expedition. The tractors were used to tow sledges, unload ships and for reconnaissance in conjunction with tracked Sno-Cats and Studebaker Weasels. The Fergusons were, for at least part of the time, equipped with rubber crawler-type tracks around the (larger than standard) front and rear wheels, with an idler wheel positioned between the axles. The output of the four-cylinder engines of the Fergusons was only 28bhp, so on occasions the tractors were used linked together to increase their abilities. They were also fitted with makeshift cabs to keep the drivers warm in Antarctic conditions. The expedition members were glad of the Fergusons' abilities on numerous occasions and drove one to the South Pole itself. The tractors were commended for their simplicity, ease of maintenance and reliability, that helped them perform well in a situation never anticipated by their designer.

■ RIGHT *A Massey-Ferguson 6150 from the 1990s. Massey-Ferguson is now part of the AGCO Corporation, but the brand name still acknowledges the contribution to agriculture of the enigmatic Irishman.*

The Trend to Specialization

Much of the early experimentation in mechanizing agriculture focused on ploughing, and steam and gasoline-engined tractors were employed as an alternative to horses. It soon became apparent that a number of other implements could be pulled behind tractors or driven from their power take-offs, such as threshers, for example. After the invention of the three-point hitch, the versatility of the tractor could be exploited more fully. As a result tractors and implements became ever more specialized to suit specific farming applications. The development followed two distinct routes. One is the evolution of the specialized machine which is essentially a tractor that incorporates equipment designed to perform a specific task. Combine harvesters are examples of this. The second type of equipment is the range of increasingly specialized implements designed to be pulled behind and driven by a tractor, such as mowers, balers and seed drills.

COMBINE HARVESTERS

■ LEFT *Prior to the development of engined harvesters, American combines were drawn by huge teams of horses such as this in Washington State.*

■ BELOW *The combine harvester became so known simply because it combined more than one harvesting operation.*

■ BOTTOM *Modern haymaking: a towed mower deposits mown hay into a trailer towed by another tractor.*

The combine harvester is an example of a tractor redesigned to do a single specialized job. The post-war years saw a plethora of such developments worldwide.

In its most general sense, harvesting is the picking or cutting and gathering of a crop. However, as crops are so many and various, the methods of harvesting also vary widely. Developments of the machine age have had to replace operations as diverse as the hand-cutting of wheat with a scythe and the hand-picking of fruit crops from trees. The machines referred to as "combine harvesters", or simply "combines", are so named because they combine two distinct operations in the harvesting of seed crops – namely, cutting and threshing. The combine harvester pulls the crop in with a reel over cutting blades, then compresses it and transports it to a thresher using an auger. In the thresher, the crop passes through a series of threshing rollers and sieves that separate the grain from the remainder. The grain is stored in a tank while the rest of

■ ABOVE *Harvesting machines, such as this John Deere 9976 designed for picking cotton, have been developed for harvesting specialized crops.*

■ FAR RIGHT TOP *The design of harvesters has progressed in recent years. This 1960s John Deere has little in the way of operator protection, while a comparable machine today would have an air conditioned cab.*

■ FAR RIGHT BOTTOM *This Claas grain combine cuts the crop and threshes it; the grain is then handled almost like a liquid as it is loaded into tractor-towed trailers that keep pace with the combine.*

the plant material is discarded. Specialized combines are designed to harvest crops such as sugar cane, cotton and tobacco.

Hay, or green foliage, as it is referred to, is mowed by combine harvesters designed to cut the crop and produce tied bales. A relatively recent innovation has been the development of combines that produce large round bales

■ RIGHT *John Deere introduced the Forage Harvester in 1969 and by 1998 when this, the 480hp 6950 model was manufactured, the type had been considerably developed and refined.*

■ LEFT *The harvesting of fruits such as blackberries is also mechanized. Here such fruit is being harvested from the rows of bushes in Oregon, USA, in the shadow of the snow-covered Mount Hood.*

■ BELOW *An image of mechanized harvesting in Britain of the 1930s, where although towed implements are in evidence the process was still considerably more labour-intensive than it is now.*

■ BOTTOM *A comparable scene from the United States showing a John Deere row crop tractor towing a John Deere 12A reaper.*

instead of smaller rectangular ones. Forage harvesters are used in making silage: they cut the crop and, by means of a spout at the rear of the harvester, deliver it into a high-sided trailer which is towed by a tractor alongside the harvester. Noted combine harvester makers currently include Case-IH, Claas, John Deere, Massey-Ferguson and New Holland Inc.

■ HARVESTING IMPLEMENTS

The various tasks associated with harvesting are dealt with by a vast range of towed implements. These include straw choppers that pick up and chop the debris from wheat

■ ABOVE *A specialized Fendt F220 GT machine from 1962 designed to harvest cabbages. It is powered by a 1410cc/86cu in displacement two-cylinder engine and has a six forward speed transmission.*

■ RIGHT *A diesel Fordson Major haymaking in Earl Sterndale, Derbyshire, England with an English-made rotary mower.*

■ BELOW *Specialized machinery has been developed for the harvesting of root crops, such as this machine for lifting carrots.*

harvesting and distribute it so that it can be ploughed in. For applications where combine harvesters are not used, towed implements are designed to carry out the same functions. These include rotary and disc mowers, rotary tedders and rakes which allow cut green crops to be aerated and dried. Towed balers are variously designed to make circular bales of everything from dry straw to damp silage. Round balers have now largely superseded the square balers, but both work on similar principles, requiring drive from the tractor's power take-off to gather up the cut crop and compress it into manageable bales to be transported from the field. Baler manufacturers include Claas, John Deere, Krone, Massey Ferguson, New Holland, Vicon and Welger.

■ ABOVE *A 1959 Fendt FL120 tractor powered by a 1400cc/85cu in two-cylinder engine, pictured in Germany with a hay rake.*

■ BELOW *A 1998 John Deere 935 MoCo. MoCo is an acronym for mower conditioner. The 935 is intended for use with 90–150 PTO hp tractors.*

■ BELOW *A 1937 Fendt Dieselross F18 with a sidebar mower attachment. The noted Dieselross tractors were powered by a single cylinder 1000cc/60cu in engine.*

PLOUGHING

■ ABOVE *Steam ploughing taking place at Uppingham, England during the 19th century.*

Once a crop has been harvested the land needs to be prepared for the next crop and many of the various machines used in preparing the land are of the pull-type – implements towed behind tractors. The process has to contend with widely varying ground conditions in different parts of the world. In many places with temperate climates, excessively wet soil is a problem. Not only can it be difficult for tractors to work without becoming bogged down, but excessive water impedes plant growth because no air can reach the roots in waterlogged soil. To contend with this, machines have been developed that can lay lengths of "land drain", perforated plastic piping, beneath the soil to drain the fields. A more basic method of draining fields is the excavation of ditches.

Ploughs are used to turn over the soil after harvest and the ploughed fields are then disced and harrowed to allow the seeds of next year's crop to be sown. The basic principle of the plough has remained almost unchanged since a single-furrow plough was towed behind horses or oxen. It still cuts the top layer of soil and turns it over. There have been enormous changes, however, in the materials from which the plough is made, the method of propulsion, the number of furrows that can be ploughed at one time and the methods of control of the plough. John Deere's self-scouring steel plough was rightly heralded as a major innovation and ploughing was one of the primary farming tasks to which early tractors were put.

The plough has to be pulled across the entire surface of the field and numerous ways of achieving this have been tried. One notable method was the use of pairs of steam "ploughing engines" that were employed for field cultivation. They worked by drawing a plough backwards and forwards between them using a winch system rather than towing it behind a single machine. This method endured in many areas until the 1930s but, once the

■ BELOW *Over the course of a century ploughing has become more straightforward, as the machines designed for it have become more advanced.*

■ BELOW RIGHT *Once proven, the gasoline-engined tractor soon superseded the horse as the motive power for ploughing and harrowing operations.*

■ LEFT *By the 1960s tractors such as the Fendt Farmer 2 were a common sight on European farms.*

■ RIGHT *A 1998 John Deere row crop ripper, designed for various field applications including ripping and bedding. It requires a 25–45 PTO hp tractor depending on soil type.*

■ LEFT *The tractor has become a vital farm tool even in countries which are perceived as less developed, such as this machine seen in an Albanian field.*

■ RIGHT *This diminutive English crawler is hitched to a Cooper tiller.*

gasoline tractor was completely viable, plough development concentrated on using tractors for propulsion. Ferguson's three-point linkage made the attachment of implements, including ploughs, more straightforward. The three-point linkage has now been so refined that the depth of furrows can be automatically controlled. The advent of the reversible plough allowed a tractor driver to turn all the soil in the same direction despite driving the tractor in opposite ways, to and fro across the field.

Preparation of the field requires more than ploughing and an array of other specialized implements has been devised to do this, including cultivators, harrows and stone clearers. A disc harrow is used to prepare a ploughed field for seeding while a cultivator can be used for a variety of tasks including stubble removal, mulching, aerating and turning in manure and fertilizer. Rollers can be used to make an even seed bed. Stone clearers remove stones that are turned up during ploughing and other operations; if left lying on the surface they can inhibit crop growth and damage machinery.

■ BELOW *Ploughing, tilling and harrowing can be dusty operations which is one reason that air conditioned and dust proofed tractor cabs have become the norm within farming.*

Another group of specialized implements for attaching on to tractors includes those that are designed for the distribution of manure, slurry or chemical fertilizers. They range from the "muckspreader" to the broadcaster, which spreads seed via a spinning disc, and injectors which force material into the ground.

Sowing, Loading and Handling

The method of planting seeds depends on the type of crop being grown. Crops such as beet, lettuce, cabbage and artichokes need space to grow and therefore require planting at specific intervals. A precision seed drill is usually employed, set to plant single seeds at a specified distance apart. Seed drills for other crops can be many times wider than the tractor used for their draft. They cut numerous parallel grooves in the soil and run a supply of seed into each groove, then fill the grooves as they pass. It goes without saying that seed drills, though they still carry out the task for which Jethro Tull's machine was devised at the beginning of the 18th century, are now vastly more technically precise. The modern seed drill that enables a precise amount of seed to be sown has now generally supplanted the broadcaster type of seed distributor.

Once a crop is sown, weeds and pests have to be controlled. To do this farmers use sprayers, normally a tank mounted on the rear of the tractor, with booms to dispense the spray. Tractors adapted for this work have tall, row crop wheels that allow crop clearance and leave only narrow tracks to minimize soil compaction and crop damage. There are numerous manufacturers of such specialized equipment around the world.

A variety of loaders have been developed, largely from the loader originally attached to the front of tractors. This purpose-built equipment includes handlers, loaders and rough terrain forklifts, all intended to speed up material and crop-handling operations for agricultural applications.

■ ABOVE *As with any agricultural equipment, technology has been applied to the planting of seeds. John Deere developed the Max Emerge series of planters that plant several rows of seeds in one pass.*

■ LEFT *How quickly this technology advanced is evidenced by this smaller 1958 Fendt F220 GT machine set up to do a similar job.*

■ OPPOSITE BOTTOM *A John Deere 1860 No-Till air drill is designed to open the soil, plant the seed and close the soil again in a single pass. Its tools adjust to soil types and depths with minimum work.*

■ LEFT *The John Deere 1560 No-Till drill is designed to speed up grain planting through tilling and seeding in one pass. It has a large capacity for grain and features low-maintenance till openers.*

■ RIGHT *Specialist high-clearance machines such as this self-propelled sprayer with a 24m/26ft boom are intended for use in fields of growing crops such as this oil seed rape.*

■ FAR RIGHT TOP *The sprayer booms are designed to fold in to the sides of the cab, as on this John Deere, to facilitate the sprayer's being driven on roads between fields. Note the high crop clearance.*

■ FAR RIGHT MIDDLE *This 1960 Fendt Farmer 2 FW 139 tractor is equipped with a hydraulic front loader suitable for loading hay and similar crops.*

■ FAR RIGHT BOTTOM *The JCB 520G is a loader that incorporates aspects of both the fork lift and front loader, and is suited for handling palletized products such as these rolls of turf.*

■ RIGHT *This specialized machine has sufficient clearance to pass over trees, which it sprays with a pesticide mist, as here in France.*

SPECIALIST TRACTORS

While row crop tricycle tractors were among the first specialized tractors, increasing specialization led to the production of tractors designed for particular tasks including vineyard work, cotton picking and orchard use. Such tractors have been built by numerous manufacturers, either as purpose-built models or as variants of their other models. Specialist tractors are designed for a range of tasks, and some are constructed to customers' specifications. One such manufacturer was Frazier, a small British company that was typical of many producers of specialized farming machinery. The company's Agribuggy was developed in 1982 and assembled from a number of proprietary components, including axles, suspension and engines, and was intended as the basis for crop-spraying and fertilizer-spreading tasks. The purpose-built machines, offered in both diesel and petrol forms, were designed to be adaptable and were available in both low ground pressure and row

■ ABOVE *One of the first specialist tractors to be developed was the tricycle-type, intended for row crop work, such as this Oliver 60.*

■ LEFT *Tractors are often used for specialist tasks such as in orchards. This Massey-Ferguson 374S is being used to collect apples.*

■ BELOW *Crop sprayers have to be suited for use in fields of part-grown crops without causing unnecessary damage to the growing plants, hence high clearance.*

■ LEFT *Sprayers are designed to be driven between rows of crops in order to minimize damage to the plants, but also require the operator to wear a mask to avoid inhaling pesticides.*

crop variants. Since 2001 the Agribuggy has been produced by a small British firm specializing in spraying, Kelland's Agricultural Ltd. Early products available in Europe included crawlers and specialist machines from the likes of Citroën-Kégresse and Latil, as well as smaller vineyard tractors.

In the United States, McCormick-Deering offered specialized orchard tractors, signified by an "O" prefix. In the early 1940s the company offered the OS-4 and O-4 models, variants of the W-4 models, for orchard work. The OS-4 had its exhaust and air filter mounted underneath in order to reduce its overall height, while the O-4 was fitted with streamlined bodywork which allowed the branches of fruit trees to slide over the tractor without damage. The concept of the compact tractor quickly established itself as a bona fide agricultural product. Similar to the Agribuggy are machines from Agrifac, Berthoud, Chafer, FarmGem, Hardi and Househam.

■ ABOVE LEFT *These specialized Frazier machines were fitted with flotation tyres to avoid soil compaction in wet conditions.*

■ TOP RIGHT *Roadless Traction enhanced the performance of many Fordson tractors, including this 1951 Fordson E1A Major, by converting them into half-tracks.*

■ ABOVE RIGHT *The lawn tractor originated as a development of a small size tractor.*

■ RIGHT *The French-manufactured Vee Pee has low ground pressure and is used for various agricultural roles.*

■ BELOW LEFT *Tobacco is another crop that requires specialized harvesting machinery such as this example seen working in Wilson, North Carolina.*

■ BELOW RIGHT *Elineau of France manufactured this machine for spraying pesticide mist on to the small trees of apple orchards. The machine has sufficient clearance to avoid damaging the trees.*

Crawler Tractors

Paralleling the developments of the steam-powered tractor were experiments with tracked machinery known as "crawlers". The first experiments involved wheeled steam engines that were converted to run with tracks. Benjamin Holt was a pioneer of this technology, and he tested his first converted steam tractor in November 1904 in Stockton, California. Holt gasoline-powered crawlers worked on the Los Angeles Aqueduct project in 1908. Holt viewed this as something of a development exercise and learned a lot about crawler tractor construction from it, simply because dust and heat took their toll on the machines. Downtime for repairs of all makes of crawler was considerable.

World Wars I and II helped speed the development of crawler machinery in several ways. During World War I the embryonic crawler technology was soon developed as the basis of the tank, now an almost universal weapon of war. American development and use of tanks lagged behind that of Europe, partially because the United States remained uninvolved in World War I until 1917. Prior to this date the US army was still steeped in the cavalry traditions of the fighting in the Old West; by the time America became involved in the European conflict, the European nations were using tanks on the Western Front. Orders went back to the United States for tanks but in the meantime US soldiers used British and French machines, namely the Mark VI and Renault FT17 respectively. These tanks were to be produced to take advantage of America's massive industrial capacity, but they had to compete for production-line space with trucks and artillery so there was some delay. It is perhaps difficult to understand this situation

■ ABOVE RIGHT *The 1904 prototype steam-powered crawler tractor made by Hornsby's of Grantham, England. The company later sold its patent to American Holt in 1912.*

■ RIGHT *Early crawlers such as this one made by the Bullock Tractor Co of Chicago were chain driven; steering was by a worm drive.*

■ RIGHT *Holt and Best were among the early pioneers of crawler technology. This early machine has a disc harrow and also belt-drive pulley.*

■ BELOW *Post-war International Harvester was among the makers of crawler tractors for agricultural use, as were Caterpillar, Fiat and Fowler.*

■ RIGHT *A diesel-engined Caterpillar crawler being used in conjunction with an elevator during haymaking in England during the late 1930s.*

■ MIDDLE RIGHT *An early 1930s Fordson Roadless crawler tractor, this was the narrow version intended for orchards and other confined areas.*

■ MIDDLE FAR RIGHT *Another version of the Fordson tractor which has been converted into a crawler.*

■ BOTTOM *The Bristol tractor was manufactured by a small English company that changed hands several times. In the late 1940s, while owned by Saunders, the Bristol 20 used Roadless tracks and a 16hp Austin car engine.*

■ RIGHT *Allis-Chalmers became involved in the manufacture of crawler tractors in 1928 when it acquired the Monarch Tractor Company. The Model 35 was a 1930s model.*

when the crawler track was already well established and there had been a couple of experiments in tank development. The experimental machines included the Studebaker Supply Tank and the Ford 3-ton tank. The French tank produced in the United States was designated the M1917 and was the only US tank to arrive in Europe before the Armistice.

Tractor and crawler technology progressed as a result of these military applications. The US army had become interested in crawlers and in half-tracks – vehicles with crawler tracks at the rear and a tyred axle at the front – and in May 1931 it acquired a Citroën-Kégresse P17 half-track for assessment. US products soon followed: James Cunningham and Son produced one in December 1932; in 1933 the Rock Island Arsenal produced an improved model; Cunningham built a converted Ford

■ LEFT *International Harvester started crawler production in 1928 when it offered the TracTracTor, which then became the T-20 in 1931.*

■ BELOW *Minneapolis-Moline made this Mopower crawler loader in 1960.*

truck later in 1933; General Motors became interested and the Linn Manufacturing Company of New York produced a half-track. In 1936 Marmon-Herrington also produced a half-track, converted Ford truck for the US Ordnance Department with a driven front axle.

■ ABOVE ***A 1941 Allis-Chalmers WM crawler tractor. Allis-Chalmers had adopted the orange colour scheme of Persian Orange back in 1929 just as the Depression began.***

Towards the end of the decade a half-track designated the T7 made its appearance at the Rock Island Arsenal: it was the forerunner of the Models M2 and M3 to be produced subsequently by Autocar, Diamond T, International Harvester and White.

■ ABOVE ***Cletrac was an acronym for the Cleveland Tractor Company which specialized in the production of crawlers including this 9-16 Model F of 1921.***

■ RIGHT ***This 1950 Fowler-Marshall VF crawler was based on the long-running and popular English Field Marshall series of tractors.***

During the 1920s Robert Gilmour Le Tourneau, an American contractor who manufactured equipment for Holt, Best and later Caterpillar tractors, developed a new system of power control that began to widen the scope of the crawler. All the control systems featured winch and cable actuation until the development of hydraulically lifted and lowered blades. One of the first British machines to be so equipped was the Vickers Vigor, developed from the Vickers VR-series crawlers. Hydraulics was just one example of the advances in technology being applied to agricultural machinery. It was first used in the late 1930s in time for bulldozers and similar machines to make a lasting impression during World War II. During the war the bulldozer earned numerous accolades and led directly to the blade-equipped tank, a type of armoured fighting vehicle still in general use.

Throughout the war years the half-track evolved and although the designs were

■ ABOVE *Converting wheeled tractors to crawlers was employed for light 4x4 vehicles such as the Land Rover. This is the Cuthbertson devised by the Scottish firm of the same name.*

■ RIGHT *The rubber tracks used on the Challenger MT765C show how the idea has been refined in five decades.*

■ ABOVE *Fowler's of Grantham, England also used the name Challenger on their crawlers in the 1950s. This 35 model predates the Challenger but is of a similar design overall.*

■ LEFT *The Track Marshall crawler was manufactured by Marshall of Gainsborough, England, which specialized in crawlers from 1960 until the 1990s, the last British maker to do so.*

■ LEFT *The Roadless RT20 crawler was powered by a Perkins P3 diesel engine. It was introduced in 1954 and intended for sales in South America.*

■ LEFT *The concept of converting wheeled machines to crawlers has endured until the present-day as this rubber tracked Toyota Landcruiser 4x4 illustrates.*

standardized, there are certain differences between the models produced by the various manufacturers. As well as the crawler conversions to wheeled tractors made by companies such as County, Roadless and Doe, there were even more specialized conversions to other machines. Trackson was a crawler track conversion offered for Fordson tractors in the late 1920s by Trackson of Milwaukee, Wisconsin. Later, Cuthbertson and Sons of Biggar, Scotland converted Land Rovers to crawler operation through the use of bogies on a subframe assembly and sprockets driven by the conventional axles. A variation of this idea has been offered by Toyota on one of its luxury four-wheel-drive vehicles.

Current crawler tractor manufacturers tend to be the bigger companies, including Claas, Case, John Deere, Kubota and AGCO, who began producing the Challenger after acquiring the brand from Caterpillar in 2002.

■ ABOVE *The Cuthbertson conversion for Land Rovers relied on toothed sprockets bolted to the driven hubs which interlock with the rubber and steel tracks.*

■ RIGHT *A surviving Cuthbertson-converted Land Rover from the early 1960s. Ground clearance was increased and ground pressure decreased.*

MILITARY TRACTORS

■ TOP *The Allis-Chalmers Model U was in production throughout the war years and among those exported to the UK to assist in the war effort.*

■ BELOW LEFT *The Minneapolis-Moline ZTX US military tractor of 1943 featured five gears that gave it a top speed of over 25kph/15mph.*

■ ABOVE RIGHT *During World War II tractors were used for a variety of non-agricultural tasks including work on airfields towing aeroplanes.*

■ ABOVE LEFT *As steam traction became viable the British army was quick to use Fowler engines as artillery tractors during the Boer War.*

During World War I Holt supplied crawlers to the allies while the English company Hornsby experimented with crawler tracks for tanks. The vast scale of World War II necessitated massive industrial production of all types and saw numerous tractors made that were designed for specific military purposes. The tractor types varied and included wheeled, half-track and full-track types.

In America an unusual military tractor was made by Allis-Chalmers. It was the M7 (T26E4) over-snow machine, a half-track tractor that used the entire 63bhp engine and transmission assembly from a Willys Jeep. Full-track tractors were made for the US army by International Harvester, Cletrac, Allis-Chalmers and the Iron Fireman Manufacturing Company. The International models included the TD9, TD18 and M5. The TD models were conventional full-track tractors powered by four-cylinder diesel engines, while the M5 was a high-speed tractor powered by a Continental six-cylinder engine that produced 207bhp. Cletrac manufactured the MG1 and MG2 models that were fitted with a six-cylinder Hercules engine that produced 137bhp. The Allis-Chalmers tractors were massive – the M4 weighed 18 tons and the M6 38 tons. Both were intended for use as artillery tractors and were powered by six-cylinder Waukesha engines.

In Britain a David Brown tractor became noted for its use by the Royal Air Force as an airfield tractor. The model was powered by an in-line four-cylinder engine of 2523cc/154cu in displacement that produced 37bhp at 2200rpm. It had a four-speed transmission and a conventional appearance.

The RAF also used a number of Roadless-converted Fordson tractors fitted with a

■ RIGHT *British Royal Engineers in the years prior to World War II landing Royal Navy equipment from a landing barge with the assistance of a Fordson tractor.*

Hesford winch for aircraft-handling duties. The Germans, Japanese and Italians made use of tractors manufactured by Latil, Somua, Hanomag, Isuzu and Pavesi. French companies Latil and Somua were captured by Germany.

There are numerous current specialist military tractors: one such specially built to meet British Ministry of Defence specifications is made by JCB. This towing and shunting tractor is designed to be manoeuvrable and offers tremendous traction and torque. It is ideal for moving aircraft and trailers and has a high specification cab.

■ LEFT *The Studebaker Weasel was a light crawler machine designed by Studebaker's engineers during World War II that exerted minimal ground pressure. It was among the first of such specialist machines.*

■ LEFT *Minneapolis-Moline produced the Model NTX as an experimental military machine. It was four-wheel-drive and used standard military wheels and tyres.*

■ LEFT *A restored example of the David Brown VIG airfield tractor manufactured for the Royal Air Force and extensively used on British airfields during the conflict.*

Bulldozers first came to the military's attention after their use by the allies in removing beach defences, and even occupied pillboxes, in both Europe and the Pacific during World War II. Later, tanks would be equipped with bulldozer blades to assist in clearing obstacles. The Caterpillar D7 saw service in all theatres of operation during World War II and General Eisenhower credited it as being one of the machines that won the war.

As for the other US auto makers, World War II interrupted civilian vehicle manufacture, and production was turned to helping win the war. One of Studebaker's products at this time was the M29C Weasel, an amphibious cargo carrier that was a light, fully-tracked military vehicle, powered by a 65bhp six-cylinder engine, with three forward gears and a two-speed driven rear axle. It was fitted with 50cm/20in wide endless tracks and exerted a low ground pressure. This machine, designed by Studebaker's own engineers, can be regarded as one of the pioneers of the light crawler-tracked vehicle. Such machines have since become popular for specialist applications ranging from vineyard work to use on small agricultural sites where a conventional tractor or crawler would be too large.

4 x 4 Tractors

■ BELOW *A County Fourdrive converted Fordson tractor being used in the Solomon Islands.*

■ BOTTOM *A mid-1980s U1700L38 model of the Mercedes Unimog.*

The 1920s saw much experimentation with four-wheel-drive tractors as an alternative to crawler machines. Wizard, Topp-Stewart, Nelson and Fitch were amongst those who manufactured machines in the United States. After World War II, companies such as Roadless Traction and County Tractors offered four-wheel-drive conversions to many tractors, often using war surplus GMC truck-driven front axles. Selene was an Italian company offering 4 x 4 conversions. As the benefits of four-wheel drive came to be seen by the larger manufacturers, including the likes of Ford, John Deere and Case, they began offering their own four-wheel-drive models. This squeezed some of the small companies offering conversions. Nowadays the 4 x 4 tractor is simply seen as another conventional tractor model, and four-wheel drive is often offered as an extra-cost option on machines that are also available in a two-wheel-drive configuration.

■ LEFT *On state-of-the-art tractors such as this Fendt machine, four-wheel drive is considered as just another conventional but useful feature in enhancing the tractor's performance.*

■ LEFT *A Massey-Ferguson tractor preparing a field for cultivation. Tractors have greatly increased in size and power in recent years by comparison.*

■ BELOW LEFT *The four-wheel-drive version of Massey-Ferguson's streamlined Perkins engined 4235 Model tractor.*

■ BELOW RIGHT *Four-wheel-drive tractors such as this tend to have larger diameter front tyres than the two-wheel-drive variants.*

■ ABOVE RIGHT *Some four-wheel-drive tractors such as this Fiatagri machine have different sizes of tyres at the front and rear.*

■ RIGHT *Modern tractors feature computerized dashboards, allowing operators to monitor engine, transmission and GPS functions.*

Compact Tractors

The concept of the compact tractor can be said to have its origin in southern Europe where it was used for vineyard work. In the years immediately after World War II, NSU sold a number of its light artillery tractor, the Kettenkrad, for agricultural use, and developments also took place in the Far East. The use of compact tractors spread quickly. In England the British Motor Corporation (BMC) offered a "mini" tractor and the major tractor makers added compact tractors to their ranges.

By the mid-1980s the Japanese firm Hinomoto was making the C174 compact, which is fitted with a 1004cc/61.2cu in three-cylinder diesel engine. It produces 20hp and has nine forward gears and three reverse. The C174 is equipped with a rear-mounted power take-off and a hydraulic linkage.

Other Japanese specialists include Shibaura, who continue to produce compact and sub-compact tractors, and once made them for Ford, and Mitsubishi made

■ ABOVE *The British Motor Corporation Mini tractor was aimed at the same market as the Ferguson TE20. The tractor was announced in 1965 but was shortlived and production had ceased by 1970.*

■ ABOVE *The BMC Mini was based around a 950cc/58cu in diesel version of a car engine of the time. It proved to be underpowered and was later uprated to 1500cc/90cu in.*

■ LEFT *The 1998 John Deere 5210 tractor is only 239.5cm/94.3in tall to the top of the rollbar and has an 205cm/80.7in wheelbase. Power is from a 2900cc/175cu in three-cylinder engine.*

■ LEFT *The compact tractor is in use worldwide as this laden example in Bhutan shows.*

machines for Cub Cadet and Case, and continue to produce small utility tractors like the MT1800. Iseki, another current Japanese manufacturer, produced machines for White, Bolens and Massey-Ferguson. In their compact category are tractors such as the TM3160 and 3265 models. They are powered by three-cylinder water-cooled diesel engines, 928cc/56.6cu in and 1123cc/68.52cu in respectively, both in four-wheel-drive forms, and accept a wide range of implements.

Kubota is a Japanese company that was founded in the last decade of the 19th century. It began manufacturing tractors in the 1960s and claimed to be the fifth largest producer during the mid-80s. One of its products then was the compact B7100DP, a three-cylinder-powered tractor that displaced 762cc/46.5cu in and produces 16hp. It also featured four-wheel drive, independent rear brakes and a three-speed PTO.

Larger companies dominate the current compact utility and sub-compact tractor market, including John Deere, New Holland and Case. A compact crawler, the Magnatrac, is made by Struck in the USA.

■ RIGHT *The International Harvester Cub Cadet was a diminutive tractor aimed at garden and grounds use rather than full-scale agriculture.*

■ FAR RIGHT *The BMC Mini tractor bore some resemblance to the Ferguson TE20 but struggled to compete in sales terms even with secondhand examples of the "Grey Fergy".*

THE SPORT OF TRACTOR PULLING

In the early years of the 20th century, when agriculture in the United States was booming, huge numbers of boulders had to be removed with the help of horses from massive acreages before they could be cultivated. Folklore has it that one farmer told another that he could remove a larger boulder than the other, and so almost inevitably a competition started. At the time of the outbreak of World War II, the mechanization of agriculture was well under way and by then tractors were being used for clearing boulders. Such boulder-pulling was seen as a challenge and informal competitions were introduced. The tractor that was needed on the farm all week was used for "tractor pulling" on Sundays. Over the years the tractors became bigger and the competition became ever more serious. Eventually the boulders also became a little too large to handle so the "dead-weight sled" was introduced. This was a sled with weights on it, connected to the tractor by means of a chain. It was all or nothing: either the tractor took off with the sled or it lost grip and spun its driven wheels, digging itself into the track. To gain more grip, the tractors were soon loaded with anything that was heavy.

■ ABOVE *Smoky Joe is a Ford 8600, based tractor puller seen here competing in an event in Warwickshire, England.*

■ ABOVE *A Fiat 1000 tractor in the same event. Tractors compete in different classes depending on engine type and modifications.*

■ LEFT *One class is for modified tractors that have to retain a relatively standard appearance and bodywork. This German Deutz machine has been prepared for such a class.*

■ RIGHT *Kevin Brian's Volvo BM T800 tractor puller. Notice that the overall profile of the machine has been altered in order to accommodate the various modifications.*

Later on came the idea of making the sled heavier during the pull. A number of volunteers stood next to the track and stepped on the sled as it went past: this was, unsurprisingly, called a "step-on sled". The greater the distance covered, the higher the position. If a tractor made it to the end of the track this was called a "full pull" and the driver qualified for the finals of the day's events. Over years of pulling, the tractors continued to grow. It became harder to recruit volunteers to step on the sled because it was going faster and faster and, naturally, safety became an issue. To solve the problem, the "weight-transfer machine" was developed. This is a sled which has wheels at the rear end. At the start of the pull the weights are placed above the wheels. As the tractor starts to pull, the weights travel forward to the sled-plate by means of a chain. The friction increases and at some point the tractor loses traction. This principle is still in use today. The best pull is made when the tractor has a quick start. At the start of the track the sled is easy to pull, so a lot of speed can be developed. As the friction increases, the speed of the sled and tractor means that the whole unit keeps powering on and goes a few metres further.

The distance covered is now measured with infra-red equipment, and the results of a pull,

■ BELOW *A Case IH tractor puller. To increase the all-important traction, much larger than standard rear tyres are fitted where class regulations permit.*

■ ABOVE *In the least restricted classes tractors are especially built with multiple engines coupled together for a massive power output.*

so calibrated, show that sometimes tractors come as little as 1cm/½in short of a full pull, or stop at exactly the same point. At tractor-pulling events, it is not only power that counts. Almost as important is the balance of the tractor. The sport of tractor pulling could be described as the world's most powerful motor sport, albeit not the fastest.

The tractors compete in a complex array of classes. Within the modified class come specially designed tractors, that compete in different weight classes. All types of component parts are allowed as long as the overall weight and size are within the rules. The numbers and types of engines are similarly limited by the rules. There are now also strict safety rules to protect the tractor, driver and spectators from danger. Usually, the specially constructed chassis in this class is fitted with the rear axle of a truck or excavator shovel. The internal components are replaced with stronger gears. The tyre size is limited to a diameter of 77.5–81cm/30.5–32in by the rules. The original tractor-tyre profile is always decreased by reducing the pressure in order to generate sufficient wheel-spin to prevent the tractor digging itself in while giving enough traction to move the sled forwards.

In the largest-capacity classes aircraft engines are often used today, as are gas-turbines. In the United States V8 racing-engines are very popular and in Europe tractors are fitted with up to nine engines, depending on the type and weight class.

The Super Standard or Super Stock classes feature heavily tuned standard agricultural tractors, weighing 4.5 tons. The basis of the tractor is a normal agricultural model but not much of the machine is left – everything that is normally needed for field operation is removed. The block, the clutch housing, the gearbox housing and the rear-axle have to be original although the insides of these components can be modified. To increase the engine's power, a maximum of four turbos can be fitted, as long as it all fits under the original tractor hood. The great amount of air that flows into the intake means that a lot of diesel can be injected into the cylinders. When the air is compressed by the turbos a great deal of heat is produced and

■ BELOW *This German Q8 sponsored machine gets its power from no less than three V12 Allison aero engines.*

■ ABOVE LEFT *When too much is never enough: this German tractor pulling special has been constructed with four jet aircraft engines.*

■ ABOVE RIGHT *It provides spectacular tractor pulling action, but unlike some of the smaller power and weight classes, bears little resemblance to anything that can be seen in a field.*

to prevent the turbos from melting, a spray of water is injected into the intakes; this water leaves the exhaust as water vapour. To make sure this massive power reaches the wide rear tyres, numerous parts of the transmission are replaced by stronger versions, while all the unnecessary gears are removed.

Alky-burners which use methanol can be fitted: methanol burns for longer than diesel, so more power is generated and the engine suffers less stress. Numerous modifications are needed but up to 2500bhp is achievable.

The Garden Puller is the ideal start-up class. Drivers may compete from the age of eight and since this class requires little more than a former lawnmower or garden tractor it is available to those with limited funds.

Mini-pullers are small modifieds, whose weight must include both the weight of the driver and its fuel. This class uses its own special, small sled and the tractors are custom-designed and built. They use mainly V8 engines and helicopter turbines. The power produced can be up to 3000bhp, though the average is about 1700bhp. Due to the enormous power-to-weight ratio, these machines are very hard to handle. The rear axles are mostly custom-engineered and the gearbox is little more than a single speed with a reverse gear.

■ RIGHT *The same can be said for some of the machines that rely on internal combustion engines too, and the team's name reflects the cost of this sport.*

29 00252

SECTION TWO

A–Z OF TRACTORS

The section that follows lists the major tractor manufacturers and their most important machines, stretching back to the beginning of the 20th century. It also illustrates how, throughout its history, the tractor manufacturing industry has been characterized by numerous mergers and amalgamations. Where once there were hundreds of minor manufacturers producing small numbers of farm machines, there is now just a handful of multinational corporations making thousands of tractors. Also apparent is how quickly innovations in tractor manufacture spread. For example, Henry Ford offered the new and innovative Fordson in 1917; within a few years his style of tractor had become the norm and the basic configuration of the Fordson is still followed by manufacturers today. Computers and global positioning systems are the latest technologies to be applied to the farm tractor, and undeniably have a place in today's modern agriculture.

■ OPPOSITE *Technology supersedes tradition in Tian Shan Province, China.*

■ LEFT *A gleaming 1951 David Brown Cropmaster.*

AGCO ALLIS

During the mid-1980s the well-known Allis-Chalmers tractor brand became Deutz-Allis under the ownership of Klockner-Humboldt-Deutz, based in the German city of Cologne. In 1990 the Deutz-Allis division was sold to the Allis-Gleaner Company (AGCO), which later reintroduced the brand as AGCO Allis tractors. The machines were produced as one of its numerous brands of AGCO farming equipment throughout the 1990s, incorporating several different series, including those that were designated as 5600, 6670, 8700 and 9700 models.

The 5600 Series models were mid-sized machines and ranged from the 45hp 5650 to the 63hp 5670. They were powered by direct injection air-cooled diesel engines. The 5600 models were designed to be capable of tight turns and to drive a wide variety of equipment from the power take-off (PTO). The given horsepower figures were measured at the PTO. The AGCO Allis 6670 tractor was a row crop tractor that produced 63 PTOhp; powered by a four-cylinder direct injection air-cooled diesel engine. Reactive hydrostatic power steering was designed to end drift and what was termed the "economical PTO" setting was designed to save fuel by reducing engine speed by 25 per cent on any jobs that did not require the full PTO power.

The 8745 and 8765 Models were large capacity AGCO Allis tractors designed for large-scale farming. The 8765 was available with a choice of all-wheel drive or two-wheel drive and

■ RIGHT *The Model 9690 is a two-wheel-drive AGCO Allis tractor manufactured in 1996. Seen here with twin rear wheels, it was one of the company's largest tractors.*

■ ABOVE *This AGCO Allis 6690 model is one of the company's 6600 Series and is powered by an air-cooled diesel engine.*

■ LEFT *The 6690 is a four-wheel-drive AGCO Allis tractor. This is a 1994 example that uses different diameter front and rear wheels.*

■ BOTTOM *A four-wheel-drive AGCO Allis 9815 model from 1996, seen in the field with a disc harrow.*

■ LEFT *Note the stylized curved hood on this four-wheel-drive 1995 AGCO Allis 9435 model.*

produced 85hp at the PTO, while the 8745 produced 70 PTOhp. Both came with 12-speed synchronized shuttle transmissions designed to offer sufficient power in all gears. These tractors had an AGCO Allis 400 Series turbocharged diesel engine providing the power under the bodywork, which was then a modern "low-profile" appearance. The larger tractors in the 8700 Series were the 8775 and 8785 Models, powered by a fuel-efficient AGCO Allis 600 Series liquid-cooled diesel. These tractors produced 95hp and 110hp at the PTO respectively. They were manufactured with a choice of all-wheel-drive and two-wheel-drive transmissions. The transmission had four forward speeds and an optional creeper gear. The tractors were also equipped with a 540/1000 "economy PTO", a durable wet multi-disc clutch and electronically controlled three-point hitch. The 125 PTOhp 9735 and 145 PTOhp 9745 Models were tractors that had been designed with styling and performance in mind. Both were available in an all-wheel-drive version or as a standard model with either four- or 18-speed transmissions.

Innovative advanced computer technology was employed in the manufacture of the AGCO Allis range. The proprietary system known as DataTouch was designed to be a compact, easy-to-read, touch-screen display, from which all the functions of the in-cab systems can be controlled. The system was designed so that there were no cables in the operator's line of sight. It was based on simple touch-screen technology that was considered by the manufacturer to be easy to use despite the complexity of the operations and data it controls.

In 2001 AGCO merged AGCO Allis with another of its brands, White, and renamed it AGCO. The AGCO Allis brand continues to be used for the South American market, with manufacturing based in Argentina where they produce tractors, harvesters and other machinery.

Allis-Chalmers

■ BELOW *From 1929 onwards Allis-Chalmers tractors were painted in a bright shade of orange. It was known as Persian Orange and was an attempt to attract new customers.*

This tractor maker has roots that stretch back to Milwaukee's Reliance Works Flour Milling Company that was founded in 1847. The company was reorganized in 1912 with Brigadier General Otto H. Falk as president. It remained based in Milwaukee, Wisconsin and, although it had no experience of steam traction, built its first gasoline tractor, the tricycle-type Model 10–18, in 1914. This had a two-cylinder opposed engine that revved to 720rpm and, as its designation indicates, produced 10 drawbar hp and 18 belt hp. It was started on gasoline but once the engine warmed up it ran on cheaper kerosene. The single wheel was at the front while the driver sat over the rear axle.

Unlike some of its competitors, Allis-Chalmers did not have an established dealer network around the United States so sales did not achieve their full potential. Between 1914 and 1921 the company manufactured and sold approximately, 2,700 10–18s. Some of these were sold through mail order catalogues, and during World War I some export sales were achieved. The French imported American tractors and sold them under their own brand names – the Allis-Chalmers 10–18, for instance, was marketed in France as the Globe tractor.

■ BELOW *The Allis-Chalmers Model B tractor was exported from the United States to Britain under the Lend-Lease policies of the war.*

The conventional Model 18–30 tractor, introduced in 1919, was powered by a vertical in-line four-cylinder engine. In the early days sales were limited, partially as a result of competition from the cheap Fordson, and only slightly more than 1,000 had been assembled by 1922, but over the course of the next seven years the total reached 16,000.

Allis-Chalmers acquired a few other companies when the end of the post-war boom led to numerous closures and mergers within the tractor industry. Among these acquisitions was the

■ RIGHT *The Allis-Chalmers Model U had a lengthy production run that extended between its introduction in 1929 and end of production in 1953.*

■ BELOW *On top of the orange paint, the A-C logo left no doubt as to which make the operator was driving.*

Monarch Tractor Company of Springfield, Illinois, that made crawler tractors. The company had started tractor production in 1917 and had reorganized twice by the time of the merger, when production of a range of six different-sized crawlers was under way. The smallest of these was the Lightfoot 6–10 and the largest the Monarch 75, which weighed 11.5 tons. Allis-Chalmers continued the production of crawlers in Springfield. Another of its acquisitions was the Advance-Rumely Thresher Company, that was taken over in 1931.

In 1929 as many as 32 companies making farm equipment merged to form the United Tractor and Equipment Corporation, which had its headquarters in Chicago, Illinois. Amongst the 32 was Allis-Chalmers, which was contracted to build a new tractor powered by a Continental engine and known as the United. The tractor was launched at an agricultural show in Wichita in the spring of 1929. The corporation did not stay in business long. Allis-Chalmers was fortunate enough to survive the collapse and continued to build the United tractor, albeit redesignated the Model U. The Model U and E tractors became the basis of the Allis-Chalmers range. Allis-Chalmers also introduced a distinctive colour scheme to attract new customers and differentiate its tractors from those of other makers. The colour chosen was called Persian Orange. It was a simple ploy but one that no doubt worked, as other manufacturers soon followed suit with brightly coloured paintwork and stylized bonnets, radiator grilles and mudguards.

The Model U later became famous as the first tractor available with low-pressure pneumatic rubber tyres. In 1932 Model U tractors fitted with aircraft-type tyres inflated to 15psi were successfully tested on a dairy farm in Waukesha, Wisconsin. Despite their proven ability, pneumatic tyres were greeted with scepticism by those who thought that such tyres would not be adequate for farming use. Allis-Chalmers indulged in a series of speed events involving pneumatic-tyred tractors to promote this latest breakthrough in tractor technology. They went as far as hiring professional racing drivers to demonstrate their pneumatic-tyred machines at agricultural shows and state fairs. In the late 1930s, Allis-Chalmers introduced its Model A and B

ALLIS-CHALMERS MODEL U	
Year	1933
Engine	Four cylinder
Power	34hp on kerosene
Transmission	Four speed (pneumatic tyres)
Weight	n/k

■ BELOW *The Allis-Chalmers Model U played an important part in the development of pneumatic tyres for tractors as the company used a number of them to demonstrate Firestone tyres.*

■ LEFT *A 1942 version of the long-running Allis-Chalmers Model U which pioneered the use of pneumatic tyres. Steel rims reappeared during World War II as a result of rubber shortages.*

tractors. The four-speed Model A replaced the Model E and was made between 1936 and 1942, while production of the Model B ran between 1937 and 1957. The Model B was powered by a four-cylinder 15.7bhp engine and more than 127,000 were made over the course of the lengthy production run. In 1936 the Model U was upgraded by the fitment of the company's own UM engine. The Model WC was introduced in 1934 as the first tractor designed for pneumatic tyres, although steel rims remained available as an option. In 1938 Allis-Chalmers offered the downsized Model B tractor on pneumatic tyres, a successful sales ploy. The tractor sold particularly well and was widely marketed. It was manufactured in Great Britain after World War II for sale in both the home and export markets. In another move to increase sales in the same year, the company increased the number of its tractor models with styled hoods and radiator grille shells.

Many established American tractor manufacturers quickly added new models to their ranges in the immediate post-war years. Allis-Chalmers introduced its Models G and WD. The Model WD-45 was fitted with a gasoline engine. In 1955 a diesel variant was offered and this marked something of a landmark for Allis-Chalmers as it was the first wheeled diesel tractor the company had launched, though it had been making diesel-engined crawlers since taking over Monarch in the late 1920s. The diesel engine selected for the WD-45 was an in-line six-cylinder of 3770cc/230cu in displacement. An LPG engine option was also made available for the WD-45 and it was the first model Allis-Chalmers offered with power steering. The WD-45 was a great success overall and more than 83,000 were eventually made.

■ BELOW *The three-point linkage, as seen on this WD-45, revolutionized the attachment of farm implements to tractors.*

■ BOTTOM *The Allis-Chalmers WD-45 was one of the first all-new post-World War II tractors.*

Allis-Chalmers produced the Model B tractor at a plant in Southampton, England, from 1948, although by then it was already considered an old-fashioned tractor. The British plant was moved to Essendine in Lincolnshire soon afterwards and the D270 went into production. This was in some ways an updated Model B, featuring high ground clearance – which made it suitable for use with mid-mounted implements – and a choice of three engines, all from later Model B tractors. These included petrol and paraffin versions of the in-line, four-cylinder, overhead-valve unit and a Perkins P3 diesel. The petrol and

■ LEFT *A restored Allis-Chalmers WD-45, with adjustable rear wheel tread.*

■ BELOW *The Model C was made between 1940 and 1948 and featured a tricycle-type wheel arrangement for row crop use.*

paraffin engines produced 27hp and 22hp at 1650rpm respectively. The D272 was a further upgraded version offered from 1959 and the ED40 was another new model introduced in 1960. Disappointing sales of these models, amongst other factors, caused Allis-Chalmers to stop making tractors in Britain in 1968.

In 1955, the company bought the Gleaner Harvester Corporation and introduced its D Series in the latter part of that decade. This was a comprehensive range of tractors that included numerous D-prefixed models including the D10, D12, D14, D15, D17, D19 and D21 machines. There were up to 50 variations in the series once the various fuel options of gasoline, diesel and LPG were considered. The D17 was powered by a 4293cc/262cu in engine that produced 46 drawbar and 51 belt hp in the Nebraska Tractor Tests. There were 62,540 Model D17s made during the tractor's ten-year production run.

In 1960 the company changed the livery used on its products, selecting an even brighter hue, named Persian Orange Number 2, which was contrasted with cream wheels and radiator grilles. The most important models to benefit from this change were the D10 and D12, tractors which had superseded the Models B and CA. Their production run lasted ten years but fewer than 10,000 were made.

The last Allis-Chalmers tractors were produced during the mid-1980s because in 1985 the company, hit by the recession, was taken over by a West German company. Klockner-Humboldt-Deutz acquired it and renamed the tractor division Deutz-Allis. It was shortlived: in 1990 the company was acquired by an American holding firm, known as Allis-Gleaner Company (AGCO), which soon renamed the tractor producer AGCO Allis.

One of the final Allis-Chalmers tractors was the Model 4W-305 of 1985. It had a twin turbo engine that produced power in the region of 305hp and a transmission that included 20 forward gears and four reverse. Production of tractors at West Allis, Wisconsin, ceased in December 1985.

OTHER MAKES

(ACME, Advance-Rumely, American Harvester, Avance, Belarus, Bolinder Munktell, Braud, Breda, Brockway, Bull)

■ LEFT
A 40-60 Advance-Rumely tractor of 1929. Noted for the manufacture of large tractors, the company was acquired by Allis-Chalmers in 1931.

■ BELOW LEFT
Early tractors such as this Advance-Rumely took many of their design features from the steam traction engines that had preceded them.

■ ACME

ACME was one of a lengthy list of short-lived tractor manufacturers founded during the boom years that followed the end of World War I. The ACME tractor was advertised as being available in both wheeled and half-track form. It is hard to say with complete certainty but it is likely that many small companies which advertised tractors, such as this one, never made more than a handful of machines after their initial prototype. This was one reason why the Nebraska Tractor Tests, started in 1920, were to become such a useful consumer aid for farmers.

■ ADVANCE-RUMELY

Meinrad Rumely was a German emigrant who set up a blacksmith's shop in La Porte, Indiana during the 1850s. His smithy was gradually expanded into a factory that built farm machines and steam engines for agricultural use. In 1908 John Secor joined the company to develop an oil-fuelled engine, and Rumely, which had primarily been a thresher manufacturer, made its first OilPull tractor in 1909 after Secor had perfected a carburettor for kerosene or paraffin fuel. A later result of this development work was the Model B 25–45 tractor that in turn was superseded by the Model E of 1911. The Model E was a 30–60 tractor, the designation indicating that it produced 30hp at the drawbar and 60hp at the belt. These figures were substantiated when the Model E was tested in the 1911 Winnipeg Agricultural Motor Competition. In 1920 the same tractor was the subject of Nebraska Tractor Test Number 8, when the drawbar figure was measured at almost 50hp and the belt at more than 75hp. The engine capable of producing this horsepower was a low-revving, horizontal twin-cylinder with a bore and stroke of 25 × 30cm/10 × 12in. The measured fuel consumption of this engine was high at almost 50 litres/11 gallons of kerosene per hour. Notable features of the engine design included the special carburettor with water injection and air cooling induced by creating a draught through the rectangular tower on the front of the tractor. The company was renamed the Advance-Rumely Thresher Company in 1915 during the production run of the Model E 30–60 OilPull, which remained in production until 1923 when it was superseded by the similarly designed 20–40 Model G. By 1931, Advance-Rumely had produced more than 56,500 OilPulls in 14 configurations.

Advance-Rumely, noted for making large tractors, entered the small tractor market in 1916 when it first advertised its All Purpose 8–16 model. The operation of the machine was described as being "just like handling a horse gang". The machine had only three wheels – a single steering rear wheel and two front wheels, one driven and the other free-wheeling. It was powered by a four-cylinder engine that ran on kerosene. The tractor was intended for drawbar towing of implements and for the belt driving of machines such as threshers and balers.

While Advance-Rumely continued to refine its own OilPull line of tractors, it acquired Aultman Taylor in 1924 but was itself sold to Allis-Chalmers in 1931. In that year it marketed the Model 6A tractor, a modern-looking machine for its time. The 6A was powered by a six-cylinder Waukesha engine and fitted with a

■ RIGHT *This large tractor was rated at 22-65hp at the drawbar and belt respectively and was made by the Advance-Rumely Thresher Company during 1919.*

■ BELOW RIGHT *Advance-Rumely was founded by Meinrad Rumely, a German emigrant blacksmith who opened a smithy in La Porte, Indiana in the mid-19th century.*

six-speed gearbox. Allis-Chalmers, however, sold the 6A only until existing stocks had been used up, and less than 1,000 were made in total.

■ AMERICAN HARVESTER

American Harvester diesel tractors were made under contract in the People's Republic of China and imported into the United States by a company called Farm Systems International. There were numerous tractor manufacturers in China, but Farm Systems International claimed to contract only with those manufacturers who were capable of matching or exceeding specified standards of quality and workmanship. The engines used in American Harvester machines incorporated features such as removable cylinder sleeves and forged pistons, aimed at ensuring the longevity of the tractors.

The Model 504 was one of a range of Compact American Harvester tractors that were engineered to last between 6,000 and 11,000 hours between overhauls, and were also designed to be sufficiently powerful though small and fuel-efficient. The 504 was fitted with a low-pollution diesel engine coupled to an eight-speed transmission with four-wheel-drive capability. Options included a two-wheel-drive transmission with an adjustable width, row crop front end. The 504 had a full-size, mechanical

■ BELOW *This Advance-Rumely Model H tractor was rated at 16-30hp in 1920, but was superseded by lighter models from 1924.*

power take-off as standard and a full-size, three-point hydraulic hitch. A range of models were available, with engines that produced from 18 to 50hp. All had a 12 volt electrical system with emergency hand crank starting, glow plugs and compression release for cold weather. There was a built-in auxiliary hand-pump to purge fuel lines.

The American Harvester Model 250 is of smaller overall dimensions and was primarily intended for use with implements

OTHER MAKES

■ RIGHT *Belarus tractors are made in the Republic of Belarus, a member of the Commonwealth of Independent States previously known as Belorussia, in the former USSR, and are widely exported.*

■ BELOW *Belarus offers around 30 models from 20 to 130bhp. Earlier machines were of a simpler design to ensure reliability.*

such as rotary cultivators, rotary disc ploughs, rotary harrows and reaping machines, as well as ordinary ploughs and harrows. To enable it to do this, it had a system of "live hydraulics" and large diameter tyres to aid traction in fields. It can also be used as the power for irrigation and drainage equipment, threshing machines and rice mills or to drive trailers.

The Model 250 is 268.7cm/105.8in long and 124cm/48.8in wide. The height to steering wheel is 143.3cm/56.4in while the wheel base is 152cm/60in. The turning circle varies depending on whether brakes are fitted to the front axle. With brakes fitted the turning circle is 2.5m/8.25ft, while without them it is 2.8m/9.24ft. The Model 250 is powered by a vertical, water-cooled, four-stroke, three-cylinder diesel. Its displacement is 1432cc/87.4cu in achieved through a bore and stroke of 8.6x9.7cm/3.4x3.8in. The Compression Ratio is 22:1 and the engine produces 25hp at 2500rpm. The engine is cooled by a pressurized system. The transmission has eight forward and two reverse gears and is assembled with a dry, single plate clutch. The gearbox is fitted with a differential lock to assist traction in wet or heavy soil. The drum brake is of the internal expanding shoe type while steering is of a traditional peg and

■ RIGHT *This Belarus 862 D is designed for high-speed field work and has a 90hp engine and a four-wheel-drive system that only engages drive to the front axle when the rear wheels slip up to 6 per cent.*

worm design. The Model 250 has 6.0x15 and 8.3x24 tyres, front and rear respectively and its hydraulic linkage has a maximum lift capacity of 1878kg/4140lbs.

■ **AVANCE**

Avance was a Swedish tractor manufacturer active in the second decade of the 20th century when tractor innovations were accruing rapidly. Avance offered a tractor of an improved design, the first semi-diesel-engined machine. All oil products had to be imported into Sweden and were expensive, so a machine that could run on as cheap a fuel as possible – including waste oil – offered clear advantages. The engineers at Avance had considered the starting procedure of diesels in some detail and developed the semi-diesel, which ignited the fuel by its injection on to a red hot bulb in the cylinder head. The Avance machine offered this new technology in a machine that was in other ways dated, relying on both a chassis and tank cooling of the engine. By the end of the decade Avance were offering two-cylinder, hot-bulb, semi-diesel tractors of two capacities, 18–22 and 20–30hp. They utilized compressed air starters with glow plugs and batteries as additional options.

■ ABOVE RIGHT *This Belarus 862 D is fitted with independent and ground speed PTO and category II live hydraulics with draught and position control.*

■ RIGHT *A Belarus 862 D powered by a 4075cc/248cu in, in-line four-cylinder engine which drives through a transmission with 18 forward and two reverse gears.*

■ **BELARUS**

Belarus Tractors are made in the Minsk Tractor Factory (MTZ) in the Republic of Belarus, a member of the Commonwealth of Independent States (CIS). The company's products have been exported widely, and it offers numerous tractors in a variety of configurations.

The Belarus Model 862 D of 1986 was powered by an engine that displaced 4075cc/248cu in and produced 90hp. It featured an automatic four-wheel-drive transmission that incorporated 18 forward and two reverse gears. Hydrostatic steering was fitted as standard.

The current Belarus range of four-wheel-drive tractors includes the 1221.3, which produces 140hp, the 124hp 1220.3, the 100hp 952.3 and the 920.3 machine, that has 90hp. The two-wheel-drive line of Belarus tractors includes the 900.3, which produces 90hp.

OTHER MAKES

■ **BOLINDER-MUNKTELL**
The Swedish tractor-maker Bolinder-Munktell was formed by the amalgamation of two Swedish companies. In 1932 the tractor manufacturer Munktell combined with its engine-maker, Bolinder, to form Bolinder-Munktell, which continued the production of the 15–22 and 20–30 tractors. Munktell is credited with having built the first tractor to be manufactured in Sweden, the BM 30–40 of 1913. It was powered by a two-cylinder Bolinder engine. The company also experimented with wood-burning tractors, because fuel was a major consideration in countries where oil had to be imported. In 1921 and 1922 the company offered a two-stroke, two-cylinder, hot-bulb engine that produced 15-22hp and, as a result, was designated the Model 22. Its engine was actually derived from a marine engine and used compressed air to start after the hot bulbs had been heated with an integral blowlamp. By 1930 the company was also offering a larger model, the 20–30, and both variants took part in the Oxfordshire World Tractor Trials of

■ ABOVE *Bolinder-Munktell later combined with Volvo to form Volvo BM, but prior to this the company's two-stroke diesel engines proved popular.*

■ BELOW *Bolinder-Munktell was a merger of the Swedish tractor maker Munktell and engine maker Bolinder. This three-cylinder diesel was one of the company's products.*

1930. Another Swedish manufacturer was Bofors, the arms manufacturer, that entered the tractor market alongside Avance and Munktell with its 40–46hp two-cylinder tractor first built in 1932.

Bolinder-Munktell offered a 31hp twin-cylinder engined tractor in 1939 and in the aftermath of World War II offered the Model 10 tractor, a 23hp machine powered by a hot-bulb engine. It was not until the 1950s that the company abandoned the hot-bulb engine, when it introduced the BM35 and BM55 models with direct injection diesel engines. These tractors also featured five-speed transmissions and an optional cab. Bolinder-Munktell later merged with Volvo.

■ BRAUD

In 1870 Braud was founded in St Mars La Jaille, in France, to manufacture threshing machines. Over a century later, in 1975, Braud produced its first grape harvester and went on to specialize in this field. In 1984 Fiatagri acquired 75 per cent of Braud. Then in 1988 all of Fiat-Allis and Fiatagri's activities were merged to form a new company, FiatGeotech, the Fiat group's farm and earthmoving machinery sector. Within this restructuring, Hesston and Braud joined forces in a new company, Hesston-Braud, based in Coex, France. It then became part of New Holland Geotech, and later CNH.

■ BREDA

Breda was active in tractor production in Italy during the 1920s, and unlike many of its competitors, produced gasoline-engined tractors. These were powered by four-cylinder engines of 26 and 40hp. During the 1930s the range of models offered was expanded to include both a conventional four-cylinder gasoline/kerosene-engined tractor and an unusual two-stroke, two-cylinder, Junkers diesel-engined machine. After World War II the company offered multi-cylinder-engined crawler tractors.

■ BROCKWAY

During the years immediately after World War II, there was an influx of new tractor manufacturers into the industry. Brockway had made bridging equipment for the US Army during the war and was one of several American companies new to tractor manufacture. Others included Custom, Earthmaster, Farmaster, Friday, General, Harris and Laughlin.

■ BULL

The Minneapolis Steel and Machinery Company was primarily a structural steel-maker, producing thousands of tons per year in the late 1800s and early 1900s. The company also manufactured the Corliss steam engine, that served as a power unit for many flour mills in the Dakotas. In 1908, Minneapolis Steel and Machinery produced tractors under the Twin City brand name.

By the outbreak of World War I, the company was one of the larger tractor producers in the world, and had diversified into manufacturing tractors for other companies. One of these was the Bull tractor for the Bull Tractor Co: the company was contracted to build 4,600 machines, using engines supplied by Bull.

The acceptance that small tractors were practical for all kinds of farming tasks quickly changed the emphasis of the tractor-manufacturing industry and threatened some of the old-established companies and their larger machines.

The Bull tractor was a small machine based around a triangular steel frame. It had only one driven wheel, thereby eliminating the need for a differential. A single wheel at the front steered the machine and the other two simply free-wheeled. An opposed twin engine produced up to 12hp and the transmission was as basic as the remainder of the machine, with a single forward and single reverse gear.

At first the little Bull tractor sold well, but after an initial success, the limitations of its usefulness, and some inherent faults in the machine's design and construction became apparent. Sales quickly declined and as a result, little was heard of the company after 1915.

■ ABOVE *This 1950 Bolinder-Munktell BM10 tractor produced 20hp from its two-cylinder, two-stroke hot-bulb engine.*

Case

Case built its first viable gasoline-powered tractor in 1911 and by 1913 had developed a practical and small-sized tractor powered by a gasoline engine, although the company's history began long before this. J. I. Case and Company was formed in 1863, in Racine, Wisconsin, to build steam tractors. It became the J. I. Case Threshing Company in 1880, and its first experimental gasoline tractor appeared in 1892, but was not a success. In 1911 the massive Case 30–60 won first place in the Winnipeg Tractor Trials. It weighed almost 13 tons but clearly found a market, as it was

■ BELOW *The new Case RC of 1935 was painted light grey in order to distinguish it from the CC models. The RC began production as a four-cylinder, engine-powered, tricycle row crop tractor.*

CASE RC ROW CROP 1935

Engine	Waukesha in-line four cylinder
Power	18-20hp
Transmission	Three forward speeds, hand clutch
Weight	1180kg/2600lbs

■ BELOW *The Case L model of 1929 ended Case's production of Crossmotor models because the L used an in-line four-cylinder overhead valve engine for propulsion.*

■ RIGHT *The Case CC was a row crop version of the Model C with a distinctive steering arm, nicknamed the "chicken perch" and "fence cutter".*

■ BELOW LEFT *The Case RC of 1939 added the rounded sunburst cast grille and Flambeau Red paintwork.*

■ BELOW RIGHT *Production of Case RC models was moved to Rock Island, Illinois in 1937 after Case had purchased the Rock Island Plow Company.*

made until 1916. A smaller version, the 12–25, was made from 1913 onwards but it was the company's 20–40 model that garnered more awards at the Winnipeg Trials in 1913. All three of these Case tractors were powered by flat twin engines (horizontally opposed twin cylinders) of varying displacements and used other components taken from the Case range of steam engines.

It was generally accepted that the future lay in smaller tractors that had more in common with automobiles than steam engines. Case experimented with small-sized machines and developed the three-wheeled 10–20 Crossmotor tractor. This was powered by a vertical in-line four-cylinder engine mounted transversely across the frame. It had a single driven wheel and an idler wheel on the rear axle. The driven wheel was aligned with the front steering wheel and the machine was capable of pulling a two-tine plough. Between 1915 and 1922 approximately 5,000 10–20s were produced. Case introduced the four-wheeled Model 9–18 in 1916 to compete with the popular Fordson. It was the 9–18 tractor that, in many ways, established Case as a major manufacturer and more than 6,000 of the two versions, 9–18A and 9–18B, had been made by 1919. The 9–18 was a lightweight tractor designed to weigh around the same as a team of horses and capable of pulling a plough or driving a

■ LEFT *When pneumatic tyres were still considered innovative, tractor makers offered customers a choice of steel wheels, or pneumatic tyres as used by this Model L.*

Case had not abandoned production of larger tractors altogether and offered the 22–40 between 1919 and 1924 and the 40–72 between 1920 and 1923. Only 42 tractors of the latter design were made. Each weighed 11 tons and when tested in Nebraska in 1923 produced a record 91 belt hp, but used fuel in huge quantities.

A new president, Leon R. Clausen (1878–1965), was appointed to head the

thresher. In 1917 the 10–18 was launched. It was similar to the 9–18 but featured a cast radiator tank and an engine capable of higher rpm. During the 10–18's three-year production run around 9,000 tractors were made. The 15–27 was a tractor designed for a three-tine plough and was the first Case tractor to have a power take-off fitted. Its capabilities matched the requirements of the market to the extent that more than 17,500 were sold between its introduction in 1919 and 1924 when it was superseded by the Model 18–32.

■ LEFT *Later the Case colour scheme was a combination of Flambeau Red and Desert Sand.*

■ BELOW LEFT *The row crop tractors' front wheels minimized crop damage.*

■ BELOW *The refined row crop Case DC included upgrades such as the streamlined cast radiator grille.*

■ RIGHT *The distinctive Case name and logo was always displayed.*

■ FAR RIGHT *What made the Case DEX different from other Case tractors from the early 1940s was that the DEX used the enclosed chain final drive system instead of gears.*

■ BELOW *A 1942 Case DEX model photographed in Yorkshire, England.*

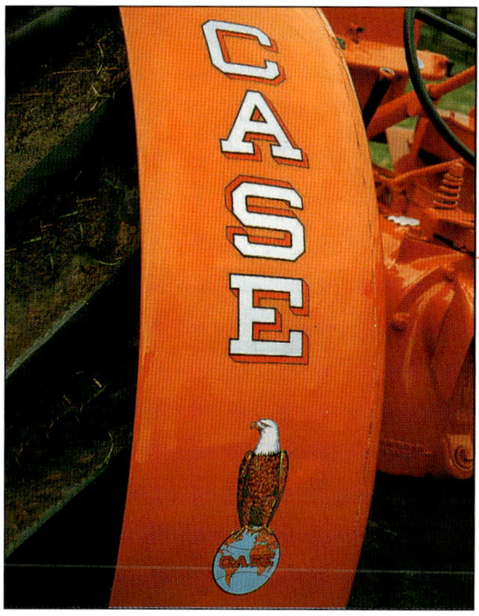

J. I. Case Threshing Machine Company in 1924. Clausen had been born in Fox Lake, Wisconsin and in 1897 had graduated from the University of Wisconsin with a degree in electrical engineering. He had experience of the tractor industry as a former employee of John Deere. He also had an antipathy towards trade unionism and some disdain for customer demands, believing that product design should be solely the province of the engineering department. He started the company working on a redesigned range of tractors.

■ CASE MODEL L

In 1929 the Case Model L went into production based around a unit frame construction. It was notable because, for the first time in 15 years, the engine was not mounted transversely but longitudinally. The angular Model L was a great success and was to remain in production until 1939 when it was replaced by the Model LA, a restyled and updated version of the L. The restyling gave the tractor a more rounded appearance typical of the time, but much of the engineering was similar to that of the Model L. The engine was a 6.6 litre, overhead valve, in-line, four-cylinder unit. Drive to the rear axle was by a pair of chains and sprockets as in the Model L. The gearbox was a conventional four-speed unit with a single reverse gear. A lever-operated overcentre-type clutch allowed selection of the required gear. The tractor stayed in production until 1955.

The Case Model C also went into production in 1929 and it, along with

CASE 385 TRACTOR

Year	1988
Engine	Three cylinder, 2536cc/155cu in
Power	45hp (33.6 kW)
Transmission	Eight forward, four reverse
Weight	(2WD model) 2430kg/5356lbs

■ RIGHT *The Case LA debuted in 1939 although under its streamlined hood and Flambeau red paint it was essentially the earlier Model L tractor, albeit more powerful.*

the Model L, was one of the tractors that helped to establish the Case brand in Great Britain. It was tested in the 1930 World Tractor Trials in Oxfordshire where, in the class for machines fuelled by paraffin, it achieved the best economy figures. The model C recorded a maximum output of 29.8hp on the belt and 21.9hp on the drawbar, figures that were almost identical to those achieved in Nebraska the previous year. The results of the tests were widely advertised by Case, which later offered the Models CC, CI, CO, CV and CD (row crop, industrial, orchard, vineyard and crawler versions respectively). Under

■ BELOW *This is a 1943 version of the Case LA tractor, which had revised wheels over the initial model. The LA was designed to pull up to five ploughs.*

■ ABOVE *The plate that identifies the tractor as Case model number 11161 LA also bears the "Old Abe" mascot and is positioned next to the oil pressure gauge.*

■ LEFT *Despite the distinctive green and yellow colour scheme that suggests John Deere, the French company SFV was acquired by Case during the 1960s.*

CASE MX100C

Year	1998
Engine	4 litre four-cylinder turbo
Power	75 kW at 2200rpm
Transmission	16 forward, 12 reverse
Weight	4750kg/10,470lbs

Clausen, progress and innovation were cautious and conservative which, in some instances allowed competitors to benefit at Case's expense. One area in which Clausen wanted to advance the company was to offer a full line of implements to complement the tractor range. To this end, Case bought out Emerson-Brantingham in 1928 and the Rock Island Plow Company in 1937. Following these acquisitions, and that of the Showers Brothers furniture factory in

Burlington, Iowa, Case moved towards production of combine harvesters. A new line of tractors appeared in 1939, the Models D and DC, which were to be followed by the Models S and V and an upgraded Model L, the LA.

The Model D was a four-wheeled tractor and was designed to pull a three-tine plough. It had a belt pulley, PTO and Case's motor lift system for the implements. The DC was a row crop tricycle with adjustable wheel spacing

■ ABOVE RIGHT *Société Française Vierzon (SFV) incorporated the blue, white and red of the French tricolor in its company logo, seen here on the right-hand side of the 302 model.*

■ RIGHT *The two-stroke semi-diesel SFV tractors featured distinctively shaped exhausts, and a transverse, leaf-sprung beam front axle.*

■ RIGHT *Case pioneered the loader backhoe to be sold as a single unit in the late 1950s and had considerable success with the resultant versatile machine. This is a 1990s version, the Case 580 SK.*

and what the manufacturers termed "quick-dodge" steering for close cultivation in uneven rows. The D Series tractors were the first Case machines to be painted in a bright hue – Flambeau Red – a colour that was to become standard for the next decade.

■ THE 1940S

As it did for most American industry, World War II changed things for Case. Between 1940 and 1945 three Case plants had made in excess of 1.3 million 155mm howitzer shells. Case also made specialized military tractors such as the Model LA1. Alongside these projects, Case made parts for army trucks, amphibious tracked vehicles and military aircraft. This war production did not adversely affect Case's tractor sales to farmers at a time when agricultural production was as crucial as armament production; in fact it ended the effects of the Depression on the company. Labour relations were not all that they might have been and in 1945 Case employees from the Racine plant went on strike for 440 days, the longest strike in the company's history. This had a disastrous effect on Case's dealers and customer base and has been credited by many historians as one of the reasons for John Deere's growth and consolidation of its position within the tractor market.

In the aftermath of both the war and the strikes, Case looked towards expansion. The company bought plants in Bettendorf, Iowa and Stockton, California, as well as the Kilby Steel Company of Anniston, Alabama. With these additional facilities Case sought to produce a wider range of farm machinery, including combine harvesters, rakes, ploughs and manure spreaders. The Alabama plant was to be used for the production of new machines, including tobacco harvesters for the south-east of the United States. In the wake of this expansion came a slump in profits for the years 1950–53, largely because many innovations that were being adopted by rival manufacturers – including the three-point hitch – were not offered on Case

■ ABOVE *The SFV 201 was one of the models made by SFV prior to the company's acquisition by Case.*

■ LEFT *Prior to the acquisition, SFV specialized in the production of two-stroke, semi-diesel engined tractors of an unusual design that proved popular in Europe.*

machines. An example of this failure to compete can be seen in Case's baling machines; in 1941 the company dominated the hay baler market because its baler had been the first to pick up the hay as it was towed along. Just before the outbreak of war New Holland introduced a baler that used twine instead of wire for baling and, more importantly, did not require two extra men to tie bales as the Case machine did. Case failed to make any improvements to its balers and sales slumped to the extent that in 1953 Case achieved only 5 per cent of sales.

■ JOHN T. BROWN

The company was in the doldrums and the situation was exacerbated when Clausen relinquished the presidency in 1948 and was succeeded by Theodore Johnson. Johnson resigned in 1953 to be replaced by John T. Brown. This change, along with impetus from the company's underwriter and a more dynamic board of directors, began to turn the company's fortunes around. New engineering practices and an acceptance of diesel engines, as well as new lines of implements including one-way disc ploughs, cotton strippers, disc harrows, Lister press drills and front loaders, all took the company forward. Most important among these advances was the 500 Series of tractors. This new line was soon followed by the 400 and the 300 Series.

These ranges of tractors were effectively the first completely redesigned Case models to appear since the 1930s. The 500 models of 1953 were powered by an in-line, six-cylinder, diesel engine that developed sufficient horsepower to pull five plough bottoms. The 500 also featured power steering, a push-button starter and live hydraulics, making them easy to operate. The 400 Series was unveiled in 1955 and incorporated all Case's new technology. Power came from an in-line four-cylinder engine with a choice of diesel, gasoline or LPG fuel, capable of pulling four ploughs. Final drive was now by means of gears and the transmission had eight forward speeds. A hydraulic vane steering system was fitted, as were a three-point hitch and suspension seat for the driver. The 400

■ LEFT *A Case tractor towing a Massey-Ferguson baler during haymaking on a hill farm in Yorkshire, England.*

■ BELOW *First seen in 1978, the David Brown 1690 was the flagship of the 90 series and was rated at 103hp. The tractor became the Case 1694 in 1983.*

■ RIGHT *The 1056XL, the largest model in the Case IH 56 Series, powered by a six-cylinder engine that produces 98hp and features a four-wheel-drive transmission.*

Series models were the first made by the company to be advertised on television. Both the 400 and 500 Series models were made at the Racine, Wisconsin plant, and a third new model line was made at Rock Island and went on sale in 1956.

■ THE 300 SERIES

The 300 Series offered customers considerable choice: diesel or gasoline engine, and transmission with four, eight or twelve speeds. The other new feature of the 300 Series was its streamlined styling, which soon became the norm across Case's entire range. The next development in styling came in 1957 and was inspired by the automobile industry: the radiator grille was squared off and inclined forwards at the top, giving a slightly concave appearance. This styling continued through the Case-O-Matics and the 30 Series tractors, introduced in 1960, and even to the massive 1200 Traction King first produced in 1964.

■ ACQUISITIONS

In France, SFV – Société Française Vierzon – had entered the tractor market in 1935 with a machine not unlike the Lanz Bulldog. Despite World War II the company endured until 1960, when it was acquired by Case. In 1957 Case merged with the American Tractor Corporation, based in Churubusco, Indiana. This corporation manufactured "Terratrac" crawler tractors and Case continued production of such machines in Indiana until 1961 when it moved the production to Burlington, Iowa. One of the results of this merger was the development of the loader/backhoe. Case's 320 loader/backhoe was the first such machine to be built and marketed as a single unit.

CASE 1255XL 1990

Engine	Six cylinder turbo 5867cc/358cu in
Power	25hp/92KW
Transmission	20 x 9 syncromesh
Weight	6225kg/13,720lbs

■ CHANGING TIMES

Case took over the British tractor-maker, David Brown Ltd, in 1972. This acquisition was seen as more than a purchase because the British company had a large distribution network in Great Britain, outlets in Europe, and even some in the United States. From then on David Brown tractors would be painted in David Brown White and Case Red. The ownership of Case itself had changed in the late 1960s. The Kern County Land Company was a majority

■ BELOW *The Case IH 1255XL, seen here harvesting, has a two speed PTO that produces 121.1hp at 540rpm and 1000 rpm. The hydraulic system has a maximum pressure of 175kg/sq cm (2488lb/sq in).*

■ RIGHT *Tractors such as the Case IH 4230 have a forward tilting hood and swing out service panel to enable convenience of maintenance.*

■ BELOW *This Case XL Plus model is fitted with transmissions that have up to 16 forward speeds as well as, in this case, a driven front axle.*

■ BOTTOM *The Case 5150 is one of many tractors equipped with front weights which are positioned to improve traction as well as reducing turning radius.*

shareholder in Case and in 1967 this company was acquired by Tenneco Inc from Texas. In 1974 new agricultural products from Case included the 2670 Traction King tractor, the 6000 Series of mouldboard ploughs and the F21 Series of wheeled tandem-disc harrows. A year later the 1410 and 1412 tractors appeared. There were further new tractors the following year, when the 1570 Agri-King and 2870 Traction King 300hp four-wheel-drive machines were announced. As it was America's bicentennial year Case also offered a limited-edition version of the Model 1570, known as the Spirit of '76. The 70 and 90 Series tractors were new for 1978 and were followed by another new line in 1983, the 94 Series.

In 1985 Tenneco Inc completed its purchase of International Harvester, after that company had been adversely affected by the recession in farming in the early 1980s. In a restructuring of Tenneco, Case IH became Tenneco's largest division. The Case IH range for 1986 included the Model 685L, with a four-cylinder engine that developed 69hp, an eight forward speed and two reverse 4x4 transmission and hydrostatic steering. A larger model in the same range was the Model 1594, with an in-line six-cylinder engine that produced 96hp and drove through a four-range, semi-automatic, Hydra-Shift transmission.

The all-new 7100 series Magnum range first appeared in 1988, consisting of three models: the 7110, 7120 and 7130. A larger 7140 appeared a couple of years later, and in 1994 the range received a facelift in the form of the 7200 series. So reliable and popular were the Magnums that further improvements were seen in 1997 when the 7200 "Pro" or US 8900 series tractors were launched. The lower-powered Maxxum tractors originally spanned from 90 to 110hp, with the 125hp 5150 model introduced in 1993. The Maxxums were badged as the 5200 series in the US, but the 5100 series in European markets. The 3200 and 4200 series tractors catered for the lower horsepower bracket. All tractors produced were badged as Case IH from 1995 onwards, a decade after the merger of Case and International Harvester. Production of the Maxxum continued until 1997 when the MX Maxxum tractors replaced the ageing range. The MX range were fitted with six-cylinder 5883cc engines and 16-speed

■ BELOW *The 7100 and 7200 series Magnum tractors first appeared in 1989 and were fitted with an 18-speed powershift transmission. Tractors ranged from 155hp up to 246hp.*

■ LEFT *The 1998 Case MX120 has sixteen forward gears, four-wheel drive and hydrostatic steering.*

transmissions, as fitted to the previous 5100 series tractors. New styling, larger cab and side mounted exhaust were all features of the new range. When the company acquired Austrian tractor manufacturer Steyr in 1997, the CS 78, 94, 110, 130 and 150 models were offered alongside existing products. The CX range replaced the smaller 4200 series in 1998 and a compact Maxxum tractor, known as the MXC was also added. The MX80C, 90C and 100C had similar transmissions and cabs, but with a lower engine horsepower. The MX Magnum replaced the previous 10-year-old design in 1999 with a five-model range. The largest 270hp MX270 has an 8.3-litre, 24-valve engine and a 175-litre/160-gallon fuel tank. The range surprisingly used 30 per cent fewer parts than its predecessor. Case IH are also well known for their harvesting machines. The 2555 Cotton Express, for example, is powered by a 280hp turbocharged diesel engine and is capable of holding 3855kg/8500lbs of cotton. The company's popular range of rotary Axial-Flow combines were updated with the 2100 series, which was launched in 1996 to replace the ageing 1600 series. Developments have seen a 2300 series with an "Exclusive" version, and the latest model is the New Axial-Flow 9230 which is currently one of the biggest combines on the market.

With an increase in popularity of rubber-tracked crawlers, Case decided to investigate the possibilities of combining their already successful Steiger articulated tractors with low compaction rubber tracks. The Quadtrac was a result of six years development and was first introduced to US farmers in 1997. A 360hp 9370 tractor was fitted with four 75cm/30in rubber tracks which gave very little compaction. The more manoeuvrable machine gave maximum traction with no soil damage while turning, and the tractors' popularity grew. The UK saw the tractor in 1998 along with a new 400hp 9380 model.

■ LEFT *Case improved the Magnum range in 1999 when they replaced it with the new MX Magnum. Models including the MX180, MX200, MX220, MX240 and the range-topping 270hp MX270.*

■ RIGHT *Case IH bought the design rights to some models from the Austrian company Steyr. The CS and CVX tractors were built at the St Valentine plant from 1997.*

■ LEFT *In 1997 Case revealed its revolutionary Quadtrac crawler design. Four separate rubber tracks were added to their existing Steiger articulated tractor. In 2005 the STX500 Quadtrac was the largest in production, but the STX series were also available with wheels.*

The STX Steiger and Quadtrac models replaced the older version in 2001, which featured new cabs and styling. The development of the 500hp STX500 saw it break the world ploughing record in 2005. Recent production has included the highest powered machine Case produces, the Steiger 600, available in both wheeled or tracked versions, with a maximum power of 670hp, making it one of the largest production tractors.

Case launched its range of Continuously Variable Transmissions (CVTs) in the form of their Austrian-built CVX tractors in 2001. Models included the 130hp CVX130, 150hp CVX150 and 170hp CVX170. They used SISU engines and were capable of a top speed of 30mph/50kph.

In 2002 Case and New Holland merged to form the CNH Company. In an agreement between the two companies, chosen ranges would be used as a platform and sold in each firm's colours as different ranges. The MXM range was thus produced and spanned from 120hp to 194hp. There was a choice of manual, semi-powershift and powershift transmission options. Another development for Case IH was the MXU tractor in 2003. Aimed at the livestock and mixed farmers, the lightweight and compact 100–135hp tractors could be specified with a headland management system for arable operations. The largest 135hp MXU135 was capable of boosting the engine to 160hp for PTO and transport duties, making it an extremely versatile machine. The MXU filled the gap between the smaller JX and JXU tractors which were released at a similar time.

■ EFFICIENT FUTURE

In 2010 Case IH introduced their Efficient Power system and began incorporating it into their current lines of Puma, Maxxum, Magnum and Steiger tractors. Designed to lower fuel consumption and increase performance, the central element in Case's engine developments is the exhaust gas cleaning system based on Selective Catalytic Reduction (SCR) that converts nitrogen oxides in the exhaust emissions into nitrogen and water. Improvements of 10 per cent in fuel saving and a 14 per cent increase in productivity have been recorded thanks to the SCR system, while the stricter EU emissions standard of Tier 4 is more readily attainable with Case's technologies.

■ RIGHT *The MXM range of tractors was built as a result of the New Holland Merger. The MXM190 was the largest and its engine was capable of boosting its power from 194hp to 227hp for PTO and transport operations.*

CATERPILLAR

■ BELOW *The Caterpillar Sixty was one of the models of crawler manufactured in the Peoria, Illinois plant from 1925 onwards. It was a post-merger version of the Best 60hp model crawler.*

During the late 19th century Benjamin Holt and Daniel Best experimented with various forms of steam tractors for use in farming. They did so independently, running separate companies, but both were pioneers with track-type tractors and gasoline-powered tractor engines. Paralleling the developments of the steam excavator were experiments with tracked machines referred to as "crawlers". Crawler technology would later diverge into separate and distinct strands of activity, although the technology employed remained essentially the same. One of these strands of activity is, of course, the crawler's agricultural application.

The initial experiments involved wheeled steam tractors which were converted to run with tracks to overcome the problem of wheels sinking into soft ground. The first test of such a machine took place in November 1904 in Stockton, California, where a Holt steam tractor had been converted to run on tracks. This was accomplished by the removal of the rear wheels and their replacement with tracks made from a series of 7.5 × 10cm/3 × 4in wooden blocks 60cm/2ft long, bolted to a linked steel chain which ran around smaller wheels, a driven sprocket and idler on each side. Originally the machine was steered by a single tiller wheel, although this system was later dropped in favour of the idea of disengaging drive to one track by means of a clutch which slewed the machine around. From here it was but a short step to gasoline-powered crawlers, one of which was constructed by Holt in 1906. By 1908, 28 Holt gasoline-powered crawlers were engaged in work on the Los Angeles Aqueduct project in the Tehachapi mountains – something Holt saw as a proving-ground for his machines. By 1915, Holt "Caterpillar" track-type tractors were being used by the Allies in World War I.

In the years after World War I, the Best Company continued the work with crawler-tracked machinery. In 1921 it introduced a new machine, the Best 30 Tracklayer. This crawler was fitted with a light-duty bulldozer blade, was powered by an internal combustion engine and had an enclosed cab. At this time there was a considerable amount of litigation involving patents and types of tracklayers, and two companies were frequently named in the litigation: Best and Holt. Holt held a patent for track-layers which put him in a position to charge a licence fee to other manufacturers of the time, including Monarch, Bates and Cletrac. During World War I, much of Holt's production went to the US Army, while Best supplied farmers. After the war the two companies competed in all markets and neither had a significant advantage over the other. Eventually in 1925, the Holt and Best companies effectively merged to form the Caterpillar Tractor Company. Holt had in fact bought out Daniel Best in 1908 but later had to compete with Best's son, C. L. "Leo" Best.

In late 1925 the new Caterpillar Company published prices for its product line: the Model 60 sold for $6,050, the Model 30 for $3,665 and the two ton for $1,975. The consolidation of the two brands into one company proved its value in the next few years: the prices of the big tracklayers were cut, business increased and sales more than doubled.

The Caterpillar Twenty was a mid-sized crawler tractor put into production by the company in Peoria, Illinois late in 1927; production continued until 1933. It was powered by an in-line four-cylinder engine that made 25hp at 1250rpm. According to its makers it could pull 2174kg/4793lb at the drawbar in first

■ LEFT *Claas introduced a new systems tractor in 1997 called the Xerion. The innovative tractor had multiple implement locations and a cab that could be automatically rotated through 180 degrees.*

■ **CLETRAC**

Rollin H. White was one of a trio of brothers who established the White name in the US automotive industry. In 1911 he designed a self-propelled disc cultivator which, although it never went beyond the experimental stage, established his interest in agricultural machines. He then worked on ideas for a crawler tractor with a differential system that allowed the machine to be steered with a steering wheel rather than the more usual system of levers. The company was based in Cleveland, Ohio, and was known as the Cleveland Motor Plow Company. The name was changed in 1917 to the Cleveland Tractor Company and then changed again in 1918 to Cletrac.

The Model R was the first commercial tractor to offer the newly developed controlled differential, that slowed the drive to one track and increased it to the other. It was effective and became standard on Cletrac tractors, later finding wide acceptance in crawler technology. Other tractors from Cletrac were the models H and W. The Model F appeared in 1920 and was made until 1922 as a low-cost crawler tractor available in high clearance row crop format. It was powered by a four-cylinder side-valve engine that produced 16hp at 1600rpm at the drawbar. Its tracks were driven by sprockets mounted high on the sides of the machine, which gave the tracks a distinctive triangular appearance. The Model F retailed for $845 in 1920.

Cletrac introduced its first wheeled tractor in 1939, the general GG. A crawler version of this model was also available and was referred to as the HG. Both were powered by a Hercules IXA engine which was an in-line four-cylinder that produced 19hp at 1700rpm, later increased to 22hp. Cletrac also made a tricycle row crop tractor, although production of this model was taken over by B. F. Avery in 1941; it was then sold as the Avery Model A. Cletrac was sold to the Oliver Corporation in 1944, which in turn was sold to the White Motor Corporation in 1960.

■ RIGHT *Claas bought Renault Agriculture in 2003 and started producing Renault tractors in Claas colour schemes. The existing Ares and Atles models were kept and their design improved.*

DAVID BROWN

David Brown manufactured Ferguson tractors in the mid-1930s as a result of Harry Ferguson approaching the company then known as David Brown Gear Cutters of Huddersfield, England, with a view to the manufacture of a tractor transmission. Brown was noted for the manufacture of gears and Harry Ferguson wanted to produce a tractor with an American Hercules engine and an innovative hydraulic lift. This machine came to be built by Brown at a plant in Meltham, near Huddersfield, after the prototype had been tested. Known as the Ferguson Model, it was at first fitted with a Coventry Climax engine and subsequently with an engine of Brown's own design. Production ceased in 1939 because Brown wanted to increase its power and Ferguson to reduce the costs.

■ **BELOW** *The successful Cropmaster tractors were superseded by the 25 and 30 models, available in gasoline or diesel.*

■ DAVID BROWN VAK-1

Harry Ferguson travelled to the United States to see Henry Ford while David Brown exhibited a new model of a tractor built to his own design. The new machine was the VAK-1 and featured

■ **BELOW** *The Cropmaster was introduced in 1947 as the replacement for the successful VAK-1 and VAK-1a models.*

■ **BELOW** *A restored David Brown tractor on display within a few miles of the original David Brown factory in Meltham, England.*

■ ABOVE LEFT *A diesel-engined Deutz 7206 tractor. This is a two-wheel-drive model so does not have open centre front tyres, but ribbed ones to assist steering.*

■ ABOVE RIGHT *This Deutz-Fahr DX 6.31 is four-wheel drive and so has open centre tyres that enhance traction at the front axle.*

■ BELOW *The unique styling of the Deutz Agrotron was first seen in 1995. In the same year Deutz-Fahr became part of the SDF group which includes Same, Lamborghini and Hurlimann. The latest tractors feature similar styling and can be specified with continuously variable transmissions.*

■ EAGLE

The Eagle Manufacturing Company was based in Appleton, Wisconsin and started tractor manufacture in 1906 with a horizontally opposed twin-cylinder engine powered machine. By 1911 it was producing a four-cylinder 56hp machine and by 1916 had a range of four-cylinder tractors in production that took it through the 1920s. In 1930 it changed course and moved from flat twins to vertical in-line six-cylinder machines. One of these was the 6A Eagle, designed for three- to four-plough use and powered by a Waukesha six-cylinder engine that produced 22 belt hp and 37 drawbar hp. Model 6B was a row crop machine and 6C a utility tractor. The Eagle stayed in production in its various forms until World War II when production ceased, not to be resumed.

■ EMERSON-BRANTINGHAM

Emerson-Brantingham was one of the pioneers of American agricultural machinery manufacturing, with roots that stretched back to John H. Manny's reaper of 1852. The company had purchased the Gas Traction Company of Minneapolis in 1912 and became heavily involved in the manufacture of gasoline-engined tractors. Its range included the Big 4 Model 30, a 30 drawbar hp 10 ton machine that was subsequently enlarged into the Big 4 Model 45. This was rated at 45 belt hp and 90 drawbar hp and was even heavier. The Model 20 of 1913 was a much smaller machine and this was followed by the Model AA 12-20 of 1918 that, in turn, was refined into the Model K of 1925.

The huge company, which was based in Rockford, Illinois, was facing financial difficulties in 1928 when it was bought by Case. This acquisition gave Case a boost as it acquired valuable sales territory in the heart of America's corn belt through a well-established dealer network, in addition to a proven line of farm implements.

Case later dropped the Emerson-Brantingham line of tractors but retained many of its implements.

Fendt

One of the simplest tractors available in Germany during the 1930s was the Fendt Dieselross, or "diesel horse". It was little more than a stationary engine equipped with a basic transmission system and wheels. During World War II Fendt was among the German tractor manufacturers that developed gas generator-powered tractors that would burn almost any combustible material in response to the fuel shortages of the war. In the post-war years Fendt reintroduced its Dieselross tractors in different capacities. A 25hp version was powered by an MWM twin-cylinder engine, while a 16hp model used a Deutz engine. Fendt was acquired by the AGCO corporation in 1997.

■ ABOVE RIGHT *A 1928 Fendt machine designed for mowing grass. It is powered by a single cylinder engine fuelled with benzine, and was assembled by Johann Georg Fendt and his son Hermann.*

■ RIGHT *A 1992 four-wheel-drive Fendt Farmer 312 tractor ploughing an English field in heavy conditions.*

■ BELOW *A 1932 Fendt Dieselross with a sidebar mower. This tractor was powered by a 1000cc/60cu in displacement single cylinder Deutz diesel engine.*

FENDT FARMER 312	
Year	1998
Engine	In-line six cylinder turbo diesel
Power	110 PTO hp, 125 BS hp
Transmission	21 forward, 21 reverse
Weight	2363kg/5210lbs

■ ABOVE *A four-wheel-drive Fendt Farmer Turbomatik, working with rollers, during the field cultivation process.*

■ LEFT *The Dieselross name was used by Fendt on several of its tractors. This 1952 model had a diminutive MWM single cylinder diesel engine of 850cc/52cu in displacement, and six forward gears.*

■ BELOW *The Fendt continuously variable transmission (Vario) was first seen on the 600 series tractors in 1988. In 1997 tractors from 170–260hp were fitted with Vario gearboxes. The 714 and 716 were the first smaller Vario tractors launched in 1998.*

■ ABOVE *A 1950s Fendt Farmer 2D diesel tractor with a two axled drawbar trailer, loaded up with logs.*

FERGUSON

The Ferguson tractor evolved from an arrangement made with David Brown and later a partnership between Harry Ferguson and Henry Ford. Originally, Harry Ferguson, who came from Belfast, had installed his innovative three-point hitching system on David Brown tractors. He subsequently made a deal with Henry Ford, through their famous "handshake agreement", although Ford and Ferguson later went their separate ways. This split led to a certain amount of litigation when Ferguson opened his own Detroit factory. The lawsuit which followed suggested that Ford's use of the Ferguson System on its 8N tractors was considered a violation of Harry's patent. The upshot was that Ferguson won

■ ABOVE *The Ferguson-Brown tractor was manufactured in the latter part of the 1930s, through the collaboration of Harry Ferguson and David Brown. Only 1350 tractors were made.*

■ LEFT *A Ferguson TE20 at work in an English field with a Massey-Harris baler. The TE20 went into production in 1946 and became a familiar sight on British farms.*

FERGUSON-BROWN TYPE A	
Year	1936
Engine	Coventry Climax E Series four cylinder
Power	18 – 20hp
Transmission	Three forward, one reverse
Weight	n/k

■ ABOVE *Ferguson tractors, converted to full track configuration for the Commonwealth Expedition to the South Pole in the Antarctic, unloading stores.*

■ BELOW LEFT *Over 300,000 TE20s were manufactured in the production run of the TE20, which paralleled production of the TO20 in the United States.*

■ BELOW *The TE20 was marketed under a slogan that read, "It's what the implement does that sells the tractor". This is a 1949 model.*

■ BELOW *TE20 Fergusons were initially available with a gasoline engine but later diesel and TVO – Tractor Vaporising Oil – versions were made available. This is a 1955 TVO model.*

■ OPPOSITE *A Ferguson TE20 ploughing the fields with a two-bottom Ferguson plough, connected to the tractor by means of Ferguson's revolutionary three-point linkage.*

FORD FERGUSON 9N

Year	1939
Engine	1965cc/120cu in displacement four cylinder
Power	16.31 drawbar and 23.56 belt hp
Transmission	Three speed
Weight	n/k

■ LEFT *A 1951 TED20. At this time production of the TE models was often in excess of 500 per week.*

■ RIGHT *The TE20 inspired great affection and was renowned for its reliability and capacity for hard work.*

■ BOTTOM *This Ferguson TE20 has the original-type, closed centre pattern, agricultural rear tyres fitted. Attached to the three-point linkage is a device for carrying, in this case milk churns.*

damages for patent infringement and loss of business from Ford.

Now on his own, Harry Ferguson set about making his own line of tractors, the TE and TO models. TE was an acronym for Tractor England while TO stood for Tractor Overseas. Both models were not dissimilar to the Fordson 9N but the Ferguson model featured a more powerful engine and a fourth gear ratio. Harry Ferguson came to an arrangement with Sir John Black of the Standard Motor Company in Britain to produce a new tractor in his factory in Coventry. Production started in 1946, using an imported Continental engine. Standard's own engine was substituted when it became available in 1947, with a diesel option being offered in 1951. The first Ferguson was the TE20, referred to as the TO20 in the United States. Over 500,000 TE20s were built in Britain from 1946–56, while some 60,000 TO20s were built in the United States during 1948–51. This tractor – the TE20 – was nicknamed the "Grey Fergy", a reference both to its designer and to its drab paintwork. It became enormously popular, to the extent of

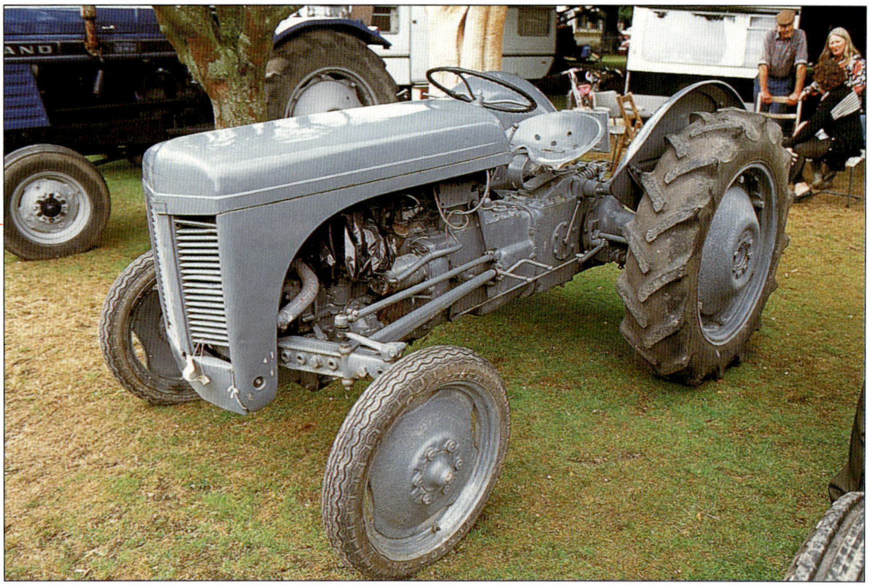

being ubiquitous on British farms. In August 1951, Harry released the TO30 Series, and the TO35, painted beige and metallic green, came out in 1954. Ferguson sold his company to Massey-Harris in 1953.

■ FERGUSON RESEARCH

Harry Ferguson then established Harry Ferguson Research Ltd and experimented with numerous engineering innovations including a four-wheel-drive system for high performance sports cars. A modified version of this later made it into production in the Jensen FF Interceptor.

Ferguson sold his company to the Canadian agricultural company Massey-Harris in 1953. This was a complex deal that saw Ferguson receive $16 million worth of Massey-Harris shares and the company become Massey-Harris-Ferguson for a period. In 1957 Ferguson resigned from involvement with Massey-Harris-Ferguson and sold his share in the company. In 1958 he was working on the possibility of another tractor development in Britain, but partially as a result of the economic trends of the

■ ABOVE *On the Ferguson TE20 the operator sat astride the gearbox, with feet placed on the footpegs to either side of it.*

■ BELOW *This Ferguson 35, intended to be a successor to the TE20, has a front loader and is towing a muck spreader.*

■ RIGHT
Ferguson's revised line of tractors, designed to supersede the TE20s, featured a much more curved hood than earlier models.

■ BELOW LEFT
A Ferguson TE20 tractor awaiting restoration in an English barn. It has been painted a non-standard red at some time.

■ BELOW RIGHT
Harry Ferguson's trademark was his surname in italic script on the top of the grille surround.

FERGUSON TE20

Year	1946
Engine	In-line four cylinder
Power	28hp
Transmission	Four speed
Weight	1 ton 2 cwt/1.12 tonnes

time it came to nothing. Despite this, the Ferguson tractor and the three-point linkage are two of the landmarks in the development of the tractor. The linkage in particular, albeit in a refined form, is the norm throughout the world and still in use on almost every working tractor.

Harry Ferguson then established a consulting engineering company based in Coventry in the West Midlands. This company experimented with numerous engineering innovations including a four-wheel-drive system for high performance Grand Prix cars. The project initially known as the Ferguson Project 99 was eventually developed into a working car and driven by Stirling Moss in 1961.

FIAT

■ LEFT *The Fiat 70-90 is one of four tractors in Fiat's Medium 90 Series that ranges from the 55-90 to the 80-90. The first number in the designation refers to the tractor's power output.*

■ BELOW *Fiat Geotech acquired Ford New Holland Inc and merged into one company – New Holland Inc – during 1993.*

Several of the European nations involved in World War I began to see the value of tractors in increasing farm productivity. In Italy the motor industry undertook experiments with tractors of its own design, and by 1918 the Fiat company had produced a successful tractor known as the 702, while the Pavesi concern introduced an innovative tractor with four-wheel drive and articulated steering.

In 1919 the first mass-produced Fiat tractor, the 702, came off the assembly line. Fiat soon became the major producer of agricultural tractors in Italy and added a crawler to its range in 1932. This was the first tractor that can be considered an earthmoving machine: the 700C was a tractor equipped with a front blade to shift earth and welded devices to load trucks. It was powered by a 30hp four-cylinder engine. Later, but before the outbreak of World War II, Fiat produced the 708C and Model 40.

After the war, in 1950, Fiat launched the Fiat 55, a crawler tractor powered by a 6500cc/396cu in, four-cylinder diesel engine that produced 55hp at 1400rpm. The transmission incorporated a central pair of bevel gears with final drive by means of spur gears. The crawler tractor had five forward speeds and one reverse. The customer could specify whether they wanted lever or steering-wheel steering. The 6 volt electrical system functioned without a battery and was reliant on a 90 watt dynamo.

In 1962 Fiat created a joint venture with the Turkish company Koa Holding in Ankara, that was known as Türk Traktor. By 1966 Fiat had created its own Tractor and Earthmoving Machinery

FIAT 70-90

Year	1986
Engine	3613cc/220cu in
Power	70hp
Transmission	n/k
Weight	n/k

■ BELOW LEFT *Like the 90 Series, the 94 models from Fiat are a range of tractors with increasing power outputs. This four-wheel-drive 88-94 model is rated at 88hp.*

■ LEFT *A Fiat combine harvester at work during the harvest. Under the Fiatagri group Fiat produced Laverda combines and Hesston forage harvesters.*

Division. This was developed until 1970 when Fiat Macchine e Movimento Terra SpA was founded and carried on the company's activities in the earthmoving sector in its new plant in Lecce, Italy. Shortly afterwards, the new company took over Simit, then the leading Italian manufacturer of hydraulic excavators. In 1974 Fiat Macchine e Movimento Terra entered into a joint venture with the American tractor manufacturer Allis-Chalmers to form Fiat-Allis. In Italy Fiat Trattori SpA was also founded and in 1975 Fiat Trattori became a shareholder of Laverda. In 1977 Fiat Trattori acquired Hesston, as a way of gaining entry into the North American market, and later took over Agrifull, which specialized in the production of small and medium-sized tractors. In 1983 Fiat Trattori entered another joint venture when it combined with the Pakistan Tractor Corporation to pursue a joint venture in Karachi, Pakistan which became known as Al Ghazi Tractors Ltd.

In 1984 Fiat Trattori became Fiatagri, Fiat Group's holding company for the agricultural machinery sector. Things changed again in 1988 when all of Fiat-Allis and Fiatagri's activities were merged to form a new farm and earthmoving machinery company, FiatGeotech. FiatGeotech acquired Benati in 1991, which was later merged with Fiat-Hitachi. Fiat also acquired Ford New Holland Inc and merged it with FiatGeotech. The new company became New Holland Inc in 1993, and part of CNH and Fiat Industrial in 1999.

■ RIGHT *A Fiat F100 tractor at work. The four-wheel-drive tractor is towing a trailer laden with circular bales previously harvested.*

FORD

In 1907 the Ford Motor Company built the prototype of what it hoped was to become the world's first mass-produced agricultural tractor. The machine was based around components – including the transmission – from one of Ford's earliest cars. As Henry Ford had grown up on his father's farm, he was aware of the labour-intensive nature of farm work and was keen to develop mechanized ways of doing things. As a result, Ford built his first tractor in 1915, and by 1916 he had a number of working prototypes being evaluated. His aim was to sell to farmers a two-plough tractor for as little as $200, and to do for farmers and farming what the Model T Ford had done for motoring.

With a number of staff, Ford designed what would later become the Fordson Model F. Its secret was its stressed cast-iron frame construction. This frame contained all the moving parts in dustproof and oiltight units, which eliminated many of the weaknesses of early tractors. It had four wheels and was compact. This gave it an unusual appearance at a time when both three-wheeled and massive tractors were the norm.

■ FORDSON MODEL F

The Fordson Model F, Ford's first mass-produced tractor, went into production in 1917. Power came from an in-line four-cylinder gasoline engine that produced 20hp at 1000rpm. A three-speed transmission was fitted with a multiplate clutch that ran in oil and the final drive was by means of a worm gear. The ignition utilized a flywheel-mounted dynamo to supply high tension current to the coil that was positioned on the engine block. The tractor retailed at $750: this was more expensive than Henry Ford had predicted, but the reputation earned by his Model T car ensured that the new tractors sold in large numbers.

Ford's prototypes, seen in action at a tractor trial in Great Britain, were considered a practical proposition and the British government requested that they be put into production immediately to assist with winning the war. Ford was preparing to do exactly that when, in the early summer of 1917, German bombers attacked London in daylight. The Government viewed this new development in the war as a serious one and decided to turn all available

■ LEFT *The Fordson F and N models were the most important tractors in the history of mechanized farming and brought benefits of tractors to a massive number of farmers.*

■ RIGHT *A group of farmers with a Roadless Traction converted E27N Fordson Major tractor.*

FORDSON TRACTOR

Year	1917
Engine	In-line four cylinder gasoline
Power	20hp
Transmission	Three speed
Weight	1225kg/2700lbs

■ OPPOSITE TOP *A restored example of a 1937 Fordson Model N. Fordson built them in Dagenham, England from 1933.*

■ ABOVE LEFT *The Fordson E27N Major was Ford's first new post-war tractor, and production started in March 1945 at Ford's Dagenham plant in England.*

■ ABOVE *The Fordson Major looked bigger and better than the Fordson Model N. A redesigned clutch, and a spiral bevel and differential drive featured in the new model.*

■ ABOVE *The E27N Major proved popular, and production soared to a peak of 50,000 made in 1948. Many were exported and production continued until 1951.*

■ LEFT *The Fordson Model N assisted Britain's war effort by helping the country grow a much higher percentage of its food requirements than previously.*

■ LEFT *The 1939 Ford Ferguson 9N was innovative because of its hydraulically controlled integral implement hitch. Rubber tyres, electric starter and a PTO were standard.*

■ ABOVE *Harry Ferguson's surname appeared on the Ford 9N as he devised the three-point implement hitch, linked to a hydraulic system.*

■ ABOVE *The Ford 9N sold well. As early as the end of 1940 more than 35,000 had been built and Ferguson's system led other manufacturers to reconsider the hitching of implements.*

■ BELOW *The English Fordson Super Major of the early 1960s, built on the success of the "new" Fordson Major that replaced the E27N Major in 1952.*

industrial production over to the manufacture of fighter aeroplanes in order to combat the German bombers. Ford was asked if he could manufacture his tractors in the United States instead. He agreed and only four months later Fordson F Models were being produced.

While this was only a temporary setback, the delay and shift in production caused Ford another problem. His plans for his new tractor became public knowledge before the tractors themselves were actually in production, and another company tried to pre-empt his success. In Minneapolis the Ford Tractor Company was set up, using the surname of one of their engineers. The rival tractor produced from this shortlived company was not a great success, but it deprived Henry Ford of the right to use his own name on his tractors. He resorted to the next best

■ BELOW *The Fordson Dexta was a Perkins, three-cylinder, diesel-engined tractor introduced in 1958 to give Fordson dealers a small, low-priced tractor to sell.*

■ LEFT *The Ford 8N was introduced in 1948 after the collapse of the agreement made by Henry Ford and Harry Ferguson.*

■ LEFT *The blue and orange Fordsons were a familiar sight in British fields during the 1950s and 1960s as this one in Hampshire indicates.*

■ BELOW *Ford celebrated its golden anniversary in 1953 and redesigned its tractors for the occasion. By 1955 the three plough 600 Series was on sale, with a redesigned grille, and red and grey colour scheme.*

thing: Henry Ford and Son, shortened to Fordson.

The Model F immediately proved popular and US sales increased exponentially from the 35,000 achieved in 1918. By 1922, Fordsons were accounting for approximately 70 per cent of all US tractor sales. By this time the post-war boom in tractor sales had ended. Ford survived by cutting the price of his tractors but his major competitors, notably International Harvester, did the same and the competition became fierce. By 1928 IH had regained the lead in sales and had achieved 47 per cent of the market total.

■ CHANGING FACTORIES

In 1919 production of the Fordson tractor had begun in Cork, Ireland. This was the first tractor to be manufactured simultaneously in the United States and Europe. Production of Fordson tractors in the United States ended in 1928 in the face of major competition from IH and in 1929 all Ford's tractor manufacturing was transferred to Ireland. In 1933 production of Fordson tractors was moved again, this time to Dagenham in England. From Ford's Dagenham factory,

■ RIGHT *The Ford Workmaster series of tractors went on sale in 1959 with a choice of gasoline, diesel or liquid petroleum gas engines. This is a 1960 601 model.*

Fordsons were exported around the world, including back to the USA. Ford produced the All Around row crop tractor in Britain specifically for the USA in 1936. The Fordson was the first foreign tractor tested in Nebraska at the noted Nebraska Tractor Tests, to which it was submitted in both 1937 and 1938. Another Fordson plant was based in the USSR where production was halted in 1932 when the factory switched to making a Soviet copy of the Universal Farmall. Production of Fordson tractors was later restarted in the USA during the 1940s.

The next important innovation – one of the most important in the history of the tractor – was the introduction of the three-point system in the late 1930s. It was to be introduced on Ford's 9N model, having been designed by Harry Ferguson, and is still used on farm tractors today. This ingenious system, combined with a variety of compatible three-point implements, made the tractor a viable replacement for the horse and horse-drawn implements. Ferguson demonstrated the system to Ford in Michigan in autumn 1938 and through the famous "handshake agreement", by which each man's word was considered sufficient to seal the business partnership, production began. At that time the three-point hitch was known as the Ferguson System and was produced in cooperation with the Ferguson-Sherman Company until 1946.

■ LEFT *This row crop 961 diesel tractor from 1959 is one of the first Ford tractors to have an American-made diesel engine.*

■ BELOW LEFT *A 601 Ford Workmaster, made in 1961, the same year as Ford introduced its largest tractor until then – the five plough 66hp Model 6000.*

The Model 9N was first demonstrated in Dearborn, Michigan, on 29 June 1939. This new agricultural concept revolutionized farming. The basic design principles and features incorporated into the 9N are still evident in many of the tractors currently being manufactured. The Ford 9N, the first of the N Series

■ BELOW *The Ford Workmaster models were offered with a choice of engine types. The Model 501 Offset Workmaster increased the versatility of the Ford range.*

■ BELOW *In Britain, Ford tractors, such as this 1962 Ford 5000 diesel, were painted in shades of blue rather than the red and grey favoured in the United States.*

tractors, went on sale complete with the first three-point hitch in 1939. It was developed as a versatile all-purpose tractor for the small farm and was exceedingly popular. The 9N was powered by an in-line four-cylinder 1966cc/120cu in displacement gasoline engine. Many of the engine's internal components, including the pistons, were compatible with parts used in Ford's V8 automobile of the time.

The 9N went through subtle changes during each year of its three-year production run. For example, in 1939 the grille had almost horizontal bars and the steering box, grille, battery box, hood, instrument panel and transmission cover were made of cast aluminium. It also had clip-on radiator and fuel caps, which were changed in 1940 to a hinged

■ BELOW LEFT *The gasoline engine used in the Ford Powermaster models between 1958 and 1961 was this 2820cc/172cu in displacement in-line four-cylinder unit.*

■ BELOW RIGHT *The 861 Powermaster, in its gasoline-engined form.*

FORD 6610 TRACTOR	
Year	1983
Engine	In-line four cylinder diesel
Power	86hp (64 kW)
Transmission	Eight forward, four reverse
Weight	n/k

■ LEFT *A Ford 5000 tractor being used with a specialized implement for the unusual, but highly colourful, task of harvesting tulips.*

type. In 1941 the grille was changed to steel with vertical bars, and many other changes were also made. By the end of 1941 Ford had made so many changes, and had so many more ideas for changes, that the designation of the tractor was changed to the Ford 2N. There were over 99,000 9Ns produced from 1939 to 1942 and almost 200,000 2Ns produced between 1942 and 1947. The 9N's selling price in 1939 was $585, including rubber tyres, an electrical system with a starter, generator and battery, and a power take-off. Headlights and a rear tail-light were optional extras.

The Ford 2N had a relatively short production run. New features incorporated in its design included an enlarged cooling fan contained within a shroud, a pressurized radiator and, eventually, sealed-beam headlights. Other changes were made here and there as a result of the constraints imposed by the war. For a while, only steel wheels were available because of the rubber shortage caused by Japanese conquests in Asia, and a magneto ignition system was used rather than a battery. When the war ended things reverted to what had been available before. Ford had made 140,000 Model N tractors in England during the war years.

■ LEFT *A Ford TW20, with a large disc harrow, in a Colorado farmyard. The TW20 is one of the high-powered TW range made in American plants.*

■ BELOW LEFT *A four-wheel-drive Ford 5095 tractor. This model has been additionally protected by the installation of tubular steel bars that extend over the cab for protection during forestry work.*

■ LEFT ***During the 1980s Ford manufactured its 10 series of tractors at Basildon in Essex, England, one of its eight plants. The 10 series consisted of 11 tractors ranging from 44 to 115hp.***

■ ABOVE RIGHT ***A 1972 diesel-engined Ford 7000 tractor, finished in the distinctive colour scheme that had become standard.***

The Ford 2N eventually evolved into the Ford 8N, a model that officially started its production run in 1947 and was to last until 1952. 1947 was also the year that the much-vaunted handshake agreement on the three-point hitch came to an end. Ford and Ferguson failed to reach an agreement when they tried to renegotiate their deal in the immediate post-war years. Ford declared he would continue using the hitch, but would no longer give Harry Ferguson any money for doing so, nor would he continue to call it the "Ferguson System". As few official business documents existed this resulted in a lawsuit which eventually awarded Harry Ferguson approximately $10 million.

By the time the lengthy lawsuit was finally settled, however, some of Ferguson's patents had expired, enabling Ford to continue production of a hydraulic three-point hitch with only minimal changes. Ferguson then started producing the TE20 and TO20 tractors, in Britain and America respectively, that were similar in appearance to the 8N and effectively competed with it.

A completely new line of implements was introduced by Ford. Some of the noticeable differences between the 8N and 2N tractors were the change in wheelnuts from six to eight in the rear wheels, a scripted Ford logo on the fenders and sides of the bonnet and finally, the absence of the Ferguson System logo which was no longer displayed under the Ford oval even though the tractor still used Ferguson's three-point hitch.

Ford's first new post-war tractor made in Dagenham was the Fordson E27N. It was rushed into production at the request of the British Ministry of

■ LEFT ***The Ford 4110 is one of Ford's English-manufactured, standardized range of 10 Series tractors. A mid-range tractor, its power output is in the region of 50hp.***

■ RIGHT *A Ford tractor, with a seed drill, planting peas. The tractor has dual wheels, front and rear, to reduce soil compaction.*

Agriculture. The basis of the machine was an upgraded Fordson N engine with a three forward, one reverse gearbox, a conventional clutch and rear axle drive. The Fordson E27N started rolling off the Dagenham production line in March 1945. Ford had made numerous improvements to this tractor over its earlier model. The new tractor featured a spiral bevel and conventional differential instead of a worm drive and a single-plate wet clutch was incorporated. The E27N was powered by an in-line four-cylinder side-valve engine that produced 30hp at 1450rpm. It came in four versions, each with different specifications for brakes, tyres and gear ratios. A variant using a Perkins engine was offered in 1948, and in that year over 50,000 E27Ns were made. Production continued until 1951, with various upgrades and options being made available. These included electrics, hydraulics and a diesel-engined version.

Ford's 50th Anniversary was in 1953 and in that year it introduced the Model NAA Jubilee. This was Ford's first overhead-valve engined tractor; it had a displacement of 2195cc/134cu in and produced 31hp. In 1958 Ford introduced the 600 and 800 Series tractors, powered by American-made diesel engines, although gasoline and LPG versions were also offered. These were followed by ranges of tractors known as Powermaster and Workmaster. The Model 8000 was the first Ford tractor to have a 100hp engine, displacing 6571cc/401cu in, while the smaller displacement Model 6000 produced 66hp.

■ RIGHT *The limited slip differential in the front axle of a four-wheel-drive Ford 6810 tractor engages automatically in difficult conditions when it senses wheel spin.*

■ CONSOLIDATION

The Basildon factory was one of eight manufacturing plants around the world and most famous for its 10 series tractors. The 11 tractor range spanned from the 44hp 2910 to the 115hp 8210. The most popular 100hp 7810 tractor was produced in a special silver livery to celebrate the Queen's Silver Jubilee in 1990. Only a small number of tractors were built and now they have become very desirable. In 1991 the Fiat Company acquired Ford New Holland Inc and merged it with FiatGeotech renaming

the company NH Geotech. The 40 series was first introduced in 1992 to replace the 10 series and was produced right up to 1998 at Basildon. The 35 series was seen a few years later replacing the smaller models in the range, and the larger 70 series appeared as well. The Versatile Farm Equipment Company became part of Ford New Holland Americas and NH Geotech changed its name to New Holland Inc in 1993. The Ford name was used up to 2001, when the tractors became known as New Holland.

■ TOP *There were many Ford conversions throughout the seventies and eighties. The most impressive was this 188hp County 1884 which was produced in very limited numbers.*

■ ABOVE *A four-wheel-drive Ford tractor, with a towed crop spraying unit, at work in Wiltshire, England. The tractor is equipped with weights at the front to improve traction.*

■ LEFT *The Doe Triple D was manufactured by Ernest Doe and Sons of Maldon in Essex, UK. The principle of connecting two Ford tractors was first seen in 1958 and around 350 tractors were produced by 1965.*

OTHER MAKES

(Frazier, Gleaner, Hanomag, Hart-Parr, Hesston, HSCS, Hurlimann)

■ FRAZIER

Frazier was a small specialist company based outside York in England, and was typical of many companies which produced specialized farming machines. The IID Agribuggy was assembled from a number of proprietary components including axles, suspension and engines, and was intended as the basis for tasks such as crop-spraying and fertilizer spreading. The machines were purpose-built and offered in both diesel and petrol forms. The diesel variant was powered by a four-cylinder Ford engine of 1608cc/98cu in displacement. Their Agribuggy was designed to be adaptable, and was available in both low ground pressure and row crop variants.

■ LEFT *A pair of Frazier IID Agribuggies. The Agribuggy is designed as a low ground pressure machine for specialist tasks.*

■ LEFT *An Agribuggy with low ground pressure tyres designed to minimize soil compaction.*

■ GLEANER

Gleaner has been a manufacturer of combine harvesters for more than 85 years. At the turn of the millenium the company offered a range of four rotary combine models as well as the C62 conventional combine, all of which are powered by Cummins liquid-cooled engines. The Gleaner rotary combines were designated as the R Series, while the C62 was a conventional combine harvester.

The R42 Gleaner Class 4 combine had a 6200 litre/170 bushel grain tank and a 450 litre/100 gallon fuel tank, with a 185hp Cummins engine. The R52 Gleaner Class 5 combine had a standard 8200 litre/225 bushel or optional 8900 litre/245 bushel grain tank. Its polyurethane fuel tank has a capacity of 450 litres/100 gallons. A 225hp Cummins engine is fitted.

The R62 Gleaner Class 6 combine offered a 260hp in-line six-cylinder engine, and had as standard an 8200 litre/225 bushel bin or as an option a 10,900 litre/300 bushel grain tank. The R62 offered accelerator rolls, chaff spreader, two distribution augers and a 680 litre/150 gallon fuel tank. The R72 Gleaner was at the time the only Class 7 combine built in North America. It featured a 12,000 litre/330 bushel grain tank and a 300hp in-line six-cylinder engine. The R72 included two distribution augers, accelerator rolls, a chaff spreader and a 680 litre/150 gallon fuel tank.

The C62 conventional combine harvester had a 10,900 litre/300 bushel grain bin and a high-capacity, turret unloading system that delivered grain into trucks and carts at a rate of 80 litres/2.2 bushels per second.

Currently there are two rotary models, the 314hp S67, a Class 6 combine, and the Class 7 S77, producing 370hp. Both are driven by an AGCO SISU in-line six-cylinder diesel engine, liquid-cooled and turbocharged. Both models have as standard a 13,750 litre/390 bushel grain tank and can carry 680 litres/150 gallons of fuel.

Gleaner is part of the AGCO Corporation – indeed AGCO is a acronym for the Allis-Gleaner Corporation.

■ BOTTOM LEFT *Gleaner is now part of the AGCO corporation. This is the S77 model.*

■ LEFT *As can be seen from this 1967 Gleaner CR combine, provision for the operator has progressed considerably in only thirty years. Air conditioned, dust-proofed cabs are now standard.*

■ **HANOMAG**

The German company Hanomag of Hanover was offering a massive six-furrow motor plough at the outbreak of World War I. It was, like other German machines of the time, intended for the plains of Germany. In the years after the war it offered a larger version with an eight-furrow plough and an 80hp four-cylinder gasoline engine. By the 1930s Hanomag was thriving, partially as a result of exports of both its crawler and wheeled machines. In 1930 it offered the R38 and R50 wheeled models and the K50 crawler. All were diesel-powered and featured a power take-off.

Hanomag contributed to the German war effort and its factories suffered extensive damage. The company resumed production of tractors in the late 1940s and offered the four-cylinder diesel R25, finished in red. A Hanomag twin-cylinder diesel engine was later incorporated in the European versions of the Massey-Harris Pony, built in France. Hanomag continued to offer its R-range of tractors, including the small R12 and R24 Models alongside larger R45 and R55 Models, through the 1960s.

A change of ownership of the company in 1971 resulted in the cessation of all tractor manufacture.

■ LEFT *Hanomag had success with export sales of both wheeled and crawler tractors during the 1930s.*

■ ABOVE *A four-wheel-drive Hanomag 35D hydraulic loader, working on corn silage in England.*

OTHER MAKES

■ HART-PARR

Charles Hart and Charles Parr were engineering students together at the University of Wisconsin and graduated in 1896. They formed a company in Madison, Wisconsin to build stationary engines. These were unusual in that they used oil rather than water for cooling, which was an asset in areas that suffered harsh winters. As oil freezes at a considerably lower temperature than water, damage to engines caused by freezing coolant could thereby be avoided. Hart and Parr moved to Charles City, Iowa in 1901 and made their first tractor in 1902. The Model 18–30 followed it in 1903. This had a distinctive rectangular cooling tower which then became a distinguishing feature of all Hart-Parr tractors for the next 15 years. The cooling system circulated the oil around vertical tubes within the tower and air flow through it was maintained by directing the exhaust gases into the tower. The engine was rated at 30hp and was of a two-cylinder horizontal design with a large displacement that operated at around 300rpm. The 17–30 was a further development, and this was followed by numerous others, including the 12–27 Oil King.

■ LEFT *Hart-Parr became the Oliver Farm Equipment Corporation of Chicago in a merger of 1929.*

■ BELOW LEFT *Early Hart-Parr tractors were characterized by the rectangular cooling tower.*

Hart-Parr redesigned its machinery for the boom after World War I. The 12–25 was one of the new models and featured a horizontal twin-cylinder engine. Later these tractors were offered with an engine-driven power take-off, but the full import of this advance was not realized until later. Oliver acquired Hart-Parr in 1929.

■ HESSTON

In 1947 the Hesston company was founded in Kansas, United States. It became a respected manufacturer of hay and forage machinery, recognized for its innovative products and with industrial and marketing offshoots in Europe. In 1977 Fiat Trattori took over Hesston in order to gain entry into the North American agricultural machinery market. In 1988 all of Fiat-Allis and Fiatagri's activities were merged to form a new company, FiatGeotech, Fiat's group farm and earthmoving machinery sector. As part of this restructuring Hesston and Braud joined forces in a new company, Hesston-Braud, based in Coex, France.

■ HSCS

Hofherr, Schrantz, Clayton and Shuttleworth was formed in Hungary after Clayton and Shuttleworth's withdrawal from the steam traction engine market in that country. Initially the company's headquarters was in Kispest but it later moved to Budapest. The company started making gasoline engines in 1919, leading to the production of its first tractor in 1923. This used a single-cylinder gasoline engine for its motive power and was assembled around a steel frame. Production versions of the HSCS tractor used single semi-diesel engines, a configuration that was popular in much of Europe but not in the UK nor the United States. The perceived advantages of the semi-diesel engine are that it is mechanically simple and will run on almost any type of fuel, including waste oil. The HSCS engine was rated at 14hp and was intended for ploughing and as a source of stationary power.

The company persevered with semi-diesels throughout the production of numerous wheeled and crawler tractors. An HSCS tractor competed in the 1930 World Tractor Trials held in Britain.

In 1951, under the auspices of the communist regime, the company name was changed to Red Star Tractor. From 1960 onwards the products were sold under the

DUTRA brand name – an amalgamation of the words "Dumper" and "Tractor", representing the company's product range. Tractors were exported to other eastern bloc countries and beyond. Later the company produced RABA-Steiger tractors under licence from Steiger.

■ HURLIMANN

Hurlimann tractors reflect the farming conditions peculiar to Switzerland, a small mountainous country. It has little room suited to the production of arable crops and Hans Hurlimann started in business to build tractors suited to the country. His first machine used a single cylinder gasoline engine, and was fitted with a power bar grass mower.

The first tractors were considered to be old fashioned but development work and upgrades through the 1930s led to a new model introduced in 1939. This was fitted with a direct injection, four-cylinder diesel engine and led to Hurlimann exporting tractors, and selling them to the Swiss military as gun tractors. These tractors proved popular, and another new model – the D-100 – was introduced in 1945.

The D-100 was equipped with a PTO, two speed belt pulley and a differential lock. It also featured both hand and foot throttles and a five speed transmission. The tractor produced 45hp at 1600rpm, and had a low centre of gravity achieved by the use of 56cm/22in diameter rear wheels. Hurlimann continued exporting tractors and later became part of the Italian Same company.

■ TOP RIGHT *A Hungarian-manufactured HSCS tractor from the 1940s. HSCS stood for Hofherr Schrantz Clayton and Shuttleworth.*

■ RIGHT *A Hurlimann S200 tractor manufactured during the 1970s. Hurlimann was one of several Swiss tractor makers at the time.*

■ RIGHT *Hurlimann's D-100 was acknowledged as a well-engineered tractor retaining a low centre of gravity through the fitment of smaller than normal diameter rear wheels.*

■ ABOVE *Hurlimann used a diesel engine in its 1930s tractors, supplied to the Swiss Army as gun tractors.*

INTERNATIONAL HARVESTER

■ BELOW *The Farmall series became popular during the 1930s, when pneumatic tyres were still only available as an extra-cost option. The range included the F-12, F-20 and F-30 models.*

The International Harvester Corporation was formed in 1902 through the merger of two small tractor makers, McCormick and Deering.

The history of International Harvester really began in 1831, when Cyrus McCormick invented a reaper which quickly became known as the "Cornbinder". The fledgling IH at first marketed two ranges of tractors, the Mogul and Titan models. The former was sold by McCormick dealers and the latter by Deering dealers. The first IH tractors appeared in 1906 when the Type A gasoline tractor was marketed with a choice of 12, 15 and 20hp engines. The Type B soon followed and lasted until 1916. IH was noted for its production of the giant 45hp Mogul tractor during the second decade of the 20th century. It followed this in 1919 with the Titan, a 22hp machine. International Harvester also produced light trucks alongside its tractors.

During World War I many American tractors were exported to Great Britain and International Harvester Corporation marketed the models from its range that were considered most suited to British conditions. These were the Titan 10–20 and the Mogul 8–16.

■ TITAN 10–20

The International Harvester Titan 10–20 was built in the Milwaukee, Wisconsin factory and was the smallest and most popular model in the Titan range. Mogul tractors were built in parallel in the Chicago, Illinois factory. Production of the 10–20 started in 1914 and lasted for

■ RIGHT *The F-12 tractor had a four-cylinder engine that operated at 1400rpm.*

■ LEFT *The Farmall F-12 was introduced in 1932. It was a row crop tractor, rated as a one to two plough tractor. One benefit was its infinitely adjustable rear hubs.*

FARMALL F-20

Year	1932
Engine	Four cylinder
Power	16.12 drawbar and 24.13 belt hp
Transmission	Four speed
Weight	n/k

■ **RIGHT** *The Farmall M was introduced in 1939 as a row crop tractor styled by Raymond Loewy. It was to become one of the classic American tractors of all time.*

■ **BELOW LEFT** *The switch from grey to red paint was made in 1936 but rubber tyres were available prior to this as this tricycle row crop model suggests.*

■ **BELOW MIDDLE** *Pneumatic tyres were offered for both the front and rear of the Farmall row crop models as seen on this tractor at a South Dakota vintage rally.*

■ **BELOW RIGHT** *Dwayne Mathies on the Farmall row crop tractor bought new by his family for their South Dakota, USA farm. Four generations of Mathies have now sat astride it.*

a decade because the simplicity of the design ensured a reputation for reliability. The 10–20 was powered by a paraffin-fuelled, twin-cylinder engine of large displacement that achieved 20hp at only 575rpm. The engine was cooled by water contained in a cylindrical 180 litre/40 gallon tank positioned over the front wheels. The Titan 10–10 was assembled on a steel girder frame. It was chain driven and had a two-speed transmission. More than 78,000 were made and it was one of several models of tractor that were to carry the company into the 1920s. Others produced in that decade included the 8–16, the 15–30 and the Farmall Regular.

■ IH 8–16 TRACTOR

The International Harvester 8–16 was produced in the United States during World War I and proved popular. It had a distinctive appearance, with a sloping hood over the engine and radiator. Production commenced in 1917 and lasted until 1922. The design, although inspired by the IH truck line, was old-fashioned at the time of its introduction as it was based on a separate frame and featured chain and sprocket final drive. However, the availability of a power take-off as an optional extra gave the 8–16 an advantage over its competitors as the tractor could be used to drive other machinery. While IH could not claim to have invented the PTO (it had been used on a British Scott tractor in 1904) it was the first company to have commercial success with the innovation. IH made it a standard fitting on its

■ **LEFT** *The Farmall F-14 replaced the F-12 in 1938. It was a slight upgrade of the earlier model with an engine that operated at 1650rpm and made 14.84 drawbar and 17.44 belt hp at Nebraska.*

■ RIGHT *It was industrial designer Raymond Loewy who gave the Farmall tractors the horizontal barred grille and rounded radiator grille shell during the 1930s.*

■ BELOW *Diesel engines were another innovation introduced to the Farmall range during the 1930s.*

McCormick-Deering 15-30 tractor introduced in 1921.

As the initial post-war wave of prosperity subsided in the early 1920s, Ford cut its prices to keep sales up and, faced with this competition, IH offered a plough at no extra cost with each tractor it sold. This had the effect of shifting all IH stock, allowing the company to introduce the 15–30 and 10–20 models in 1921 and 1923 respectively. These machines were to give Ford competition in a way that that company had not experienced before. The new IH models were constructed in a similar way to the Fordson, around a stressed cast frame, but incorporated a few details that gave them the edge on the Fordson. These included a magneto ignition, a redesigned clutch and a built-in PTO, setting a new standard for tractors.

■ MCCORMICK-DEERING

The International Harvester 10–20 of 1923 was said to offer "sturdy reliability" and power, and it went on to become an outstanding success in the United States where it was generally known as the McCormick-Deering 10–20. It remained in production until 1942, by which time 216,000 machines had been sold. The styling of the 10–20 owed a lot to the larger 15–30: both models were powered by an in-line four-cylinder petrol and paraffin engine with overhead valves that were designed for long usage with replaceable cylinder liners. A crawler version of the 10-20 was unveiled in 1928 and was the first crawler produced by International Harvester; known as the TracTracTor, it was to become the T-20 in 1931.

In 1924 the company progressed further with the introduction of the Farmall, the first proper row crop tractor. It could be used for ploughing but could also turn its capabilities to cultivation.

■ ABOVE *The Farmall M was offered on pneumatic tyres as standard at the time of its introduction, although steel wheels were a lower cost option. An electric starter and lights were also optional extras.*

■ LEFT *A mix of famous brands as a red Farmall row crop ploughs using a two-furrow plough in the familiar yellow and green colour scheme that shows it was made by John Deere.*

It was suitable for use along rows of cotton, corn and other crops. It was refined and redesigned for the 1930s, when the Farmall Regular became one of a range of three models as the F-20, with the F-12 and F-30. These machines were similar but had different capacities.

In 1929 the 15–30 had become the 22–36 and was subsequently replaced by the W-30 in 1934. The 10–20 had a long production run, being made until 1939. IH dropped its hitherto traditional grey paint scheme during the 1930s and replaced it with red. The effect of this was twofold: first, it allowed the tractors to be more visible to other motorists as they became more widely used on public roads; secondly they were more noticeable to potential buyers. In the USSR at Kharkov and Stalingrad the International Harvester 15-30 went into production as the SKhTZ 15-30 and engines based on Caterpillar units were produced at Chelabinsk in the Ural Region.

The first IH wheeled, diesel-powered tractor appeared in 1934, designated the WD-40. It was powered by a four-cylinder engine and the numerical suffix referred to its power, in the region of 44bhp. The engine was slightly unorthodox in that it was started on petrol and once warm switched to diesel through the closure of a valve.

■ ABOVE LEFT *Later International Harvesters were fitted with additional equipment such as the front loader on this Farmall model.*

■ ABOVE RIGHT *A restored example of the Farmall Super FC-D tractor. It retains the adjustable rear wheel spacing and the streamlined Raymond Loewy design.*

■ BELOW *This Farmall M is the tricycle row crop type and is fitted with a hydraulic front loader.*

■ THE W-MODELS

The International Harvester W6 was announced in 1940 as part of a range of new tractors. The range also included the W4 and W9 models and all were powered by an in-line four-cylinder engine that produced 36.6hp when running on gasoline and slightly less on paraffin. A diesel version was designated the WD6.

■ LEFT *The Farmall A was also new in 1939, it was a small machine with adjustable tread front wheels and an engine and transmission offset to the left of the tractor.*

■ RIGHT *Clearly visible on this standard tractor is the steering arrangement to the front axle and the infinitely adjustable rear track by means of the splined hubs.*

■ RIGHT *The International 584 tractor, seen with a muck spreader on an English winter's day.*

■ BELOW *The International 955 was a four-wheel-drive model, made before Tenneco Inc merged Case and International Harvester.*

In the late 1930s the industrial designer Raymond Loewy redesigned IH's trademark before moving on to deal with the appearance of the company's range of tractors. It was he who gave them their rounded radiator grille with horizontal slots. The new styling initially appeared on the crawler tractors but soon after the Farmall M models were restyled in the same way.

During World War II IH manufactured a range of machinery for the war effort, including half-track vehicles for the allied armies. The company produced more than 13,000 International M-5 half-tracks at its Springfield plant. It also made a number of "essential use" pick-ups for civilians who required transport in order to assist the war effort.

■ RIGHT *International Harvesters from different decades. International Harvester suffered during the United States farm crisis of the early 1980s.*

■ BELOW *Hay bales being loaded by hand on to a farm trailer on a Yorkshire Dales farm in England.*

■ OVERSEAS OPERATION

The W6 was improved in the first years of the 1950s, when the model was redesignated as the Super W6 and Super M, from International Harvester and Farmall respectively. The bore was increased slightly to give the tractors an extra 10hp. The more established American tractor manufacturers quickly added new models to their ranges in the immediate post-war years and IH was no exception. The company replaced the Model A with the Super A, which gained a hydraulic rear-lift attachment as hydraulics began to be more widely used.

In the post-war years IH was one of the three large American tractor manufacturers to establish factories in Britain. It opened a factory in Doncaster,

■ RIGHT *International Harvester still manufacture harvesting machinery including combine harvesters such as these.*

■ FAR RIGHT TOP *The Farmall Cub was the smallest tractor in the range, built throughout the years between 1949 and 1979.*

■ FAR RIGHT MIDDLE *A 1965 International Cub.*

South Yorkshire, while Allis-Chalmers opted for Hampshire and Massey-Harris for Manchester, although it moved to Kilmarnock, Scotland in 1949. IH was the only company to have noteworthy commercial success, assembling the Farmall M for the British market.

■ DIESEL TECHNOLOGY

In 1959 the American tractor manufacturers adopted industry standards for the increasingly popular three-point hitches to make farm implements more versatile by increasing their interchangeability between makes. To meet this standard, IH offered new tractors for 1960 – the 404 and 504 models – that offered the first American-designed, draught-sensing three-point hitch. The 504 also came with power steering while both models featured dry air cleaners and a means of cooling the hydraulic fluid. The 1960s saw increasing refinements made to the diesel engine as turbochargers and intercoolers were developed. IH embraced the new technology and developed better transmissions and four-wheel-drive systems as farming became more mechanized. By the 1970s the Farmall 966 was a 100hp machine with 16 forward and two reverse gears and a 6784cc/414cu in displacement engine.

The economic crisis of the early 1980s was to have far-reaching consequences within the American agricultural industry. International Harvester was a casualty of the recession. In the 1980 financial year the company's losses exceeded $3,980 million and the following year they were similarly high. In 1982 the situation worsened as losses totalled more than $1.6 billion. Despite this catastrophe the losses were reduced to $485 million for 1983, but IH could not survive. In 1984 Tenneco Inc, which already controlled Case, bought IH's agricultural products division and formed Case IH.

■ RIGHT *The IH 2+2 pivot design first appeared in 1979 with the launch of the 3388 and 3588 tractors. The tractors used an IH 466 turbocharged engine producing 160hp and 180hp respectively.*

JCB

■ BELOW *A JCB 1115 Fastrac, spreading granular fertilizer from an Amazone N1209 spreader. The 1115 produces 115hp and can haul as much as a 24 tonne gross train weight.*

The British plant manufacturer JCB currently produces a comprehensive range of machines including the famous "digger", with a front loader and backhoe. JCB also produces wheeled and tracked excavators. It is the company's range of crawler tractors, the Fastracs, that are wholly designed for agricultural applications.

■ JCB FASTRAC

The JCB Fastrac is a modern high-speed tractor. The Fastrac features a unique all-round suspension system and a spacious ROPS (rollover protective structure) and FOPS (falling objects protective structure) cab with air-conditioning and passenger seat as standard. It has four equal-sized wheels. The Fastrac has a three-point implement mounting position and the optional JCB Quadtronic four-wheel steering system is available on the 2000 series Fastrac models. This automatically switches between two-wheel and four-wheel steering for quicker headland turns. Power comes from turbo diesel engines that produce 160–300hp. The 3000 and 8000 series use a Sisu Power six-cylinder engine, 7.4 litres and 8.4 litres respectively, with Selective Catalytic Reduction (SCR) technology to reduce emissions and improve fuel consumption. The 2155 and 2170 use a 6.7-litre Cummins engine.

The suspension and chassis use equally advanced technology, including a three-link front suspension that allows the tyres to tuck in against the chassis for a tight turning circle. Self-levelling on the rear suspension compensates for the additional weight of implements and

JCB FASTRAC 2150	
Year	1998
Engine	Perkins 1000 Series turbo diesel
Power	133 PTO hp, 150hp
Transmission	54 forward, 18 reverse
Weight	6365kg/14,032lbs

■ LEFT *The JCB Fastrac is designed to be versatile. It operates both at the slow speeds required in fields, and at up to 72kph (45mph) on roads. Many of the machine's functions are controlled by computer.*

■ RIGHT *The Fastrac design has been improved over 20 years and the latest model has a 306hp engine with a continuously variable transmission. This 220hp Cummins-powered 3220 is pulling a tanker with a slurry injection system.*

self-levelling from side to side assists boom stability which is useful when working on hillsides. Optional adjustable wheel-slip control, working in conjunction with a radar sensor that measures true ground speed, helps reduce tyre wear and soil smearing. Air over hydraulic disc brakes are fitted on all four wheels and the external disc brakes allow cooling.

■ TRANSMISSION

Inside the cab, the JCB electrical monitoring system (EMS) provides a performance assessment of the numerous machine functions on the dashboard. It includes the engine rpm, PTO rpm, selected Powershift ratio and a full range of warning indicators, such as one indicating whether the front or rear PTO is selected. The 3000 and 8000 series use touch-screen technology to give the driver greater control.

The axle drive shafts have double seals on the bearing cups to retain more grease for longer life. Improved axle drive shafts and cross serrated drive shaft location is designed to ensure durability and longer component life. The heavy-duty front axles feature a solid bearing spacer between the pinion bearing for improved durability. Soft engage differential-lock, fitted as standard to the rear axle, can be selected when wheels are spinning. It engages smoothly to protect the drive train and then automatically disengages when four-wheel steering is operated or when the "differential-lock cut-out" is selected.

■ RIGHT *A JCB Fastrac 150, working with a Claas Quadrant 1200 square baler. Unusually for a tractor, the Fastrac cab has room to accommodate a passenger, and a seat has been fitted for them.*

OTHER MAKES

(HST, Iseki, Ivel, Jeep)

■ H.S.T. DEVELOPMENTS

H.S.T. Developments was formed as Taylor Engineering Developments Ltd in 1972 and changed its name in 1989. The company pioneered what it refers to as the Trantor, an acronym for Transport Tractor. The Trantor is designed to offer off-tarmac farm use as a normal tractor but to offer greater versatility on the road where a high percentage of farm products need to be transported.

The Trantor has been designed, through a sprung drawbar, to tow a ten tonne load on road and have a top speed of 55mph. In the field the Trantor has the capability to pull an eight tonne load. The Trantor 904 has a 90hp diesel engine which drives through a ten forward speed transmission (with two reverse gears). It has a two speed PTO that can be operated at 540 and 1000rpm, an independent PTO clutch and a Category Two three-point linkage. Power steering, a differential lock and fully suspended pick-up hitch are all fitted. The 904 has air brakes on all four wheels – 71cm/28in diameter rear and 41cm/16in front – and an air-operated hand brake. There are a variety of cab options, power ranges and transmissions on offer. The initial models were unveiled in the late 1970s at British agricultural shows and a revised version, the fully suspended Trantor Mk II, was made in limited numbers. Production is now underway in the UK and plans are being developed to market and manufacture Trantor tractors in third world countries. In these countries within Asia and South America, the requirements for a tractor are less specialized and sophisticated than in North America and western Europe.

■ ISEKI

Iseki is a Japanese manufacturer of both compact and larger conventional tractors. In the former category are tractors such as the TM3215 and 3265. They are powered by three-cylinder water-cooled engines of 1123cc/47.3cu in and 1498cc/91.5cu in respectively, both in four-wheel-drive forms and are suited for use with a range of

■ ABOVE *Engineer's sketches of the Trantor range prepared in the 1980s after the production of a prototype.* LEFT *The Trantor tractor was designed to offer versatility, and is shown here with a canvas tilt over the rear load area.* MIDDLE *The Trantor tractor features a three-point rear linkage for implement applications.*

■ LEFT *A 1982 Trantor Mark II tractor in a Welsh farmyard.*

■ RIGHT *The CJ5 Jeep such as this 1973 model was one of the last Jeeps intended for agricultural use. The company then moved to sport utility production.*

■ BELOW RIGHT *The CJ2A Jeep, introduced in 1945, was a civilian version of the wartime Jeep, and was aimed at farmers and ranchers.*

implements. One of Iseki's larger machines is the Model TJW117 which is powered by a 4398cc/268cu in four-cylinder water-cooled diesel engine. The transmission uses the AT Shift system and offers twenty-four forward and reverse gears, with a maximum speed of 35kmh/22mph, as well as automatic four-wheel drive.

■ IVEL AGRICULTURAL MOTOR

In England in 1902 Dan Albone patented something he termed the "agricultural motor": it was of a tricycle tractor design and went into production in 1903 in a Biggleswade, Bedfordshire factory. Albone called it the Ivel after a river near his home, and the production Ivel tractor developed 20bhp at 850rpm. The Ivel weighed 1650kg/3638lbs and was a viable machine.

Albone died in 1906 and little further work was done on his patented machine: in fact, the company gradually declined without his impetus and went into receivership in 1920. The legacy Albone left to agriculture, however, is a rich one. He demonstrated that agricultural motors were to be the farming power source of the future and paved the way for the acceptance of the new machines.

■ JEEP

As World War II drew to a close it was apparent that the four-wheel-drive Jeep would be invaluable to farmers, so Willys-Overland began to manufacture civilian Jeeps designated as CJ models. The first was the CJ2A. Initially the Jeep CJs were marketed for agricultural purposes, equipped with power take-offs and agricultural drawbars. They were promoted for a variety of farming tasks, such as towing ploughs and disc rotavators. The second of the CJs was the CJ3A. This Jeep went into production in 1948 and was built until 1953. In 1953 the CJ3B was introduced and would stay in production until the 1960s: a total of 155,494 were constructed. Gradually Jeeps became more refined and were sold as transportation rather than as farming vehicles. Currently, Jeep is a trademark of the Chrysler Corporation and the vehicles so named can best be described as sport utility vehicles.

JOHN DEERE

■ BELOW *Soon after its introduction, the John Deere GP tractor was offered in a variety of configurations. These included the tricycle row crop, and its derivatives the Models A and B.*

The history of the massive John Deere company starts in 1837. In that year John Deere, a 33-year-old pioneer blacksmith from Vermont, designed and made a "self-polishing" steel plough in his small blacksmith's shop in Grand Detour, Illinois. He made it from the steel of a broken saw blade and found that the plough was capable of slicing through the thick, sticky prairie soil efficiently without becoming stuck or forcing itself out of the ground. As it cut the furrow it became polished and this ensured that the soil would not stick. It was a major breakthrough in farming technology and became the first commercially successful steel plough in America. The plough was fundamental in opening the American Midwest to agriculture and ensuring high levels of crop production.

■ EXPANSION

With a succession of partners, John Deere made an increasing number of ploughs each year. The supply of broken saw blades was of course limited, so at first Deere had steel shipped from England. In 1846 the first plough steel ever rolled in the United States was made to order for John Deere in Pittsburgh. In 1848 Deere moved his

■ RIGHT *The John Deere GP model: the designation GP stood for General Purpose. It was introduced in 1928 and was designed as a three-row cultivating tractor.*

■ BELOW *A restored John Deere GP Model A, with a two-furrow plough. The Model A was introduced in 1934 and most were like this tricycle row crop version.*

JOHN DEERE MODEL A	
Year	1934
Engine	Two cylinder, 5047cc/308cu in
Power	18.72 drawbar hp, 24.71 belt hp
Transmission	Two speed
Weight	1840kg/4059lbs

operation to Moline, Illinois, to make use of the Mississippi River to power his factory's machinery and for distribution of his products. By 1852 Deere, Tate and Gould were making approximately 4000 ploughs per year. This partnership did not last long – in fact Tate later became a competitor – and by 1856 John Deere's son Charles was working at the company. In 1868 it was incorporated as Deere & Company.

■ ABOVE *Steel lugged wheels gave traction while in the field, but meant the tractor was not permitted to run on roads.*

■ LEFT *The advent of the pneumatic agricultural tyre can be considered a major step on the road to the modern complex tractor.*

Charles Deere went on to expand the company established by his father. He was reputed to be an outstanding businessman, and established marketing centres, called branch houses, to serve his network of independent retail dealers. During the 1880s John Deere was able to offer financing to retail customers for its agricultural products. By the time of Charles Deere's death in 1907, the company was making a wide

■ RIGHT *For all the technological advances that have been made within tractor technology, some things have changed remarkably little. In John Deere's case the brand name and colour scheme of the tractors have remained constant.*

■ LEFT *The John Deere Model B was introduced in 1935. It was smaller than the Model A and rated at 11.84 drawbar and 16.01 belt hp in the Nebraska Tests.*

■ BELOW LEFT *Industrial designer, Henry Dreyfuss, redesigned the Model A and B tractors to give them aesthetically pleasing lines, and to keep up with the competition.*

■ BELOW RIGHT *The Model A and B GP tractors both featured infinitely adjustable rear wheel tread.*

■ BOTTOM *In excess of 322,200 John Deere Model B tractors were made between 1935 and 1952.*

range of steel ploughs, cultivators, corn and cotton planters, and other farming implements.

■ ACQUISITION

In 1911, under Deere & Company's third president, William Butterworth, six farm equipment companies were acquired and incorporated into the Deere organization, going a long way to establishing the company as a manufacturer of a complete range of farm equipment. In 1918, the company purchased the Waterloo Gasoline Engine Company in Waterloo, Iowa, and this put it in the tractor business. Tractors, of course, went on to become one of the most important parts of the John Deere business and meant that the modern era of the John Deere Company had begun.

■ RIGHT *A Dreyfuss-styled, John Deere tricycle row crop tractor, with a two row planter. The success of the design ensured a long production run for this tractor.*

■ RIGHT *New for 1937 was the John Deere Model G, capable of pulling a three furrow plough. The Model G produced 20.7 drawbar and 31.44 belt hp.*

At the time of the acquisition, the Waterloo Gasoline Traction Engine Company was making its Model N tractor and under John Deere's supervision this model was kept in production until 1924. It was the subject of the first ever Nebraska Tractor Test in 1920. The Model N was rated as a 12–25 model when the tests confirmed outputs of 12.1 drawbar and 25.51 belt hp.

■ RIGHT *A 1935 John Deere Model A, with the more utilitarian pre-Dreyfuss styling. Numerous variants of the Model A were produced, including orchard models.*

■ JOHN DEERE MODEL D

During the 1920s the company introduced its two-cylinder Model D tractor. Many other tractor-makers were offering four-cylinder machines at the time but Deere's engineers, aware that the post-war boom in tractor sales was over, considered the economics of both manufacture and maintenance and designed the two-cylinder engine. History showed that their decision was correct as the Model D was a particularly successful machine. It was Deere's interpretation of the cast frame tractor, powered by a two-cylinder

■ LEFT *The provision of a belt drive pulley on tractors was originally as important as the fitment of a drawbar, as it enabled the farmer to drive a variety of equipment.*

kerosene/paraffin engine and fitted with a two forward and one reverse speed gearbox. From this basic machine a production run of sequentially upgraded tractors continued until 1953, by which time more than 160,000 had been made. The scale of upgrades can be gauged from the fact that the 1924 model achieved a rating of 22–30hp when tested in Nebraska while the 1953 model achieved 38–42hp in the same tests. The distinctive exhaust note made by these two-cylinder machines earned them the nickname of "Johnny Poppers".

JOHN DEERE 4010 TRACTOR

Year	1959
Engine	In-line six cylinder
Power	73.65 drawbar hp
Transmission	Eight speed
Weight	3175kg/7000lbs

■ JOHN DEERE GP

John Deere brought out a row crop tractor in 1928 known as the GP. In the same year, Charles Deere Wiman, a great-grandson of John Deere, took over direction of the company. During the period when modern agriculture was developing, his strong emphasis on engineering and product development resulted in rapid growth. The GP designation indicated General Purpose. It was designed as a three-row row crop machine and was the first John Deere tractor with a power lift for raising attached implements. Sufficient crop clearance was achieved by having a curved front axle and step-down gearing to the rear wheels. Unfortunately it did not prove as successful as had been hoped, so John Deere's engineers went back to the drawing board and produced the GPWT. The WT part of the designation indicated Wide Tread and the machine was of a tricycle configuration. In subsequent years a number of variants of this model were produced, including models for orchard use and potato farming – the GPO and GP-P models.

■ FAR RIGHT *The power take-off (PTO) shaft and linkage for hitching up implements are clearly visible on the rear of this restored row crop John Deere.*

■ RIGHT *A restored example of a 1931 John Deere GP. The engine flywheel is clearly visible on this side, and the belt pulley is on the other.*

■ BELOW *The row crop tricycle tractor was one of the first specialist designs of tractor to be developed, and it found appreciative customers in a short space of time.*

Through the Great Depression, and despite financial losses in the early 1930s, Deere elected to carry debtor farmers as long as was necessary. The result was a loyalty among the primary customer base that extends across three generations to the present day. Despite the setbacks of the Depression, the company achieved $100 million in gross sales for the first time in its history in 1937, the year of its centennial celebration.

■ JOHN DEERE MODEL A

The Model A was a John Deere machine produced between 1934 and 1952. It was a tricycle row crop tractor that incorporated numerous innovations.

■ ABOVE *Although John Deere came late to the tractor manufacturing business, after its acquisition of Waterloo Boy, the company wasted no time in catching up and developing new models.*

■ BELOW *The size and scale of prairie farming in the United States led to the development of larger tractors with much more powerful engines.*

The wheel track was adjustable through the use of splined hubs and the transmission was contained in a single-piece casting. The first Model A was rated at 18 drawbar and 24 belt hp but this output was subsequently increased. By the time production of the Model A was halted in 1952 over 328,000 had been made. Another tractor to have a long and successful production run was John Deere's Model B, manufactured between 1935 and 1952. It was smaller than the A and rated at 11 drawbar and 16 belt hp. It was later produced in numerous forms including the model BO and the crawler-track equipped version of the 1940s. The MC model made later was purpose-built as a crawler tractor.

■ ECONOMIC RECOVERY

By 1937 the American economy was well on the way to recovery and in 1938 the company unveiled a range of tractors

■ ABOVE *A row crop 630. The 30 Series was the last range of two-cylinder John Deere-engined tractors.*

■ LEFT *The new diesel-powered Model R was Deere's most powerful tractor when introduced in 1949.*

■ LEFT *The two tone 20 Series made its debut in 1956, and featured a yellow stripe on the sides of the hood and radiator shell. The engines of tractors such as the 620 had redesigned cylinder heads to increase their power.*

■ RIGHT *A John Deere tractor in preservation. It is easy to understand the high regard in which these iron beasts of burden are held after years of reliable service.*

■ BELOW *The Model G Series was in production between 1942 and 1953.*

■ BOTTOM *A restored John Deere tractor at a summer vintage machinery rally in South Dakota, United States.*

that had been redesigned by the industrial designer, Henry Dreyfuss. The company's management was conscious that the John Deere line had changed little between 1923 and 1937, while many of its competitors were moving towards stylized tractors and taking their design cues from the automobile makers of the time. The Models A and B were the first restyled tractors, although mechanically the Model B was similar to the one originally introduced in 1935. They were followed by the similarly styled D and H Models in 1939 and the Model G in 1942. The Model H was a lightweight two-row tricycle tractor and in excess of 60,000 were made. The Model G was a three-plough tractor rated at 20–31hp. It was the most powerful tractor in John Deere's line-up at the time. By the time of its manufacture pneumatic tyres were supplied as the standard fitment, although the rubber shortages caused by World War II caused the maker to return to steel wheels.

■ POST-WAR YEARS

John Deere's factories produced a wide range of war-related products, ranging from tank transmissions to mobile laundry units. Throughout this period John Deere nonetheless maintained its emphasis on product design, and developed a strong position for the post-war market through the efforts of Messrs Wiman and its wartime president, Burton Peek. Before Wiman's death in 1955, the company was firmly established as one of the nation's 100 largest manufacturing businesses. Through the first post-war decade, from 1946 to 1954, many new products and innovations were introduced, including the company's first self-propelled

■ BELOW *John Deere unveiled its new generation of power tractors in 1959. From then on, the size and power output of agricultural tractors continued to increase.*

■ BELOW *The 5010 tractor was a large diesel-powered machine, more than capable of pulling a forage harvester and drawbar trailer, as seen here.*

combine harvester, cotton picker and combine corn head. The latter was one of John Deere's most successful harvesting innovations. The company also made electric starting and lights standard on its post-war tractors.

■ JOHN DEERE MODEL M

All the more established American tractor manufacturers quickly added new models to their ranges in the immediate post-war years. John Deere was no exception and replaced the Models H, LA and L with the Model M in 1947. This was followed by two derivatives, the Models MC and MT, a crawler and tricycle, in 1949. The Model M was made between 1947 and 1952 while the MT was made between 1949 and 1952. Production of both models totalled more than 70,000. The MC was John Deere's first designed and constructed crawler machine and in the Nebraska Tractor Tests it achieved a rating of 18–22hp. A variety of track widths was made available to customers and more than 6,000 tractors had been made by 1952. The MC and the industrial variant of the Model M, the MI, went on to become the basis of John Deere's Industrial Equipment Division.

John Deere's first diesel tractor was produced in 1949 and designated the Model R before the company switched to

■ LEFT *During the 1960s John Deere developed products that were aimed at specialist markets, such as this ride-on lawn mower.*

■ BELOW *A John Deere No 45. The operator is in the open, exposed to all the dust and noise of harvesting.*

■ OPPOSITE BELOW *A John Deere Model 55-H sidehill combine in Wenatchee, Washington, USA during 1954.*

■ LEFT *The modern combine harvester contrasts with the earlier machine, not least because of the increased level of comfort afforded to the operator, which inevitably has a positive effect on productivity.*

a numerical designation for its tractors. The Model R was the replacement for the Model D and was based on engineering and design that had been started during the war years. It was a powerful machine that gave 45.7 drawbar and 51 brake hp in the Nebraska Tests. The large displacement diesel that powered the Model R was started by means of an electric start, two-cylinder gasoline engine. More than 21,000 Model Rs were built between its introduction in 1949 and 1954 when production ceased.

■ **JOHN DEERE 20 SERIES**

John Deere switched to a system of numerical designations for its tractors in 1952 and the machines that followed were the 20 Series of the mid-1950s, the 30 Series introduced in 1958 and the 40, 50, 60, 70 and 80 Series that followed in sequence through the 1950s and 60s. The 50 and 60 Series, for example, replaced the Models B and A respectively in 1952 while the 80 Series replaced the Model R.

In 1956 the John Deere 20 Series tractors were announced as a range of six different machines designated sequentially from 320 to 820. Of these, the 820 was the largest and was the only diesel model. Despite this it had a horizontal twin-cylinder engine – John Deere's established configuration. The 820, in many ways an upgraded Model R tractor, produced 64.3hp at 1125rpm, meaning that it was the most powerful machine John Deere had built up until that time. The engine displaced 7726 cc/471.5cu in through a bore and stroke of 15.5 × 20cm/6.125 × 8in. Starting was by means of a small-capacity V4 gasoline engine. The 820 was fitted with a hydraulic lift as standard although PTO

■ RIGHT *This John Deere tractor has been fitted with a hydraulically operated bale and silage grapple, one of six different units that can be fitted on John Deere's hydraulic front loader.*

was an optional extra. The 820 weighed in excess of 4 tons and was, according to its manufacturer, capable of pulling six 35cm/14in furrows. This tractor had a short production run that ended in 1958, but it was one of the first in the trend towards ever larger and more powerful tractors.

■ WORLDWIDE MARKETING

In the mid-1950s manufacturing and marketing operations had been expanded into both Mexico and Germany, marking the beginning of the company's growth into a major multinational corporation. In 1958 Deere's Industrial Equipment Division was officially established, suggesting future diversification. In fact, Deere had

■ LEFT *John Deere's first four-wheel-drive tractor was added to the company's range in 1959. This is a later 2130 model.*

■ BELOW *The John Deere Pro-Series offers up to 24 row spacing configurations.*

■ RIGHT *The 1956 John Deere 20 series comprised of six tractors ranging from the 320 to the 820.*

■ BELOW *The 20 range featured a two-tone colour scheme, a revised layout of the controls, and a sprung seat to make operation of the tractor easier for the driver.*

been doing business in industrial markets since the 1920s, providing machines for road maintenance, light earthmoving and forestry work. In the same year the John Deere Credit Company was established and currently John Deere Credit is one of the 25 largest finance companies in the United States of America.

■ MULTI CYLINDERS

The 30 Series tractors of 1958 were the last two-cylinder machines to be made by John Deere. The company introduced its first four-wheel-drive tractor – the 8010 – in 1959 and then for 1960 it launched a completely new line of multi-cylinder engines capable of meeting the growing demands for more powerful tractors. These new John Deere tractors were unveiled in Dallas, Texas in August 1959.

There were four models, 1010, 2010, 3010 and 4010, and they were completely new. The smaller models were powered by in-line four-cylinder engines and the larger ones by an in-line six-cylinder engine.

■ JOHN DEERE 4010

The six-cylinder 4010 and four-cylinder 3010 were offered as diesels, although both gasoline and LPG versions were available. The tractors were designed to have higher operating speeds and a

JOHN DEERE 9976 PRO-SERIES COTTON PICKER

Year	1997
Engine	Six-cylinder 8144cc/497cu in turbocharged diesel
Power	300hp (224kW)
Transmission	Three speed
Weight	17,975kg/39,630 lbs six row

■ BELOW *Contemporary John Deere loaders have a lift height of up to 3.5m (11ft 5in) and a reach of up to 109.2cm (43in).*

better power-to-weight ratio to increase productivity. The 4010 produced more than 70 drawbar hp while the smaller 3010 achieved more than 50hp. Power steering, power brakes and power implement raising were up-to-the-minute features and an eight-speed transmission enhanced the versatility of the machines. The smaller models in the range, the 1010 and 2010, had features such as adjustable track to make them suitable for row crop work. The tractors were immediately greeted with acclaim and sales were very successful. The new range accounted for a significant increase in John Deere's market share over a five-year period. In 1959 John Deere had 23 per cent of the US tractor market and by 1964 the figure had increased to 34 per cent. This pushed Deere into the position of market leader.

In 1963, in a move to a related, if smaller, type of machinery, Deere

■ TOP *The John Deere 7520 was developed by John Deere during the 1960s and relied on the economies of scale offered in large acreage farming.*

■ ABOVE *A two-wheel-drive John Deere 3040 tractor in an English farmyard. It features a curved windscreen for enhanced visibility for the operator.*

■ LEFT *A 1990s John Deere, equipped with an hydraulic front loader and the standard rear three-point linkage to maximize versatility.*

■ LEFT *A four-wheel-drive John Deere 7520 fitted with dual tyres.*

■ LEFT *A hard worked John Deere tractor, fitted with a Farmhand bale and silage grapple.*

■ BELOW *A John Deere 4055 tractor towing a forage harvester, which is blowing hay into the trailer it is also pulling.*

entered the lawn and grounds care business. During the second half of the 1960s the company's industrial equipment line was expanded to include motor graders, four-wheel-drive loaders, log skidders, backhoe loaders, forklifts and excavators. New models of elevating scrapers, utility crawler dozers and loaders were all introduced. In 1969 John Deere entered the insurance business with the formation of the John Deere Insurance Group, which also offers credit-related insurance products for John Deere dealers.

■ THE 1970S

From 1970 onwards there were broad expansions throughout the equipment divisions of John Deere, with major advancements in all product lines, worldwide market development, and a programme of capital investment to enlarge and improve facilities. More than $1.5 billion was invested in this programme between 1975 and 1981.

At this time the 40 Series tractors were becoming more popular as by now they were being assembled with V6 turbocharged diesel engines that produced in excess of 100bhp. This figure was exceeded by the end of the next decade, when John Deere's 4955 Model tractor produced 200bhp. The 7800 has dual rear wheels at each side and a 7636cc/466cu in engine that produces 170bhp and drives through a 20 speed transmission. In 1978 sales had reached $4 billion, which represented a quadrupling of sales over the previous ten years. Expansion of the credit business continued in 1984 with the acquisition of Farm Plan, that

■ RIGHT *One of the important design considerations with four-wheel-drive tractors, such as this John Deere, is the turning radius. This figure is the official SAE standard for measuring tractor turning, so making comparisons between models.*

offered credit for agricultural purchases, including, for the first time, non-John Deere products.

■ THE 40 SERIES

The 1986 John Deere Model 2040 was powered by an engine of 3900cc/238cu in displacement using diesel fuel and producing power in the region of 70hp. It was one of the 40 series of three tractors: the 1640, 2040 and 2140 models. Also made in the same year was the John Deere Model 4450 of 7600cc/464cu in displacement that produced 160hp and featured a 15-speed transmission with a part-time 4×4 facility. Diversification continued in 1987 when John Deere entered the golf and turf equipment market and again in 1988 when the company diversified into recreational vehicle and marine markets. In the same year a worldwide Parts Division was established to increase sales of spare parts to owners of both John Deere and other makes of equipment. In 1989, John Deere Maximizer combine harvesters were introduced. In 1991 the worldwide Lawn and Grounds Care Division was established as a separate division within the company, in order to distinguish the specialist products from those of the agricultural equipment business.

■ LEFT *In the early 1960s John Deere diversified into the lawn and grounds care business.*

■ BELOW *The 1998 John Deere 7810 model is powered by a turbocharged diesel engine.*

■ THE 8000 SERIES

The 1990s were auspicious. 1992 saw the introduction of an entirely new line of 66 to 145hp tractors, the 6000 and 7000 Series, designed from the ground up as a complete range of products to meet the varying demands of worldwide markets and to facilitate on-going product updates quickly and at minimum cost. In 1993, the company's 75th year in the tractor business, the

tractor line spanned a range from 40 to 400hp. Under a distribution agreement reached in 1993 with Zetor, a tractor manufacturer in the Czech Republic, Deere became the distributor of a lower-priced line of 40 to 85hp tractors in emerging markets, starting with selected areas of South America and Asia.

The 8000 Series tractors set new standards for power, performance, manoeuvrability, visibility, control and comfort in 1994. The 8400 was the world's first 225hp row crop tractor.

■ ABOVE *A Cotton Picker picking the cotton off the plants with the spindle units and transferring the balls into the basket.*

■ BELOW LEFT *John Deere tractors feature a curved tempered glass area.*

■ BELOW *Late 1990s John Deere tractors are equipped with what the manufacturers describe as the ComfortGard cab. It is ergonomically designed so that controls are conveniently positioned.*

■ LEFT *Dual tyres as fitted on this 8850 model have to be weighted, balanced and correctly inflated to increase productivity, reduce soil compaction and optimize minimum fuel consumption.*

■ BELOW *A two-wheel-drive 65hp (49.2kW) John Deere 6110 model, fitted with the ComfortGard cab. It is also available with an open operator station.*

In the same year Deere acquired Homelite, a manufacturer of hand-held and walk-behind power products for both the home-owner and commercial markets. Then in 1995 the company introduced a new line of mid-priced lawn tractors and walk-behind mowers branded as "Sabre by John Deere" for distribution through John Deere dealers and national retailers. In that year it also announced the "GreenStar Combine Yield-Mapping System" as the first in a series of precision-farming systems that was designed to help measure crop yield in different parts of a field.

■ STOCKS AND SHARES

The company made significant financial moves in 1995 when stock was split three-for-one from 17 November, 1995. The previous stock split had been a two-for-one split in 1976. In this year the company's consolidated net sales and revenues exceeded $10 billion. Financial moves continued in 1996 when the Board authorized a $500 million share repurchase. For the year

■ ABOVE *The 8400 tractor is the largest model in the John Deere 8000 Series.*

■ RIGHT *The John Deere Advantage Series of tractors. From the left, they are the 7405, 6605 and 6405 models producing 105, 95 and 85hp respectively.*

■ BELOW *The John Deere 1860 No-Till Air Drill's no-till opener features no-tool adjustments and minimum maintenance.*

■ LEFT *The John Deere 9610 row crop combine harvester is one of the company's Ten Series of combines and is powered by a six-cylinder, turbocharged diesel engine of 496cu in (8.1 litres) displacement.*

Deere's consolidated net sales and revenues were a record $11.2 billion. In the same year the Lawn and Grounds Care Division name was changed to Commercial and Consumer Equipment Division. 1995 was successful for tractor and harvester manufacture too, with both the largest introduction of new agricultural products in the company's history and the largest single John Deere agricultural sale ever. This was an order worth $187 million for combine harvesters to be supplied to the Ukraine. Although John Deere is an American tractor manufacturer, the company has production plants in other countries, including Argentina, Australia, Germany, Mexico, South Africa and Spain.

■ BELOW LEFT *John Deere's range of machinery includes self-propelled foragers, such as this 7950i model in the field.*

■ DEERE'S LEGACY

The importance of John Deere's contribution to agriculture (and America's development) is indicated by the degree of veneration attached to the site of his original smithy in Grand Detour, Illinois. In 1962, an archaeological team from the University of Illinois unearthed the exact location of the blacksmith's shop where John Deere developed his first successful steel plough in 1837. The location has been preserved in an exhibit hall which shows how the dig was performed and contains artefacts found on the site. The centre contains numerous exhibits, including a reconstruction of John Deere's blacksmith shop enhanced with the sounds of horses' hooves on the treadmill, hammers on the anvil and

■ RIGHT *The John Deere 7020 series were an all new design in 2003, replacing the older 10 series. The 7720 and 7820 had a choice of multiple transmissions, while the largest 200hp 7920 came with the AutoPower gearbox only.*

conversations between workers. It was in a place such as this that John Deere developed the self-polishing steel plough that opened the prairie to agriculture.

Existing ranges saw updates in the early 2000s, such as the 6020, 7020 and 8020 series, for example, seen first in 2002, while following years saw the introduction of numerous new tractors, including the 3020 series. In 2007 the company brought out over thirty new machines, including extensions to the 5000 series and the 530hp 9630, also available in a tracked version.

■ LEFT *The quest for increased productivity in agriculture has led to the development of computer guidance systems such as the iTEC (Intelligent Total Control) system from John Deere.*

■ BOTTOM *The 9400 can be fitted with dual (seen here) or triple tyre combinations that offer optimum traction and minimum soil compaction.*

JOHN DEERE 9400 TRACTOR

Year	1997
Engine	In-line six-cylinder turbo diesel
Power	425hp (316kW)
Transmission	12 speed (24 speed optional)
Weight	13,295kg/ 33,770lbs

OTHER MAKES

(Kirov, Komatsu, Kubota)

■ KIROV

Kirov was based in the former USSR and among its products of the mid-1980s were the K-701 giant tractors. These were 12-ton machines powered by a liquid cooled V12 four-stroke diesel that produced 300hp and had a liquid vibration dampener on the front end of the crankshaft. The engine oil pump is electrically driven and switched on prior to firing up the engine in order to build the lubrication system up to operating pressure. The gearbox is driven through a semi-rigid coupling and a reduction unit which can be disconnected to facilitate engine starting in cold weather. The planetary gearbox is mechanically controlled and features hydraulically controlled friction clutches. The frame of the K-701 is articulated to aid traction and manoeuvrability, and to increase fuel economy the rear axle drive can be disconnected when not required.

■ KOMATSU

Komatsu is a long-established Japanese crawler manufacturer with a factory in the Ishikawa Prefecture of Japan. Like Caterpillar, much of Komatsu production has been directed to the manufacture of bulldozers. Production of the company's D50 series started in 1947 when the D50A1 was manufactured. It was a conventionally designed machine and was powered by the company's own 60hp 4D120 diesel engine. By June 1970 Komatsu had made 50,000 D50 machines. The current Komatsu range encompasses 23 crawlers, including the world's largest, the Komatsu D575A-2 Super.

■ KUBOTA

Kubota is a Japanese company that was founded in the last decade of the 19th century. It began manufacturing tractors during the 1960s and claimed to be the fifth largest producer in the mid-1980s. One of its products was the compact B7100DP, a three-cylinder powered tractor that displaces 762cc/46.5cu in and produces 16hp. It also featured four-wheel-drive, independent rear brakes and a three-speed PTO. The company offers a range of grounds maintenance equipment, mowers and implements, a series of ride-on mowers and a range of compact tractors. In the current range of ride-on mowers are models including the 597cc/36.4cu in T1880 and the G series including the 988cc/60.2 cu in G23 and the G26 with 1001cc/61cu in. Both use Kubota 3-cylinder egines. One of the current four-wheel-drive compact tractors is the B3030, which is powered by a 30hp four-cylinder liquid-cooled diesel engine. The largest Kubota compact tractor is the STV-series of STV32, STV36 and STV40 models. Of these, the latter is the largest, with an engine displacement of 1826cc/111.4cu in that produces 40hp. Kubota also manufacture a range of mid-size and larger agricultural tractors, including the MGX series featuring the 110hp M110GX displacing 3769cc/229.9cu in and the 130hp M130GX with 6124cc/373.7cu in. Both use a 4-cylinder turbocharged engine with Tier 3B emission levels.

■ BELOW ***Kubota manufacture a full range of tractors and a line of implements. This 135hp turbocharged 4-cylinder M135GX is using a Kubota front loader.***

■ ABOVE *A Kubota B8200 compact tractor, it has a diesel engine and four wheel drive capability.*

■ BELOW *Kubota manufacture a range of mowers, including those based around their compact tractors (left) and ride-on tyres (right).*

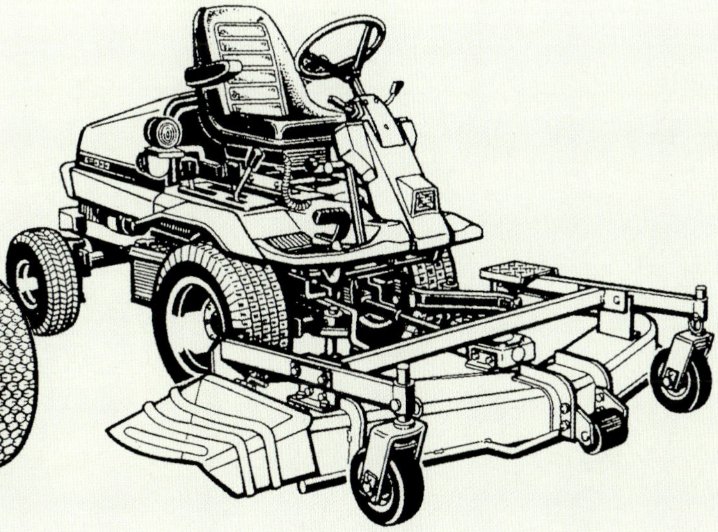

LANDINI

■ LEFT *The Velite of the 1930s was one of the Landini company's first successful tractors. It was powered by a 7222cc/440cu in single-cylinder semi-diesel engine.*

The illustrious Landini company – the oldest established tractor manufacturer in Italy – was founded by Giovanni Landini, a blacksmith who set up his own business in Fabbrico in Italy's Po Valley. As early as 1884, Giovanni Landini began a mechanical engineering concern in that small Emilian town. His business was successful and gradually he progressed from simple blacksmithing to fabricating machinery for local farms. He produced winemaking machinery, then steam engines, internal combustion engines and crushing equipment. In 1911 Landini built a portable steam engine and from here he progressed to semi-diesel-engined machines. The way forward to a modern and mechanized agricultural industry in Italy was clear and Landini started work on his own design of tractor. His death in 1925 prevented his completion of the first prototype Landini tractor.

Giovanni Landini's sons took over the business and saw the completion of the tractor project. In 1925 the three sons built the first authentic Italian tractor, a 30hp machine. It was a success and was the forerunner of the viable range of Landini 40 and 50hp models which appeared in the mid-1930s and were to become renowned under the names of Velite, Buffalo and Super. The first production tractors were powered by a

■ ABOVE LEFT *In the post World War II years Landini manufactured the L25 tractor. It was powered by a 4300cc/262cu in semi-diesel engine, producing 25hp.*

■ LEFT *This is a 1954 model Landini L25. The semi-diesel engine was capable of running on remarkably poor grade fuels including vegetable oil, creosote and used engine oil.*

■ RIGHT *The 130 Legend incorporates state-of-the-art engine and transmission management techniques.*

■ BELOW *A 1996 Landini 9880 model with a 3870cc/236cu in displacement engine which produces 88hp.*

40hp semi-diesel engine which was a two-stroke single-cylinder unit. The company continued to produce semi-diesel-engined tractors until 1957, since this type of engine was popular in many European countries, including Germany. For a period Landini and other Italian makers, such as Deganello and Orsi, produced Lanz machines under licence.

In the early 1930s the Landini brothers designed a more powerful tractor which they named the Super Landini: in 1934 it was the most powerful tractor on the Italian market. It produced 50hp at 650 rpm through an engine displacement of 1220cc/74.4cu in. The tractor was driven through a three-speed transmission with a single reverse gear and it stayed in production until the outbreak of World War II.

Following the war the Fabbrico factory both redesigned its range of tractors and expanded the company's output. In the post-war years the L25 was announced, a 4300cc/262.3cu in displacement semi-diesel engined tractor that produced 25hp. It was made in a new Landini factory in Como, Italy. Production of the 55L model, the most powerful tractor to be equipped with the single-cylinder "Testa Calda" (hot-bulb) engine, started in 1955.

Another key aspect of this redesign was the replacement of the "Testa Calda" engine used until then, with English manufactured multi-cylinder Perkins diesel power units. It marked Landini's first step towards becoming an international concern. This was later consolidated further through the agreement signed with Massey-Ferguson in 1960, by which Landini became part of the Massey-Ferguson company. As the trend towards full diesel engines continued, Landini entered an agreement with the British company Perkins in 1957 to produce its diesels in Italy under licence. This agreement between Landini and Perkins Engines of Peterborough has endured, as they are still used and are now fitted across the entire Landini range.

In 1959 the C35 model was the first Landini crawler tractor to be manufactured and the precursor of another tradition – crawler machines – that continues to the present time. The renowned 6500, 7500 and 8500 Series models were introduced in 1973 with a redesigned transmission. With the launch of the 500 Series of two- and four-wheel-drive machines in the same year, Landini advanced its wheeled tractors by applying engineering that was to remain standard for years to come. Once the four-wheel-drive models were proven, work began on the design

■ LEFT *The current Landini tractor range encompasses 50 different models that range in power from 43 to 123 PTO hp. This is the Advantage 65F model.*

■ BELOW *Landini has constructed a number of compact tractors, and collaborates with Iseki of Japan.*

of high-powered machines, aimed at producing power in excess of 100hp using in-line, six-cylinder Perkins engines. The range was widened to give tractors with power outputs from 45 up to 145hp. In 1977 production of this new series of tractors commenced.

The 1980s saw the company diversifying its products as well as specializing. Having identified the requirements of the growing wine and fruit production sector, Landini started production of the Series Vineyard, Orchard, Standard and Wide models, the V, F and L machines. Landini soon had a 25 per cent share of the worldwide market and was established as a leading manufacturer of these products. In 1986 Landini launched a new Vineyard tractor range which allowed the Fabbrico factory to become the sole supplier of orchard and vineyard versions of both crawler and wheeled tractors branded as Massey-Fergusons. In 1988 the company launched a redesigned series of tractors, the 60, 70, 80 Series. It achieved a sales record that year for the Fabbrico factory, retailing more than 13,000 tractors.

In 1989 Massey-Ferguson sold 66 per cent of its Landini shares to the Eurobelge/Unione Manifatture holding company. This company later sold the controlling interest in its affairs to the Cameli Gerolimich Group. The move took Landini SpA into Unione Manifatture and into the 1990s at the forefront of the tractor industry, both in Italy and worldwide. Landini redesigned its tractors and offered a new range with the launch of the Trekker, Blizzard and Advantage Series. The result was that for the first time, sales of Landini tractors exceeded 3000 units in the company's export markets.

In February 1994 Valerio and Pierangelo Morra, as representatives of the Argo SpA family holding company, became president and vice-president of Landini SpA respectively. They and Massey-Ferguson contributed to a substantial recapitalization of Landini and in March 1994 Iseki joined Landini SpA. In December of the same year, Landini SpA announced a net profit of 7 billion lire and an increase in tractor sales of more than 30 per cent over the previous year. Change continued into the following year when in January 1995 Landini acquired Valpadana SpA, a prestigious trademark in the Italian agricultural machinery sector. During the following month the company made an agreement for the distribution of Landini products in North America through the established AGCO sales network, and renewed the agreement for

SUPER LANDINI

Year	1934
Engine	1219cc/74.4cu in
Power	50hp at 650rpm
Transmission	Three speed, one reverse
Weight	n/k

the sole supply of specialized wheeled and crawler tractors to AGCO. Overseas markets were not ignored, and in March 1995 Landini Sud America was opened in Valencia, Venezuela. This company was aimed at promoting the Landini brand in Latin America, a market that was considered to have potential for sales of tractors. In 1995 Landini sales, including those of imported Massey-Ferguson tractors and the Valpadana tractors manufactured in the San Martino plant, reached a total of 14,057 units, of which 9415 machines were sold under the Landini name.

In 1996, in order to meet the growing demand for the Legend Series of tractors, a significant investment was made when assembly line Number 2 in the Fabbrico factory was dismantled and replaced with a new assembly line, designed to double the factory's production capacity. In San Martino a new factory was opened in 1996, entirely dedicated to machining operations, gear manufacture and prototype component assembly. The presidents of both the Landini and Iseki companies were at the opening of the new plant, signalling agreement between the two companies on long-term technological co-operation between Landini and Iseki.

The current Landini range includes numerous models, with power outputs ranging from the compact 22 PTO hp 1 25 Series powered by a Daedong engine from South Korea, to the top-powered 7 Series including the 225 PTO hp 230 Model. Other series include the Mistral, Alpine, Rex, Powermondial and Trekker crawler models.

■ ABOVE *This compact Landini is working with a round baler on a hill meadow.*

■ LEFT *Traditionally narrow tractors have been used in vineyards, and this Landini Discovery, with a specialist loader, is suitable for between rows.*

■ BELOW *McCormick Tractors International is part of Argo SpA and began production again at the old Case IH Doncaster factory in 2001, before tractor manufacturing ceased in 2007. The rights to the MX, MXC Maxxum and CX models meant the company had a complete mid-horsepower range.*

OTHER MAKES

(Lamborghini, Land Rover, Lanz, Laverda, Leyland)

■ LAMBORGHINI

This company is perhaps better known for the production of sports cars than of tractors. Ferruccio Lamborghini was born in Renazzo di Cento, near Ferrara, on 28 April, 1916. His enthusiasm for machinery led him to study mechanical engineering in Bologna, after which he served during World War II as a mechanic in the Italian army's Central Vehicle Division in Rhodes. On his return to Italy at the end of the war, Lamborghini began to purchase surplus military vehicles which he then converted into agricultural machines. Three years after the end of the war, the Lamborghini tractor factory was designing and building its own tractors.

It is hard to say what made Lamborghini turn his attention from agricultural machinery to luxury sports cars. He may have been motivated by the success of his neighbour, Enzo Ferrari. Folklore suggests that the idea came to him after a discussion with Enzo Ferrari, when Lamborghini complained about the noisy gearbox in his Ferrari. Ferrari's reply was allegedly that Lamborghini should stick to tractors and let Ferrari build sports cars.

Ferruccio Lamborghini extended his interests into various fields of engineering, including heating and air conditioning systems and even helicopter design. While the cars, which were added to the Lamborghini line in 1963, were extremely successful and are still in production, the attempts to manufacture helicopters were hindered due to complex bureaucratic controls imposed by the government, and as a result, the idea was abandoned.

■ LEFT AND BELOW *By the time the Lamborghini 950 Premium tractor was manufactured, the car-and tractor-making portions of Lamborghini's business had been sold to separate companies.*

The Lamborghini 5C was a crawler tractor unveiled at the Paris Agricultural Show in 1962. The tractor was unusual in that, as well as crawler tracks, it had three rubber-tyred wheels that allowed use on the road as the wheels lifted the tracks clear of the road surface. The tracks were driven from the rear sprockets and it was to these sprockets that the wheels were attached for driving on the road. The small front wheel was effectively an idler and steering was achieved by moving the same levers that slewed the tractor around when using tracks. The 5C was powered by a three-cylinder diesel engine that produced 39hp.

When it became clear to Ferruccio Lamborghini that his son Antonio had little interest in the automobile business, he began to contemplate retirement. In 1973 Lamborghini sold all his companies and retired to his vineyard in Umbria, dedicating the last twenty years of his life to the production of fine wines. It was here, at the age of 77, that Lamborghini died on 20 February 1993.

In 1972 the car and tractor portions of Lamborghini's business had been split. The tractor production operations were taken over by Same which has continued to develop the Lamborghini range and increased the volume of production.

■ BOTTOM LEFT *This R30.EVO Lamborghini tractor is powered by a turbocharged 4-cylinder Deutz diesel engine.*

■ ABOVE ***The prototype Land Rover with its centre steering position, operating a Massey-Harris elevator during the construction of a haystack, in 1947.***

■ LAND ROVER

In the years after World War II Rover, which had a reputation for building quality motor cars, was in a difficult position because of the shortage of steel. Rover engineers Maurice Wilks and his brother Spencer considered building a small utility vehicle with an aluminium body and four-wheel drive. The intention was that the machine, specifically intended for agricultural use, would merely be a stopgap until sufficient steel was available for the company to return to building luxury cars.

The Wilks brothers delegated much of the design work of the utility machine. The first prototype Land Rovers had a tractor-like centre steering wheel to enable them to be sold in either left- or right-hand drive markets. Because a conventional chassis would have required expensive tooling, the engineer Olaf Poppe devised a jig on which four strips of flat steel could be welded together to form a box-section chassis.

The first Land Rover, with a 2m/80in wheelbase, was shown to the public at the 1948 Amsterdam Motor Show. Orders flowed in, especially when early Land Rovers were displayed at agricultural shows around Britain, and the company began to look seriously at export markets. The vehicles were demonstrated ploughing and driving mowers. Power take-offs and winches were optional extras and between 1948 and 1954 numerous details were refined and improved. To make the vehicle more capable it was redesigned for 1954: the wheelbase was increased by 15cm/6in and the rear overhang increased by 7.5cm/3in. This enabled the rear load area to be increased. A long wheelbase variant, at 2.7m/107in, was also made available as a pick-up and these models had the 1997cc/121.8cu in engine which had been available in the later 2m/80in models. Changes were again made to the Land Rover for 1956 when both models were stretched another 5cm/2in to give wheelbases of 2.24m/88in and 2.77m/109in. The diesel engine was introduced in June 1957 and by 1958 Rover had produced in excess of 200,000 Land Rovers. In April 1958 the company introduced the so-called Series II Land Rover. The Series II featured a redesigned body that was 4cm/1½in wider than its predecessors, together with other minor improvements including more modern door hinges and bonnet (hood) latches.

While Land Rover products are still made and widely exported, the emphasis of the range is now on sport utility vehicles, with the exception of the Defender 90 and

■ BELOW ***A Series II Land Rover, adapted to tow an especially designed swan-neck articulated trailer, seen here loaded with a Perkins diesel-powered tractor.***

■ LEFT ***The most modern version of the Land Rover is the Defender 90, still widely used by farmers, although the company's more luxurious models are considered as sport utility vehicles (SUVs).***

OTHER MAKES

110 Models, which are refined versions of the original Land Rovers and are still popular for agricultural applications. Numerous specialized agricultural conversions have been made to Land Rover vehicles during the course of their production to suit them to specific tasks, such as carrying and operating implements, in the manner of the Mercedes Unimog.

■ LANZ

In Germany, Lanz produced Bulldog tractors including the Model T crawler and the L, N and P wheeled models offering 15, 23 and 45bhp respectively. The machines were imported into Britain and were popular because of their ability to run on low-grade fuel, including used engine and gearbox oil thinned with paraffin. In 1924 Ford upped the ante when the Fordson F tractor went on sale in Germany, meaning that German manufacturers had to compete. The differing types of fuel employed by Ford and the German manufacturers illustrated a divergence of ideas about tractors. The German companies, such as Stock and Hanomag, compared the Fordson's fuel consumption unfavourably with that of their own machines, which were moving towards diesel fuel. Lanz introduced the Feldank tractor, that was capable of running on poor fuel through its use of a semi-diesel engine.

The initial Bulldogs were crude. The HL model, for example, had no reverse gear: the engine was stalled and run backwards to enable the machine to be reversed.

■ ABOVE *Lanz built farm machinery from 1859 and its Bulldog tractor was regarded as a simple, reliable machine. Prior to World War II Lanz was one of the two major German tractor makers.*

■ LEFT *Lanz Bulldog production was resumed after World War II, despite the company's factory being razed to the ground by Allied bombing. The post-war political situation in Germany affected Lanz's sales adversely.*

Power came from a single horizontal-cylinder two-stroke semi-diesel engine that produced 12hp. The HL was gradually improved, becoming the HR2 in 1926. Lanz was later acquired by John Deere.

■ **LAVERDA**

Laverda was founded in 1873 in Breganze, Italy, and by the beginning of this century had become the leading Italian manufacturer of threshing machines. The company is also noted for its production of motorcycles. In 1975 Fiat Trattori became a shareholder in Laverda, then in 1984 Fiat Trattori became Fiatagri, the Fiat group's holding company for the agricultural machinery sector.

■ **LEYLAND**

In Great Britain, Morris Motors eventually became part of the British Leyland conglomerate. This company was concerned by poor sales of Nuffield tractors, so renamed the brand as British Leyland. Along with this renaming, a new two-tone blue colour scheme was adopted for the tractors.

British Leyland built tractors such as the 270 and 344 models. However, the tractor maker did not have sufficient funds to develop its products and it was gradually overtaken in sales by other tractor makers. Leyland tractors was sold in 1981 and joined with Marshall as a part of the Nickerson organization.

■ ABOVE *A late-1970s British Leyland 344 tractor, in the two-tone blue colour scheme favoured by BL after it had acquired Nuffield as part of the merger with Morris Motors.*

■ RIGHT *The British Leyland badge on the front of this 344 tractor could also be seen on a variety of cars during the 1970s.*

■ BELOW LEFT *Lanz Bulldogs were manufactured in Mannheim, Germany, but when John Deere had acquired the company production of the long-running model was halted.*

■ BELOW *This decaying British Leyland tractor retains its factory-fitted safety cab.*

MASSEY-FERGUSON

■ LEFT *A 1970s Massey-Ferguson 135 photographed in Cappadocia, Turkey.*

In 1953 Harry Ferguson merged his company with the Massey-Harris company. As the deal was being finalized, there arose the question of which exchange rate was to be used. Harry suggested settling the matter with the toss of a coin. He lost the toss, and about a million dollars, but appeared not to care, no doubt realizing that his patents and equipment were in capable hands.

Once Harry Ferguson had sold his tractor company to Massey-Harris the face of tractor manufacturing was profoundly altered. Before the merger the Massey-Harris company had been competing with both Ford and Ferguson. For a while the newly formed Massey-Harris-Ferguson company produced two

MASSEY FERGUSON MF 362 4WD	
Year	1998
Engine	Perkins four cylinder diesel
Power	60 PTO hp, 62bhp
Transmission	Eight forward, two reverse
Weight	2666kg/5877lbs

■ ABOVE LEFT *Massey-Harris was noted for the manufacture of self-propelled combine harvesters, and neglected tractor development to a degree. To catch up they merged with Ferguson in 1953.*

■ LEFT *The 1970s styling of the Massey-Ferguson range was much more angular than that which went before, as evidenced by the line of hood and grille on this MF135 model.*

■ RIGHT *A little modified, probably repainted more than once, but still working more than 30 years after it was made.*

■ LEFT *The two-wheel-drive MF 399 has 41cm/16in diameter front wheels, and 97cm/38in diameter rear ones. It is powered by a six-cylinder Perkins diesel, and has a 12-speed transmission.*

■ BELOW LEFT TOP *The four-wheel-drive version of the Massey-Ferguson MF 362. This tractor is powered by a naturally aspirated, four-cylinder Perkins A4.236 engine.*

■ BELOW LEFT BOTTOM *A dilapidated MF 20 during a break from haymaking.*

■ BELOW RIGHT *A four-cylinder, Perkins diesel-engined Massey-Ferguson 375, donated by the World Business Council to farmers in Tanzania, East Africa.*

separate lines of tractors, continuing with both the Massey-Harris and the Ferguson makes, as both tractors had loyal followers amongst dealers and customers. The MH 50 and Ferguson 40 had different bodywork but were mechanically identical as both models were based on the Ferguson 35. In November 1957 the now Massey-Ferguson Company produced its first "Red and Grey" tractor, the Model MF 35 powered by Perkins engines.

The company was Canadian-based and produced tractors all around the

MASSEY FERGUSON MF 32 CONVENTIONAL COMBINE	
Year	1998
Engine	Valmet 620DSL
Power	129kW (175 DIN hp)
Transmission	Hydrostatic
Weight	10,299kg/22,706lbs

■ ABOVE *Combine harvesters are required to cut the standing crop, then lift it on to the conveyor which takes it to the rasps, which then remove the grain from the straw.*

■ RIGHT *This Massey-Ferguson combine from the 1960s carried out the same task, but the styling of combines and provision of operator comfort were still ahead in the future.*

■ LEFT *This Massey-Ferguson 530 S combine harvester features an open operator station, something that is becoming rarer as cab technology continually progresses.*

■ BELOW *This MF 31 combine was the largest one in the Massey-Ferguson range in 1986 and was powered by a 153hp, turbocharged Perkins engine.*

■ ABOVE *Combines, like tractors, need to maintain traction in fields, but rely on hydrostatic transmissions connected to their large capacity diesel engines.*

■ RIGHT *For harvesting on fields with slopes of up to 11 degrees, Massey-Ferguson has devised the Auto Level system, designed to keep an even spread across the machine's grain-separating components.*

■ ABOVE LEFT *A Massey-Ferguson 3070 tractor, with a Cambridge roller, preparing the land for the next year's crop.*

■ ABOVE RIGHT *A four-wheel-drive Massey-Ferguson tractor, equipped with a hydraulic front loader. This is a versatile and perennially popular farmyard tool.*

■ LEFT *Two generations of Massey-Ferguson tractors at work. The older model is being used to load round hay bales on to the trailer, pulled behind the newer four-wheel-drive model.*

■ BELOW *The Massey-Ferguson 2775 tractor of the 1980s features a V8 Perkins engine of 10,488cc/640cu in displacement.*

■ RIGHT *The four-wheel-drive MF 6180, of 1998, is powered by a Perkins 1006-6T engine, a six-cylinder turbo diesel unit that drives through a gearbox offering 16 forward and reverse gears.*

world. The all-new MF 35 was followed by a range of tractors including the MF 50, MF 65 and MF 85. In 1976 Massey-Ferguson introduced new tractors, the 1505 and 1805 Models, both powered by the 174hp Caterpillar V8 diesel engine.

In the mid-1980s the 3000 Series of Massey-Ferguson machines was made available with a turbo-diesel, 190hp, six-cylinder engine. A smaller Massey-Ferguson tractor was the MF 398, powered by a 3867cc/236cu in diesel engine and featuring a 4x4 transmission. Two Massey-Ferguson tractors from 1986 were the Models 2685 and MF 699. The former had a 5800cc/353.8cu in Perkins turbo-diesel engine that produced 142 hp and was one of the 2005 Series of three tractors: 2645, 2685 and 2725. Each had a four-wheel-drive transmission that incorporated 16 forward and 12 reverse gears. The MF 699 was the most powerful in the MF 600 Series of four tractors, MF 675, 690, 698T and 699. It was powered by a 100hp engine.

Massey-Ferguson itself became part of AGCO in 1994. According to the manufacturer, "For 33 straight years more people have purchased MF tractors than

■ LEFT *A 1993 MF 3095 Autotronic. This is one of the 3000 series of tractors that was among the first Massey-Ferguson tractors to make extensive use of electronics.*

■ BELOW *The Massey-Ferguson MF 3690 Autotronic was another of the 3000 series of tractors of 1993.*

■ LEFT *The 8200 series appeared in 1999; the 8280 had an 8.4-litre engine giving 260hp. An 18-speed powershift gearbox was fitted with "Power Control" which gave left-hand control of direction and changes. A new Continuously Variable Transmission has become available on a few models thanks to the acquisition of Fendt by AGCO.*

■ LEFT *The MF 844 loader is one of the 800 series loaders, designed to be used in conjunction with 60–90hp tractors. It can lift 1700kg/3748lbs to a maximum height of 3.75m/12.3ft.*

MASSEY-FERGUSON MF 4245 4WD TRACTOR

Year	1998
Engine	Perkins 1004-4T
Power	75.8 PTO hp, 88bhp
Transmission	Eight forward, eight reverse
Weight	4330kg/9548lbs

■ RIGHT *A four-wheel-drive Massey Harris 4245 tractor, haymaking with an MF 146 variable chamber round baler.*

■ RIGHT *The MF 7499, seen here pulling an MF Hesston series 2170 square baler, is powered by a six-cylinder diesel engine producing 220hp.*

■ BELOW *The MF 2660 HD was introduced in 2010. The HD stands for Heavy Duty, with a focus on the tractor's power and reliability over technology and comfort.*

■ BELOW MIDDLE *The MF 8670 is a 2009 model tractor powered by an AGCO SISU 6-cylinder turbocharged engine that uses Selective Catalytic Reduction to cut down on the nitrogen oxides emitted.*

any other brand." Massey-Ferguson's current range is comprehensive and includes tractor series offering 22.5–25 hp, 25–60 hp, 38–97 hp, 75–115 hp, and 100–340 hp. Massey-Ferguson also offer a range of conventional combine harvesters, rotary combine harvesters, loaders and balers.

The 22.5–25 hp tractors in the GC Series are designed as sub-compact tractors, while the compact 1500 and 1600 Series cover the 25–60 hp range and specialize in ground care duties. The 2600 Series, both Heavy Duty and standard, are classed as Utility machines covering the 38–97 hp range. The 5400 Series offers power from 75 to 115 hp, while those classed as high-horsepower include the 6400, 7400, 7600 series, and the top-powered 8600 Series ranging from 240 to 340 hp, with a 6-cylinder turbocharged engine displacing 8.4 litres.

■ BELOW *A 1998 six-cylinder 114hp MF 4270 tractor working in conjunction with a Massey-Ferguson Forage Harvester during haymaking.*

MASSEY-HARRIS

■ BELOW *One of the earliest four-wheel-drive tractors was the Massey-Harris General Purpose of 1930. A 226cu in displacement engine powered it.*

■ BOTTOM *The Massey-Harris 101 was introduced in 1938 as a streamlined row crop tractor. It is powered by a high compression, gasoline-fuelled Chrysler six-cylinder engine.*

Massey-Harris was formed in 1891 in Toronto, Canada from the merger of two companies who manufactured farm implements. Daniel Massey had been making implements since 1847 while A. Harris, Son & Company were competitors for the same market. The Model 25 was a popular tractor through the 1930s and 40s. Another Massey-Harris tractor of this era was the 101 of 1935. This machine was driven by a 24hp Chrysler in-line six-cylinder engine. A third was the Twin Power Challenger powered by an I-head four-cylinder engine that produced approximately 36hp. The company chose a red and straw-yellow colour scheme for its tractors in the mid-1930s.

After World War II, Massey-Harris introduced the Model 44 based around the same engine as the pre-war

■ BOTTOM *The Massey-Harris Challenger of 1936 was the last from the company to have the Wallis tractor-style boiler plate unit frame. The rear wheels were adjustable to cater for different row widths.*

■ RIGHT *A Massey-Harris combine in Britain during the 1950s.*

■ BELOW RIGHT *The Challenger was rated as a 26-36hp tractor, power came from an in-line, four-cylinder, gasoline engine.*

Challenger and using a five-speed transmission. The company brought out a new range in 1947 which still included the Model 44, to which were added the Models 11, 20, 30 and 55. The Model 30 featured a five-speed transmission and more than 32,000 were made before 1953 when the company merged with Ferguson.

The tractor built in the largest numbers by Massey-Harris prior to the merger was the Massey-Harris Pony. This was a small tractor and proved more popular in overseas markets than in the United States and Canada, where it was considered too small for many farming applications. It was produced in the Canadian Woodstock plant from 1947 and at the Marquette factory in France from 1951. A decade later the production total exceeded 121,000.

MASSEY-HARRIS MODEL 101

Year	1939
Engine	Chrysler L-head T57-503 gasoline
Power	23.94 drawbar hp
Transmission	Three speed
Weight	2597kg/5725lbs

■ LEFT *The Massey-Harris Pony was produced in Massey-Harris's French and Canadian plants and production eventually totalled in excess of 121,000.*

The first version of the Pony was powered by a four-cylinder Continental engine driving a three-speed transmission with one reverse gear. Its top speed was 11kph/7mph and it produced 11hp. The Pony was basic in its initial form, but was refined over its production run. Canadian production was halted in 1954, but in 1957 the 820 Pony was offered from the French factory with a five-speed gearbox and a German Hanomag diesel engine. It was further refined for 1959, when it was redesignated the 821 Pony. Around 90,000 of the Pony tractors manufactured were built in the French factory and this was Massey-Harris's first real European success. The post-war Model 44 had been a success for the Massey-Harris company in the United States, where 90,000 were made in Racine, Wisconsin. It featured the rounded pre-war styling but was mechanically new. The customer had a choice of four-cylinder engines that used either petrol, paraffin or diesel fuel. A hydraulic lift system for implements was introduced in 1950. The company chose the Model 44 as its tractor to enter the British market and started by manufacturing them in Manchester in 1948, although operations were later moved north to Kilmarnock, Scotland. This was largely an assembly process because the components were imported from Racine. The models offered included row crop, high clearance and Roadless-converted

■ LEFT *Many European manufactured Massey-Harris 820 Ponys were fitted with diesel engines made by Hanomag.*

■ BELOW LEFT *A distinctive feature of the 820 Pony was its rounded radiator grille.*

MASSEY-HARRIS MODEL 44	
Year	1949
Engine	Four cylinder I-head
Power	27.75 drawbar hp
Transmission	Three speed
Weight	2307kg/5085lbs

■ ABOVE *Massey-Harris started production of the 744 PD tractor in Manchester in 1948. Production was later moved to Scotland and the tractor redesignated as the 744D.*

■ BELOW *The Massey-Harris 33 was made between 1952 and 1955. It was an upgraded version of the two plough 30 that had been introduced in 1947.*

half-track versions. Around 17,000 were made in total and in later years approximately 11,000 of a Perkins-engined variant – the 745 – were made before production was halted in 1957. In that year, after the merger with Ferguson, the company was renamed Massey- Ferguson and another new line of tractors was introduced.

The following three examples of results from Nebraska Tractor Tests give an illustration of how the Massey-Harris tractor range progressed in the post-war decades. Nebraska Test Number 306 was on the Massey-Harris Model 101 S made by the Massey-Harris Co, Racine, Wisconsin, and tested between 22 and 26 May 1939. The tractor's equipment consisted of 10–36 rear tyres, 5.00–15 front tyres, a six-cylinder L-head Chrysler T57–503 engine, run at 1500 and 1800rpm, 3.125in bore × 4.375in stroke, and an Auto-Lite electrical system. The tractor's weight was 1726kg/3805lb on steel wheels and 2597kg/5725lb on rubber tyres.

The Test H Data obtained with rubber tyres was as follows: gear: 3, speed: 7.27kph/4.52mph, load: 901.3kg/1987lb, rated load: 23.94 drawbar hp, fuel economy: 9.85hp hours per gallon. The Test H Data on steel wheels was as follows: gear: 2, speed: 5.92kph/3.68mph, load: 844kg/1862lb, rated load: 18.29 drawbar hp, fuel economy: 7.46hp hours per gallon. The fuel economy at 1800rpm maximum with a load of 36.15 belt hp was 10.89 hp

hours per gallon. Fuel economy at 1500rpm with a rated load of 31.5 belt hp yielded 11.86hp hours per gallon.

Nebraska Test Number 427 was carried out on the Massey-Harris 44K Standard made by the Massey-Harris Co, Racine, Wisconsin, and tested between 29 September and 14 October 1949. The tractor's equipment included a four-cylinder I-head engine, 1350rpm, 3.875in bore × 5.5 in stroke, a 6 volt Auto-Lite electrical system, a Zenith 62AJ10 carburettor. The tractor's weight was 2306kg/5085lb and the Test H Data obtained was as follows: gear: 3, speed: 4.29mph, load: 1182kg/2608lb, slippage: 4.4 per cent, rated load: 27.7 drawbar hp, fuel economy: 10.42hp

■ ABOVE *Despite the familiar colours of this tractor on a French beach it is not a John Deere, but a repainted Massey-Harris Pony from the French Marquette factory.*

■ LEFT *The Massey-Harris 745 was a Perkins diesel-powered tractor intended as an improved version of the 744. Approximately 11,000 were made between 1954 and 1958 in the Kilmarnock, Scotland plant.*

■ BELOW *A hard-worked example of a French built, Massey-Harris Pony, more than forty years after it was made. The mudguards and seat are not the originals.*

■ BELOW *A gasoline-engined version of the European-manufactured Massey-Harris Pony. The engine is an in-line four-cylinder unit.*

hours per gallon. 506kg/1116lb of ballast was added to each rear wheel for tests F, G, and H. Test G resulted in a low-gear maximum pull of 2128kg/4692lb. Fuel economy at Test C maximum load of 35.66 belt hp was 11.3hp hours per gallon. Test D rated load of 33.64 belt hp yielded 11.19hp hours per gallon. Tractor fuel was used for the 45.5 hours of engine running time.

Nebraska Test Number 603 was carried out seven years later on a Massey-Harris 333 made by Massey-Harris-Ferguson Inc, Racine, Wisconsin, and was tested between 25 October and 3 November 1956. The tractor's equipment included a four-cylinder I-head engine, 1500rpm, 3.688in bore × 4.875in stroke, 12–38 rear tyres, 6.50–16 front tyres with a tractor weight of 2685kg/5920lb. The Test H Data recorded was: gear: 3, high range, speed: 7.94kph/4.93mph, load: 1026kg/2262lb, slippage: 3.76 per cent, rated load: 29.71 drawbar hp, fuel economy: 10.69hp hours per gallon. 466kg/1028lb of ballast was added to each rear wheel for tests F, G and H. Test G resulted in a low-gear maximum pull of 2452kg/5407lb at 2.1kph/1.31mph with a slippage of 12.08 per cent. Fuel economy at Test C maximum load of 39.84 belt hp was 12.37hp hours per gallon.

■ BELOW *One reason that production of the Massey-Harris Pony was continued in Europe, after being halted in Canada, was that the size of the tractor proved more suitable to the smaller scale farms of Europe than those of North America.*

Mercedes-Benz

Benz started building tractors in 1919 when it offered the 40 and 80hp gasoline-engined "Land Traktors", but the Benz-Sendling S7 of 1923 was the first diesel-engined tractor manufactured by Benz. It featured power from a 30hp two-cylinder, vertical engine. The machine itself was a three-wheeled tractor with a single driven rear wheel, although outriggers were supplied to ensure stability during use. A four-wheeled machine, the BK, quickly superseded the S7.

■ BENZ AND DAIMLER

In 1926 Benz and Daimler merged, adopting the name Mercedes-Benz. During the 1930s the company

■ ABOVE *The MB-trac 1500 Mercedes Benz tractor is fully reversible which means it can be used as a dual directional tractor by rotating the controls, instruments and seat through 180 degrees in the cab.*

■ LEFT *The dual directional nature of the MB-trac 1500 means it can be used to push or pull implements where appropriate. A 150hp turbo diesel engine of 5673cc/346cu in displacement provides ample power.*

MERCEDES-BENZ U1200 UNIMOG

Year	1998
Engine	OM 366 A in-line six cylinder 5958cc/ 363cu in
Power	125hp
Transmission	Eight forward, eight reverse
Weight	8500kg/18,739lbs

■ RIGHT *Mercedes-Benz Unimogs are supplied in numerous configurations, and have been manufactured for several decades, offering four-wheel drive.*

produced the OE model that was powered by a horizontally arranged single-cylinder, four-stroke diesel engine that produced 20hp. One of these machines competed in the 1930 World Tractor Trials held in England. Prior to World War II tractor production in Germany was relatively small in scale, and even in the coming conflict the German army was to rely heavily on horse-drawn vehicles, in stark contrast to the mechanized armies of the Allies.

In the post-war years two of the first popular and successful tractors were of a four-wheel-drive configuration. One was the MAN 325, that remained in production for two decades until the company shelved tractor production in favour of trucks. The second was the Boehringer Unimog, which was later sold to Mercedes-Benz. Mercedes-Benz has continued to produce this machine, still known as the Unimog, for several decades in a variety of configurations, including models designed for agricultural use as implement carriers.

■ ABOVE *A short wheel base platform variant U900 Unimog from the mid-1980s. The Unimog is designed to accept a variety of specialist implements.*

■ MERCEDES UNIMOG

The Unimog has evolved into the Unimog System of vehicle and implements, based on a wide range of vehicles and an almost unlimited number of implement attachment options. Several ranges are offered, from compact to heavy-duty models, and each has at least three standard implement attachment points and a hydraulic system that ensures implement operation. The Unimog has been designed so that its wheels distribute pressure evenly on the ground in order to minimize soil compaction. It is of all-wheel-drive configuration to ensure optimum traction.

Another advanced Mercedes-Benz tractor was the MB-trac 1500, introduced in 1986. This tractor featured a turbo-diesel engine of 5675cc/346cu in displacement that produced power in the region of 150hp. The MB-trac was designed as a dual-direction tractor.

■ RIGHT *To enhance ground clearance, the Unimog, such as this 1990s U1200 model, are based on portal axles.*

OTHER MAKES

■ MINSK

The Minsk Tractor Works sells its tractors through agricultural machine distributors in 60 countries around the world. Tractor production has included models such as the MTZ-320, MTZ-682, MTZ-1221 and MTZ-920.

MINNEAPOLIS-MOLINE

■ BELOW *The Minneapolis-Moline Universal Model J was a row crop tractor with infinite rear wheel adjustment, capable on rubber tyres of 12.2mph (19.5kph).*

In the hectic 1920s, many new tractor-making companies were formed while others merged to form new corporations. In 1929 three extant companies, Minneapolis Steel and Machinery, the Minneapolis Threshing Machine Company and the Moline Implement Company, all merged and Minneapolis-Moline Power Implement Company was the result. Amongst these companies' assets were Twin City Tractors and Minneapolis Tractors, and in the wake of the merger came the rationalization of their products and factories. The Twin City tractor range was chosen as the one to spearhead the Minneapolis-Moline push into the market, with production continuing in the Minneapolis factory. Initially the machines were marketed as Twin City tractors with the Minneapolis-Moline name added, but as the range evolved, the Twin City brand name was reduced in prominence and Minneapolis-Moline became the brand name. The constituent companies are detailed here.

■ BELOW *The Minneapolis-Moline Model R was a two-plough tricycle, row crop tractor, manufactured between 1939 and 1941.*

■ **MOLINE UNIVERSAL**

In 1915 the Moline Plow Company had purchased the Universal Tractor Company of Columbus, Ohio. The product line was moved to Moline, Illinois and a new building was constructed for the production of the Moline Universal Tractor. This was a two-wheel unit designed for use with the farmer's horse-drawn implements as well as with newly developed Moline tractor-drawn implements. The Universal was commonly referred to as the first row crop tractor. It was equipped with electric lights and a starter, components that were considered advanced for the time.

After World War I, a number of automobile manufacturers wanted to produce tractors and the Moline Plow Company was courted by manufacturer John N. Willys. Willys purchased Moline from the owners, the Stephens

■ LEFT *The Minneapolis-Moline Model U was available in both row crop tricycle and standard tread forms. The UDLX was available with a cab, but was only made in small numbers.*

MINNEAPOLIS-MOLINE UNIVERSAL MODEL J	
Year	1935
Engine	F-head four cylinder
Power	16hp
Transmission	Five speed
Weight	2222kg/4900lbs

family, and subsequently his automobile company began producing the Universal tractor. Willys had as his partners in the tractor trade George N. Peek, a well-known farm equipment executive, and General Hugh Johnson. Willys continued to produce the Moline Universal tractor into the 1920s. In this decade the tractor boom subsided; Willys withdrew from the Moline Plow Company and sold out to his partners. General Johnson became president and R. W. Lea

■ BELOW *The Model U was tested in the Nebraska tractor tests in 1938 and produced 30.86 drawbar and 38.12 belt horsepower at 1275rpm.*

■ LEFT *The Minneapolis-Moline Model V was a compact tractor. This example was produced in 1944.*

■ BELOW *The Minneapolis-Moline Model Z was introduced in 1937 as a row crop tractor, painted in the new Prairie Gold colour.*

became vice-president of the Moline Plow Company. When they retired their associates took over and operated the business as the Moline Implement Company, which it remained until joining the Minneapolis-Moline organization in 1929.

■ TYPES A AND B

The Minneapolis Threshing Machine Company began producing steam traction engines in 1889 just west of Minneapolis, where the town of Hopkins was founded, and flourished solely because of the company. In 1893, a Victory threshing machine and steam engine built by the company won several medals at the World Exposition in Chicago. By 1911 the Minneapolis Threshing Machine Company was building tractors under the Minneapolis name and went on to build many large tractors before the Minneapolis-Moline merger, but these tractors were better suited to sod-breaking than for row crop applications. After building a couple of row-type tractors the company marketed its Minneapolis 17-30 Type A and Type B. These were cross-motor row crop tractors and remained in production even after the merger. During the 1920s, even before the Minneapolis-Moline organization, the company's products were advertised as being part of "The Great Minneapolis Line".

In the late 1800s and early 1900s the Minneapolis Steel and Machinery Company was primarily a structural steel producer, turning out thousands of tons per year. The company also produced the Corliss steam engine, that served as a power unit for many flour mills in the Dakotas. In 1910 Minneapolis Steel and Machinery produced a tractor under the Twin City name, the Twin City 40. At the outbreak of World War I, the company was one of the larger tractor producers. It also manufactured a number of tractors under contract, such as the Bull tractor for the Bull Tractor Co. Through the 1920s, Twin City tractors were promoted with slogans such as "Team Of Steel" and "Built To Do The Work". After 1929, this line was still produced in the

■ LEFT *Minneapolis-Moline came about from the merger in 1929 of three companies involved in the production of farm machinery.*

■ RIGHT *The UTS, like others in the Minneapolis-Moline range, was equipped with red-painted wheels.*

MINNEAPOLIS-MOLINE MODEL U	
Year	1938
Engine	In-line four cylinder
Power	30.86 drawbar and 38.12 belt hp
Transmission	Five speed
Weight	n/k

■ RIGHT *Although the M-M logo stands for Minneapolis-Moline, the tractor manufacturers lost no time in using it to suggest that M-M made Modern Machinery.*

■ BELOW *The Minneapolis-Moline UTS was a wartime model in the U-series of tractors. The similar UTU was a tricycle row crop tractor.*

old Minneapolis Steel and Machinery Lake Street Plant under the Minneapolis-Moline Twin City tractor banner.

In the new Minneapolis-Moline Power Implement Company, two of the major historic agricultural machine-producing cities were represented. After the merger, the Minneapolis-Moline Power Implement Company Officers for 1929 were as follows: J. L. Record (MSM) Chairman of the Board; W. C. Macfarlane (MSM) President and Administrative Officer; George L. Gillette (MSM) Vice-President of Sales; Harold B. Dineen (Moline) Vice-President of Production and Design; N. A. Wiff (MSM) Vice-President; W. C. Rich (MSM) Secretary; W. S. Peddle (MSM) Treasurer. In reality most of the top officers of the three companies were content to retire instead of becoming involved in Minneapolis-Moline Power Implement, preferring that the younger generation take over.

After experiments with the luxury UDLX tractor with an enclosed cab,

■ ABOVE *This 1947 Minneapolis-Moline GTA tractor of 1947 was designed to run on liquid petroleum gas (LPG).*

■ LEFT *Minneapolis-Moline tractors were restyled in the immediate post-war years. This is a restyled, row crop tricycle Model Z from 1949.*

■ LEFT *One of the last new tractors to be added to the M-M range before the outbreak of World War II was the GT, a standard tread tractor that was tested at Nebraska in 1939.*

MINNEAPOLIS-MOLINE M-5	
Year	1960
Engine	5506cc/336cu in Diesel
Power	58.15hp at 1500rpm
Transmission	Six speed
Weight	n/k

Minneapolis-Moline launched the GT as a five-plough tractor in 1939. In the Nebraska Tractor Tests its measured power output was 55hp at the belt, despite being rated at only 49hp by its manufacturer. Powered by a gasoline-fuelled in-line four-cylinder engine, it developed its maximum power at 1075rpm. Later, in the aftermath of World War II, increased power versions, the G and GB Models, were offered.

The White Motor Company purchased Minneapolis-Moline in 1963. AGCO purchased White Tractors in 1991, and in doing so acquired the rights to the Minneapolis-Moline name.

■ ABOVE LEFT ***By the time this 1969 M670 tractor had been made, Minneapolis-Moline had been owned by White for six years. The company was later acquired by AGCO.***

■ RIGHT ***The fact that this 1970 Minneapolis-Moline G1050 tractor, of 504cu in displacement, is designed to run on LPG gas, is made clear by the provision of a tank in front of the radiator.***

NEW HOLLAND

The New Holland Machine Company was founded in 1895 in Pennsylvania and specialized in the manufacture of agricultural equipment. It endured until 1940 when New Holland changed owners and, following a company reorganization, began production of one of the first successful automatic pick-up hay balers. In 1947 the Sperry Corporation acquired the New Holland Machine Company and formed Sperry New Holland. In 1964 Sperry New Holland purchased a major interest in Claeys, which was by this time one of the largest combine manufacturers in Europe. Sperry New Holland launched the haybine mower-conditioner, Model 460. This was capable of accomplishing what had previously required two or three machines to do and was perceived as a significant innovation in hay-harvesting technology.

FORD NEW HOLLAND 8830	
Year	1998
Engine	6571cc/401cu in, diesel
Power	170hp
Transmission	18 forward, nine reverse
Weight	6804kg/15,000lbs

■ BELOW ***New Holland is a noted manufacturer of an automatic pickup hay baler. The company expanded its operations by buying a major interest in Claeys, an established European company.***

■ MERGER

In 1986 the Ford Motor Company acquired Sperry New Holland and merged it with Ford Tractor Operations, naming the new company Ford New Holland. In 1991 Fiat acquired Ford

■ RIGHT ***During the 1970s companies such as Case, Claas and New Holland began to dominate the increasingly international European market.***

New Holland Inc, merged it with FiatGeotech and named the new company N. H. Geotech. In 1993 this company was renamed New Holland. At its second worldwide convention held in Orlando, Florida, New Holland launched 24 tractor models in three different ranges alongside the Fiat-Hitachi Compact Line.

The articulated tractors in the Versatile 82 Series are high-powered machines designed for the biggest of fields and the heaviest applications. The range includes the Models 9282, 9482, 9682 and 9882, all of which are powered by six-cylinder engines of varying horsepower with twelve-speed transmissions in both two- and four-wheel-drive configurations. The Series 70 tractors have power outputs that range between 170 and 240hp. They incorporate New Holland's own "PowerShift" transmission which offers single lever control of the 18 forward

■ ABOVE ***A New Holland 8070 combine harvester loading a trailer with the grain which has been threshed and separated in the combine.***

■ RIGHT ***This New Holland combine is the CR980, seen here with a TG285 tractor. The TG series shares many of the same components as the Case IH MX Magnum to help reduce production costs within the CNH Company.***

and nine reverse gears. They are manufactured in Winnipeg, Canada and marketed worldwide. The tractors are available with or without cab, or with ROPS (Rollover Protection Structure). The third range of New Holland tractors is the 90 Series, whose models have a range of transmissions. The 100–90 and 110–90 Models are manufactured in Jesi, Italy, while the 140–90, 160–90 and 180–90 Models are manufactured in Curitiba, Brazil.

In 1997 New Holland completed its purchase of Ford Motor Credit Company's partnership interests in the two joint ventures that provide financing for New Holland's products in the United States. New Holland also signed an agreement with Manitou for the design and production of a New Holland range of telescopic handlers. In India in 1998 New Holland completed the construction of a new plant for the manufacture of tractors in the 35–75hp range, and had produced 150,000 machines by 2012.

In 1999 the TS and TM series replaced the 35 and 40 series. New Holland merged with Case IH in 2002 to produce CNH.

The Basildon plant ceased producing the T series in 2008. In 2010 the T4000 range and some of the T5000 were replaced by the T4 series. Also introduced were the T8 and T9 series, with emission-reduction systems.

NEW HOLLAND NH 6635

Year	1996
Engine	Turbo diesel
Power	85hp (63 kW)
Transmission	Optional with creeper
Weight	n/k

■ TOP *The 40 Series of New Holland tractors such as this model 7840 of 1996 can be considered state of the art, with its ergonomically designed cabs and modern four-wheel-drive systems.*

■ LEFT *A 1996 New Holland 7740 tractor from the 40 Series, with a New Holland 640 round baler in tow. The baler is capable of producing circular bales of up to 1.5m/5ft diameter.*

■ LEFT *The New Holland T5.115 meets the latest Tier 4 emissions with its 115hp 4-cylinder engine.*

■ ABOVE *A Ford New Holland 8340, one of the last to bear the Ford name.*

■ BELOW *New Holland also manufactures self-propelled forage harvesters. This 533hp Caterpillar-powered FX60 is accompanied by a TM175 tractor in 2005.*

NUFFIELD

William Morris made his reputation as the force behind Morris cars, which became one of the British motor industry's most renowned names. As early as 1926 he had become interested in the tractor market and produced a small crawler tractor based on the track mechanism of a light tank. This project was later abandoned, but not forgotten, and work was progressing on another machine as the world moved towards the end of the war in the mid-1940s. A dozen prototypes were being tested in Lincolnshire by 1946 and, boosted by the success of these machines, plans for full-scale production at the Wolseley car factory were made. So Nuffield entered the tractor market with the Universal, which it unveiled at the 1948 Smithfield Agricultural Show.

The Universal was offered in two versions: the M4 was a four-wheeled tractor and the M3 was a tricycle type for row crop work. The engine was derived from the wartime Morris Commercial engine, a four-cylinder side valve, and its tractor application was started on petrol and run on paraffin. It produced 42hp at 2000rpm. Later a diesel variant was offered, initially with a Perkins P4 unit, then later with a 3.4 litre British Motor Corporation (BMC) diesel following the Austin and Morris merger. In 1957 came the Universal 3, a three-cylinder diesel-engined tractor. The Universal 4/60 was announced in 1961. This was a 60hp tractor and the increased power had been achieved by boring out the existing 3.4 litre engine to 3.8 litres.

Production was eventually moved to the Bathgate plant in Scotland via the Morris Motors plant at Cowley in Oxfordshire. The Nuffield tractors were

■ ABOVE LEFT *Sir William Morris was the man behind Nuffield tractors, allegedly after being asked to build tractors in the UK to compete with the numerous imported models available in Britain after World War II.*

■ BELOW *The Nuffield Universal was introduced to British farmers at the 1948 Smithfield, London show.*

■ LEFT *This is a restored version of the 1955 M4, powered by a version of the Morris Commercial truck engine that had been proven in numerous Morris vehicles during the war years.*

■ RIGHT *A diesel version of the Nuffield M4. The engine was initially sourced from Perkins, then a 3.4 litre displacement British Motor Corporation diesel was used.*

■ BELOW *The early Nuffield M4 was regarded as a viable British alternative to imported American models. It had a five-speed transmission and a truck engine, and was noted for speed.*

■ BELOW *The 1949 M4 had a three-point linkage, drawbar and rear PTO drive.*

given a facelift in 1964 and became the 10–60 and 10–42 models. The tractors were redesigned for 1967, but before they could find widespread acceptance, Nuffield was involved in the merger that created the British Leyland Motor Corporation, making Nuffield tractors into Leylands. In 1981 Leyland was sold to the Nickerson organization.

NUFFIELD M4	
Year	1948
Engine	Morris Commercial ETA
Power	42hp at 2000rpm
Transmission	Five speed
Weight	n/k

OLIVER

Many of the major tractor manufacturing corporations were formed from the merger of numerous small companies, and Oliver is an example of this. In 1929, Hart-Parr, Nichols and Shepard and the American Seeding Machine Company all merged with the Oliver Chilled Plow Company to form the Oliver Farm Equipment Sales Company. The company then began to design a completely new line of tractors. Oliver itself dated back to 1855 and bore the name of its Scottish-born founder, James Oliver, who had developed a chilled steel plough. He had patented a process that gave the steel used in his ploughs a hard surface and tough consistency.

Once the Oliver Farm Equipment Sales Company was formed, the original Oliver company's prototype row crop models Models A and B could go into production. Oliver was the first company to use laterally adjustable rear wheels to suit the differing row spacings of different crops, but other manufacturers soon followed. These tractors were powered by a 18–27 four-cylinder engine that was also fitted to the company's line of conventional tractors, the Oliver Hart-Parr standard models. These were available in Standard, Western, Ricefield and Orchard versions and built until 1937. With a choice of four- or six-cylinder engines, these models became the Oliver 90 during the late 1930s. This was a three-speed 49hp machine.

■ ABOVE AND RIGHT *The Oliver Row Crop 60 made its debut in 1940 as a compact version of the already extant Row Crop 70.*

OLIVER 60 ROW CROP

Year	1940
Engine	1894cc/115cu in
Power	n/k
Transmission	Four speed
Weight	907kg/2000lbs

■ BELOW *An Oliver Model 70 from 1937, by which time Oliver had dropped the Hart-Parr name.*

■ ROW CROP 70 HC

The company achieved unexpected success with the Oliver Hart-Parr Row Crop 70 HC, which was introduced to the farming public in October 1935. This streamlined machine was fitted with a high compression, gasoline-fuelled, six-cylinder engine and was noted as being quiet and smooth running. By February 1936 Oliver had

■ ABOVE LEFT *The Oliver 80 was another new model for 1940 although it did not have the streamlined styling of the 60 and 70 models.*

■ ABOVE RIGHT *The 80 was available with a gasoline engine, seen here, or one suited to running on kerosene distillate.*

sold in excess of 5000 examples, which was 3000 more than anticipated. An electric starter and lights were options.

In 1937 the Hart-Parr suffix was dropped from the company name so that the Model 70 Row Crop models carried only the Oliver name on their streamlined hoods. In the Nebraska Test the high-octane-fuelled, six-cylinder Row Crop 70 produced 22.64 drawbar hp and 28.37 belt hp. The Models 80 and 90 followed in 1938. The 80 had the angular look of earlier models while the 90 was run on kerosene. Oliver made both 90 and 99 Models between 1938 and 1952. After this date both were referred to as Model 99s. In 1940 the company introduced a smaller tractor, the 60, in a row crop configuration and in 1944 it acquired Cletrac.

■ FLEETLINE MODELS

In 1948 Oliver unveiled a line of tractors to mark its 100th year in business. They were known as Fleetline Models 66, 77 and 88 and identified by a new grille and sheetmetal. Each was fitted with a power take-off and the range of engines offered something for every customer. Engine displacements ranged from the 2113cc/129cu in diesel to 3784cc/231cu in diesel installed in the 99 Model. Other diesel options in the new range included the 77 and 88 Models; otherwise the tractors used four-cylinder gasoline and paraffin engines. PTO equipment was standard but hydraulic lifts were not.

These models were followed by the Super Series of 44, 55, 66, 77, 88 and 99 Models. The Super 44 was the smallest model in the range, powered by a four-cylinder Continental L-head engine that was offset to permit the operator better visibility for field use. The Super 55 was a compact utility tractor which on gasoline produced 29.6 drawbar hp and 34.39 belt hp. Production of the Oliver 55 continued after Oliver was taken over by White. The Super 99 of 1954 was available with a three-cylinder, two-stroke, supercharged, General Motors diesel engine with a displacement of 3770cc/230cu in or an Oliver diesel. It was equipped with a three-point hitch and a cab was an extra-cost option.

In 1960 White Motor Corporation bought Oliver and later Cockshutt and Minneapolis-Moline. All eventually merged as White Farm Equipment.

■ LEFT *The Oliver 1955 model featured an angular cab, and was built during the 1970s, more than a decade after Oliver had been acquired by White. Both companies later became part of AGCO.*

RENAULT

■ BELOW *A Renault 145.54. This is one of a modern range of different capacity tractors, of a similar design, powered by turbocharged diesel engines.*

In the early days of European tractor production France lagged behind the main European countries; tractor production was confined to the Renault Car Company although some Austin tractors were assembled in France. In the years immediately after World War I Renault (along with Peugeot and Citroën) announced the production of a crawler tractor. Renault's crawler was based on its experience of tank manufacture during the war. The tractor was subsequently designated the GP. It used a four-cylinder 30hp gasoline engine and a three-speed transmission with a single reverse gear; steering was by means of a tiller. An upgraded version, the H1, went on sale in 1920. Renault then developed the HO, a wheeled version of the H1. These models were powered by a four-cylinder engine that produced 20hp at 1600rpm and featured epicyclic reduction gears in the rear wheels. All these tractor models were based around a steel girder frame and the engine was enclosed within a stylish curved bonnet (hood) that bore a close resemblance to Renault's trucks and cars of the time. The PE tractor was introduced in 1922 and was considerably redesigned from the earlier models. Renault introduced the VY tractor in 1933, powered by a 30hp in-line, four-cylinder diesel engine. It had a front-positioned radiator and the engine was enclosed. This model was painted yellow and grey and became the first diesel tractor to be produced in significant numbers in France. Renault

■ BELOW *The four-wheel-drive Renault Ceres 610RX, along with the smaller 85hp 95X, was part of a range with a similar streamlined design.*

RENAULT 106.54 TRACTOR	
Year	1996
Engine	Six cylinder turbo diesel
Power	100hp, 75kW
Transmission	12 forward, 12 reverse
Weight	n/k

■ RIGHT *Renault produces general tractors, such as this one seen ploughing in England, and specialist machines for orchard use.*

■ BELOW LEFT *A Renault tractor equipped with a French-manufactured hydraulic front loader.*

■ BELOW RIGHT *The Renault 106.54 is a four-wheel-drive 100hp tractor. The dual tyres and four-wheel drive help traction in heavy clay soils.*

was also the major force in the World War II French tractor industry and had built in excess of 8500 tractors by 1948. Many of these were of the 303E model, although Renault followed this with the 3042 in 1948.

Renault became popular thanks to its 14 series tractors, with the 145-14 TZ leading the company's line-up before 1989. The range was updated with the launch of the 54 Series in 1989 when the flagship became the 155hp 155-54 TZ. A few years later the the larger 160hp 160-94 TZ and 180hp 180-94 TZ were introduced. Ceres and Ares tractors appeared in 1997 alongside existing models. The 197–250hp Atles range was launched in 2000 and had three models: the 915, 925 and 935. In 2003 the Claas Company bought Renault Agriculture and started producing Ceres, Ares and Atles in Claas livery. The current Claas range includes the Nexos, Elios, Axion and Xerion tractor series.

ROADLESS TRACTION LTD

In the UK, Roadless Traction Ltd of Hounslow designed numerous half-track bogie conversions for vehicles as diverse as a Foden steam lorry and a Morris Commercial. It later devised tracked conversions for various makes of tractor, including the Fordson E27N and forestry tractor conversions for Land Rover.

■ PHILIP JOHNSON

The company name Roadless Traction Ltd was registered on 4 March 1919 by Lieutenant Colonel Henry Johnson. Johnson was born in 1877 and attended the King Edward VII School in Birmingham before studying engineering at the Durham College of Science. After Durham he gained work experience in the heavy industries of South Wales before the outbreak of the Boer War in 1899. Johnson volunteered for the army, but was not selected because of defective eyesight, and found his way to South Africa by working his passage on a cattle boat. Once in Cape Town he was able to get seconded to a steam road transport company of the Royal Engineers as a result of his experience with steam engines. The unit was responsible for towing howitzers and field guns as well as ammunition, mostly behind Fowler steam engines. It was here in South Africa that Johnson was able to study the use of mechanized transport in off-road situations. Johnson returned to England in 1906 and took up employment with the Leeds-based firm of Fowler and Compan. This required him to assist in the export of steam engines and involved a period of living in India. There Johnson is reputed to have delivered many Fowler engines under their own steam to the remotest parts of the sub-continent.

Johnson returned from India in 1915 to take up a wartime post with the Ministry of Munitions. He spent much of those war years working on tank development and went out to France to the Front once the tanks were being used in combat. His tank development work, including that with rubber tracks and a spring and cable suspension system, continued after World War I.

Johnson's military duties ended in 1918 and during the 1920s he started converting Foden and Sentinel team lorries to half-tracks by substituting the driven rear wheels with tracks and bogies. It is estimated that the company invested £50,000 in the development of its products in the seven years following 1921. The company moved into Gunnersbury House, a former nunnery, in Hounslow, Middlesex in 1923. Johnson bought the house, leasing part to the company and living in the remainder.

Motor lorries of varying sizes were also converted to half-track in this period, including those from Peugeot,

■ RIGHT
A 1941 Fordson N Roadless, equipped with a front-mounted, chain drive, Hesford winch.

■ OPPOSITE BOTTOM ***A Fordson Roadless half-track, in service with the Royal Air Force during World War II, towing a refuelling trailer. A group of WAAFs are refuelling a Hawker Hurricane.***

■ BELOW
A Fordson E27N converted to a half-track through the installation of Roadless DG4 tracks.

Vulcan, Austin, Guy, Daimler, FWD and Morris Commercial. These were sold to customers in places as diverse as Scotland, Sudan and Peru. One of the company's first major commercially successful orders was for a batch of lorries for the Anglo-Persian Oil Company for use in connection with oil exploration in Iran. Roadless supplied converted Morris Commercial lorries to fulfil this order.

FORDSON N ROADLESS TRACTOR

Year	1944
Engine	In-line four cylinder gasoline
Power	20hp
Transmission	Three speed
Weight	1225kg/2700lbs plus track bogies

■ CRAWLER TRACTORS

Following on from this growing success, the company turned its attention to tractors and potential agricultural applications for its technology. One of the first machines to be converted was the Peterbro tractor, manufactured by the Peter Brotherhood Ltd of Peterborough, Cambridgeshire.

This tractor used a four-cylinder gasoline-paraffin engine of Ricardo design that produced 30hp. Few of these tractors were made and even fewer – possibly only one – converted to half-track configuration using the Roadless components. Roadless also cooperated with another Peterborough-based firm, Barford and Perkins Ltd, to produce a half-track tractor. This was based on that company's THD road roller and powered by a rear-mounted, vertical, two-cylinder McLaren-Benz engine driving through a three-speed forward and reverse transmission. It utilized Roadless tracks and had a drawbar pull rated at 6858kg/17,419lb, but as it weighed 11 tons it was of limited use off-road and the project was abandoned.

The development of rubber-jointed tracks eventually enabled Roadless to

produce viable agricultural machines. Its system, known as "E tracks", was easily adapted to many tractors and required little maintenance, so endearing it to farmers. The company converted AEC-manufactured Rushton tractors to full-tracks using E3 rubber-jointed tracks that were skid-steered, Ferodo-lined and differential-braked. Rushton Tractors was formed as a subsidiary of AEC in 1929 to manufacture Rushton and Roadless Rushton tractors. There were two variants of the Roadless Rushton with different lengths of track: the standard version had two rollers on each side while the other had three. These tractors were amongst those successfully demonstrated at the 1930 World Agricultural Tractor Trials held at Wallingford, Oxfordshire. The tractor was a success and sold in both the UK and export markets, although Rushton went out of business after an Algerian customer defaulted on payment for 100 tractors shipped there for use in vineyards.

The Fordson tractor was gaining in popularity and in 1929 the first Roadless conversion on a Fordson tractor was carried out on a Fordson Model N. It was successfully demonstrated on Margate Beach early in 1930, when it hauled 3 tons of seaweed off the beach. Roadless-converted Fordsons soon became popular and were offered in two track lengths. Fordson tractor production was moved from Ireland to Dagenham in 1931 and Fordson approved the conversion for use with its machines. The association between Ford and Roadless Traction would endure from then until the 1980s.

■ ABOVE ***This 1950 Roadless Model E is powered by a TVO engine. It is thought that a total of only 25 machines were ever made.***

ROADLESS FULL-TRACK MODEL E

Year	1950
Engine	Fordson TVO or diesel option
Power	40hp
Transmission	Three speed
Weight	n/k

Another major tractor maker to take advantage of Roadless crawler technology was Case of Racine, Wisconsin. A number of Case tractors, including the Models C, L and LH, were converted and, unlike the other conversions, the Case tractors retained their steering wheels. Roadless built experimental machines for McLaren, Lanz, Bolinder-Munktell, Mavag and Allis-Chalmers, although many never progressed beyond prototypes. Forestry and lifeboat hauling were two tasks that were ideally suited to the Roadless converted machines.

The war years saw Roadless building a variety of machines for the British Air Ministry to use as aircraft tugs. Despite being almost blitzed out of its factory, the company's production was entirely devoted to war requirements, whether it was experimental work or track conversions to imported American tractors from manufacturers such as Case, Massey-Harris and Oliver.

In the immediate post-war years Roadless converted a large number

■ BOTTOM LEFT *The full-track Roadless Fordson used the company's E3 rubber jointed tracks, but even after considerable development, production of the machines was very limited.*

■ BOTTOM RIGHT *Roadless put the Model E into production in 1950 when this TVO variant was manufactured.*

of the popular Fordson E27N tractors, that were sold through advertisements in many Ford publications. The conversion received an accolade when it was awarded a silver medal at the 1948 Royal Show in York. Subsequently several versions of the E27N were built and exported widely.

Through the 1950s the company diversified, turning its attention to full-track and four-wheel-drive tractors. This and its connections with the forestry industry would ultimately lead to the Roadless-converted Land Rover. In the same way as the company's half-tracks were built by converting wheeled tractors, so too were the full-track models. The Fordson Model E was converted and later the Fordson Diesel Major was converted as the Roadless J17. At the same time the company also developed a row crop tricycle conversion for the Fordson E27N Major for sale in the United States and this stayed in production until 1964.

The first Roadless 4×4 Tractor appeared in 1956, overseen by Philip Johnson who was now running the company. He travelled widely to see his company's products in use. While in Italy to visit Landini he met Dr Segre-Amar who had founded the Selene company, based near Turin. Selene converted Fordson tractors to 4×4 configuration using a transfer box and war surplus GMC 6×6 truck front axles. A working relationship between the two men developed that ultimately led to the Roadless company producing the 4×4 Fordsons in Britain. This tractor was a great success and subsequently Roadless converted the Power Major of 1958 and the later Super Major in large numbers, together with a small batch of Fordson Dextas. International Harvester also marketed a Roadless converted 4×4 tractor known as the B-450, that was constructed in International's Doncaster factory in England. It stayed in production until 1970.

■ ROADLESS ROVERS

Around the end of the 1950s the Hounslow company focused its attention on the light 4×4 Land Rover which had now been in production for a decade. The Forestry Commission was experiencing some difficulty with its use of conventional Land Rovers, which were prone to getting stuck on rutted forest tracks and were hampered by fallen trees in cross-country use. The Machinery Research Officer for the Forestry Commission, Colonel Shaw, suggested that tractor-type 25 × 70cm/10 × 28in wheels should be fitted to the Land Rover. A prototype was built and evaluated in the Alice Holt Forest in Hampshire, England. The verdict was that the machine had potential but required further development in order to be viable. A 2.77m/109in wheelbase Land Rover was despatched to the Hounslow premises of Roadless for a redesigned and properly engineered conversion to be effected.

Roadless used a combination of components to make the machine functional: it retained the original gear- and transfer boxes and coupled them to a pair of Studebaker axles with GKN-Kirkstall planetary hub reductions and the same 25 × 70cm/10 × 28in wheels that had been used before. The front axle had a track 35cm/14in wider than the rear in order to facilitate sufficient steering lock to retain the vehicle's manoeuvrability. The turning circle was approximately 12m/40ft. In order to accommodate the large wheels and tyres

■ RIGHT *To convert the Rover Company's Land Rover to the Roadless specification, with 28in diameter wheels, it was necessary to alter the front wings (fenders).*

■ BOTTOM LEFT *The Roadless conversion to the British Land Rover was approved by the Rover Company from 1961 onwards. This steel rear body was an extra option.*

the normal Land Rover front wings (fenders) were removed and replaced with huge flat wings while the rear ones were fabricated in the manner of tractor rear wheel arches. With the change in gear ratios and wheel diameter the complete machine was capable of approximately 48kph/30mph.

This machine was despatched to the Forestry Commission's test site at the Alice Holt Forest. Roadless prepared a second prototype that was sent to the Special Projects Department of the Rover Co Ltd. It was thoroughly tested – reportedly at the Motor Industry Research Association (MIRA) cross-country course at Lindley. Roadless made some further modifications to the Land Rover, including strengthening the chassis and altering the axle clearances, and after a couple of years of tests Rover approved the conversion. This approval meant that the converted Land Rover could be marketed as the Roadless 109 from 1961. In December of the same year the 2286cc/139cu in gasoline engine model retailed at £1558 and the diesel variant at £1658. A special pick-up body was listed as an extra at £172. The Roadless was capable of returning 35kpg/10mpg and had a 68 litre/15 gallon tank. Tests showed that the machine understeered when cornering at 24kph/15mph, the steering was heavy at low speeds and that the machine was capable of wading in up to 75cm/2½ft of water. This latter fact was one of the features that Roadless Traction Ltd mentioned in its advertisements, also pointing out that the wide track ensured stability on side slopes – a useful asset for forestry work.

The Land Rover project was something of a side-show for Roadless, as by the mid-1960s the major portion of its business was the production of four-wheel-drive tractors. Approximately 3000 Roadless four-wheel-drive Fordson tractors had been manufactured when production of the Fordson Super Major ended in 1964.

■ ROADLESS 4X4s

Over the next decade things would change considerably for the company. The first major change was brought about by the death of Lieutenant Colonel Philip Johnson on 8 November 1965 at the age of 88. Johnson had been active in Roadless right into his last years and had only relinquished the managing director's post in 1962. His death meant that a reshuffle took place. Four-wheel-drive tractor production continued, with Roadless conversions being supplied for Ford's new range of 2000, 3000, 4000 and 5000 tractors. The 5000 was the most powerful, a 65hp unit with a choice of eight- or ten-speed transmissions and in Roadless converted form known as the Ploughmaster 65, still using a GMC front axle. This was followed by the Ploughmaster 95.

These tractors, like their predecessors, had smaller front wheels than rear ones but the technology employed in the Land Rover had taught lessons, because in the mid-1960s the company had drawn up plans for four-wheel-drive tractor conversions that had equal-sized wheels all round, like the Roadless 109. The Roadless 115 was one of the first tractors of this design to be produced.

Successful demonstrations of Roadless' products at the Long Sutton Tractor Trials in Lincolnshire meant that through the 1970s the company was not

short of work. Increasingly stringent legislation affected Roadless' tractors, and from the end of the 1970s the company was required to fit its machines with "Quiet Cabs".

In 1979 the company relocated from its original premises in Hounslow to Sawbridgeworth in Hertfordshire, England. Sales of Roadless 4×4 tractors had started to slacken simply because of increasing competition from other 4×4 tractor makers, including cheaper machines from Same, Belarus and Zetor from Eastern Europe, as well as machines from the other international major tractor makers.

Roadless then diversified into the manufacture of log-handling machinery and forestry tractors, but with hindsight it appears that Roadless had had its day. A combination of circumstances and the recession of the early 1980s forced the companies that made up Roadless into voluntary liquidation.

ROADLESS 109 LAND ROVER	
Year	1961
Engine	In-line four cylinder diesel
Power	67bhp (50kW) at 4000rpm
Transmission	Eight forward, two reverse
Weight	3052kg/6728lbs

■ TOP AND LEFT ***The Roadless Traction conversion was made to the 109in wheelbase Land Rover models. This is a diesel-powered Series II version, and the conversion was aimed at forestry work. The conversion involved swapping both the front and rear axles for Studebaker ones that increased ground clearance and track.***

OTHER MAKES

(Same, Somua, Steyr)

■ ABOVE *This Diamond 270 is the highest powered tractor from Same, using a Deutz turbocharged engine.*

■ SAME

Same is an Italian company that was founded in 1942 and currently owns the Lamborghini and Hurlimann brands, and became known as SAME Deutz-Fahr after purchasing the German tractor brand in 1995. One of the company's earliest tractors was the 4R20M of 1950 which was powered by a 2hp, twin-cylinder, gasoline and kerosene engine. Same production included the Condor 55 and Models 90 and 100 of the mid-1980s. The Condor 55 was a conventional tractor powered by a 2827cc/172.4cu in 1003P, direct-injection, air-cooled diesel with three cylinders that produced 55hp. The 90 and 100 Models use numerical designation approximates to the number of horsepower that they produce.

■ LEFT *Same was founded by Francesco Cassani in 1942. This is a Same Antares 100 from 1990.*

■ BELOW *The Same Silver 90 of 1995 is a four-wheel-drive tractor from a range of similar tractors with different outputs.*

■ BELOW *The Same Silver 90 has a turbo diesel engine that produces in the region of 90hp.*

■ RIGHT *Somua was one of the numerous French manufacturers that produced agricultural tractors in the inter-war decades. This one is working at Courtelin, France.*

■ **SOMUA**

Somua was a French manufacturer of agricultural machinery in the inter-war years and among its products was a machine with a rear, power-driven rotary cultivator. Other French makes of similar machines included Amiot and Dubois. The former was a machine with an integral plough while the latter was a reversible motor plough.

■ LEFT *An earlier Somua tractor in use on the Normandy coast of France for transporting fishing boats from the water across the long, sloping beach.*

■ **STEYR**

The Austrian manufacturer Steyr entered the tractor market in 1928 when it announced an 80hp machine of which only a few were made. After World War II Steyr returned to tractor manufacture with the Model 180, a two-cylinder diesel, in 1948 and the smaller Model 80 in 1949. These were followed during the 1950s by the models 185 and 280, three- and four-cylinder diesel tractors respectively. The company was based in St Valentin, Austria and through the 1980s and 90s offered a range of row crop and utility tractors ranging from 42 to 145hp.

In 1996 the Case Corporation acquired 75 per cent of the shares in Steyr Landmaschinentechnik GmbH (SLT) from Steyr-Daimler-Puch AG.

■ LEFT *Austrian Steyr resumed tractor manufacture after World War II, and has manufactured tractors ever since. This is a modern, four-wheel-drive example of the company's products.*

STEIGER

The first Steiger tractor was built in North Dakota in the late 1950s. Named after the brothers who designed it, this tractor is reputed to have gone on to achieve more than 10,000 hours of field time and is now on display in the museum at Bonanzaville in West Fargo, North Dakota. The first Steiger manufacturing plant was a dairy barn on the Steiger brothers' farm near Thief River Falls in Minnesota. By the late 1960s, the company had been incorporated and moved into larger facilities in Fargo. Several moves and several years later, Steiger tractor manufacturing arrived at its current Fargo location. The distinctive lime-green Steiger tractors were constructed around engines that produced up to 525hp. The tractors were named after animals including Puma, Bearcat, Cougar, Panther, Lion and Tiger, and each name denoted a specific horsepower class.

In 1986, Steiger was acquired by Case IH. To consolidate the merger, both companies' four-wheel-drive tractor lines were unified in both colour and name. The name Steiger was associated with high-power tractors, and in a survey of farmers in four-wheel-drive tractor markets, this name was cited as the most popular and well-known four-wheel-drive tractor brand. As a result, the name was later revived for the Case IH 9300 Series tractors which were then claimed to be the industry's leading line of four-wheel-drive machines. For a period, a Hungarian tractor-making company produced RABA-Steiger tractors under licence from the Steiger company.

The 1996 range, the 9300 Series of massive four-wheel-drive tractors from Case IH, consisted of ten Steiger

■ LEFT *Steiger tractors were finished in a distinctive shade of lime green, and named after animals. This Cougar II is one such tractor.*

■ ABOVE *Steiger built large tractors for other manufacturers including this, the Allis Chalmers 440 of 1973, which was followed by the 4W-305 of 1986.*

■ ABOVE *This 1992 Steiger Case IH 9280 is fitted with triple tyres and has been specifically designed for the needs of the large acreage farmer.*

■ LEFT *Case IH acquired Steiger in 1986. Following the merger, both companies' tractors bore the red and grey of Case IH. This 9280 model dates from 1992.*

STEIGER 9310 4WD TRACTOR

Year	1996
Engine	Case 6TA, six cylinder
Power	207 PTO hp, 240 bhp
Transmission	12 forward, three reverse
Weight	9537kg/21,026lbs

machines. The models ranged from 240 to 425hp, with two row crop special models and the Quadtrac tractor which featured four independent crawler tracks. The 9300 Series tractors were designed and manufactured in Fargo, North Dakota.

Four-wheel-drive tractors have the perceived advantage of superior flotation compared to two-wheel-drive tractors. Weight and pull are evenly distributed with less slippage, less rolling resistance and more drawbar pull. The 9300 Steiger tractors offered fuel efficiency through the use of the Case 8.3 L, Cummins N14 and Cummins M11 engines. These were engineered to provide the optimum balance of torque rise, power curve and fuel economy. The 9300 Series models ranged from the 240hp 9330 to the 425hp 9390.

In 2007 the STX500 Quadtrac set a world ploughing record. The Steiger name continues today with the Case IH Steiger range introduced in 2011. Models range from 350hp to 600hp, with the 450, 500, 550 and 600 also available in Quadtrac versions. The engines are fitted with Case's Selective Catalytic Reduction system to meet Tier 4 emission standards.

■ ABOVE *The diesel-powered Steiger ST-310 Panther has a Cummins engine, as does the larger Tiger ST-470.*

■ BELOW *The Steiger Panther ST-310 has a 855cu in displacement, six-cylinder, diesel engine, which produces 310bhp.*

OTHER MAKES

(Tung Fung Hung, Twin City, Universal, Ursus, Valmet, Versatile, Volvo, Waterloo Boy)

■ **TUNG FUNG HUNG**

Tractor production has always had a place in Chinese agriculture despite the availability of a huge pool of labour. Tung Fung Hung is one of several Chinese manufacturers. During the 1950s the company built a tractor known as the Iron Buffalo and a crawler in state factories. It also built a version of the MTZ tractor from the Minsk Tractor Works. A number of Chinese factories produce tractors for export, and these machines are marketed under a variety of other names, such as American Harvester.

■ ABOVE *Both conventional tractors and crawlers have been widely built in China.*

■ TOP *In China agriculture is not as reliant on technology as in other parts of the world, although compact tractors such as this machine in Nanking are widely used.*

■ ABOVE *Small farm machines, such as this in the Hunan Province of China, rely on small engines with tractor-type tyres.*

■ ABOVE *A machine in the Yixing Province of China used for a plethora of tasks.*

■ RIGHT *Over the years the Universal name has been used by a variety of tractor makers both as a brand and a model designation. This is a UTB Universal 530.*

■ **TWIN CITY**

Twin City was the brand name used by the Minneapolis Steel and Machinery Company which produced tractors for a time. In 1910 it introduced the Twin City 40. Its steam engine influences were obvious: it had an exposed engine in place of the boiler, a cylindrical radiator and a long roof canopy. The Twin City 40 was powered by an in-line four-cylinder engine and its larger cousin the 60–90 by an in-line six-cylinder of massive displacement. The 90 suffix indicated 90hp at 500rpm. The machine also had 2.1m/7ft diameter rear wheels and a single speed transmission which made it capable of 3kph/2mph. In 1929 Minneapolis Steel and Machinery became part of Minneapolis-Moline.

■ **UNIVERSAL**

In 1915 the Moline Plow Company purchased the Universal Tractor Company of Columbus, Ohio. The product line was moved to Moline, Illinois and a new building was built for the production of the Moline Universal Tractor. The Moline Universal Tractor was a two-wheel unit design for use with the farmer's horse-drawn implements as well as newly developed Moline tractor-drawn implements. It was commonly referred to as the first row crop tractor, and was equipped with electric lights and a starter, which was very advanced for its time.

■ ABOVE *The UTB Universal 600 is a diesel-engined tractor made in Brasov, Romania, where production started in 1946. Like other Eastern Bloc tractor makers UTB considered exports important.*

■ LEFT *The UTB logo indicates that the 600 model, seen here at a European vintage machinery rally, was made by Universal Tractors of Brasov.*

OTHER MAKES

■ ABOVE *Ursus tractor manufacture started in Poland, with a design based on that of the Lanz Bulldog, and then a standardized Eastern Bloc tractor. This much later 106-14 is working in Ireland.*

■ LEFT *An Ursus tractor, photographed in the Kielce province of Poland. Exports of Ursus tractors were made to the United States as well as much of Europe.*

■ OPPOSITE TOP *The Valmet 8450 is a modern, four-wheel-drive tractor, powered by a 140hp turbocharged diesel engine.*

■ OPPOSITE *Canadian company Versatile offered massive articulated tractors from 1966 onwards. The 895 is a 310hp 14,010cc/855cu in displacement machine that articulates behind the cab.*

■ **UNIVERSAL**

Another company to use the Universal brand name was a Romanian company based in Brasov. They began production in 1946 and exported widely. A mid-1980s product was the Model 1010 which is powered by a 100hp 5393cc/329cu in six-cylinder diesel engine. In the United States the Romanian Universal tractors are marketed under the Long brand name.

■ **URSUS**

Ursus was a state-owned Polish tractor maker whose tractors were very similar to those from other State-owned companies elsewhere in the Eastern Bloc including 1950s models from the East German (DDR) ZT concern and Czechoslovakian Zetor. Tractors were also produced in Bulgaria under the Bolgar name.

■ **VALMET**

Valmet is a Finnish tractor maker which was amalgamated with Volvo BM from Sweden in 1972. The company has specialized in forestry tractors such as the Jehu 1122. This machine is a wheeled tractor although provision has been made to install tracks over the tyres to improve traction in deep snow. Volvo BM Valmet also made the 2105, a 163hp six-cylinder, turbo diesel tractor as part of a range.

■ **VERSATILE**

In 1947 the Hydraulic Engineering Company was formed in Toronto, Canada and began production of small-size agricultural implements under the Versatile name. In 1954 the Hydraulic Engineering Company launched its first large machine,

OTHER MAKES

an innovative self-propelled swather. The Hydraulic Engineering Company was incorporated in 1963 as a public company, adopting the name Versatile Manufacturing Ltd. Then in 1966 Versatile, operating out of Winnipeg, Canada, became involved in the manufacture of huge four-wheel-drive tractors that produced power in excess of 200hp. Versatile Manufacturing Ltd changed ownership in 1976 and changed names in 1977, becoming the Versatile Farm Equipment Company, a division of Versatile Corporation. In 1991 it became part of Ford New Holland Americas before being sold to current owners Buhler Industries Inc, who reintroduced the red colour scheme in 2000.

■ LEFT *Versatile is a Canadian tractor maker who from the early 1970s specialized in the production of large four-wheel-drive tractors such as the 895.*

■ BELOW *In 1991 Versatile became part of Ford New Holland which led to machines such as the articulated four-wheel-drive 946 model being produced in Ford's blue colours.*

■ **VOLVO**

The Sweden-based Volvo group is a massive motor manufacturer and a long-established tractor maker. During the 1920s it produced tractors alongside Munktells who it later acquired.

Volvo tractors have a history of diesel engine fitment: during the 1950s the T30 model used a Perkins L4 engine, for example. Another Scandinavian merger occurred in 1972 when Volvo began to cooperate with Finnish Valmet in the manufacture of tractors, offering the Nordic range specifically designed for Scandinavian countries. During the 1980s Volvo manufactured the 805 model in two forms: the 805 was a two-wheel-drive tractor, while the 805-4 was a four-wheel-drive variant. Both were powered by a 95hp four-cylinder turbocharged diesel engine. A larger tractor from the same era was the 2105 model. Volvo was among the first to design and fit safety cabs to its tractors. Its machines have been exported widely around Europe and to the United States.

■ **WATERLOO BOY**

John Froelich built a machine powered by a Van Duzen single-cylinder engine in Iowa that many consider as the first practical tractor. The engine of the machine was mounted on the Robinson chassis from a steam engine and Froelich devised a transmission system. He was experienced in the agricultural business and had worked as a threshing contractor, so was aware of the requirements of mechanized harvesting.

Froelich bought a large Case thresher and transported it together with a wagon for the crew to live in, by rail to Langford, South Dakota. It is reported that hundreds turned out to see the machines at work, as over a seven-week period his crew threshed wheat full time. His machinery suffered no breakdowns and as a result many were convinced of the benefits of mechanization. As a result Froelich gained backing from a group of Iowa businessmen and they formed the Waterloo Gasoline Traction Engine Company. In 1893 the company built four more tractors, of which only two were fully workable, and others in 1896 and 1897. The company dropped the word "Traction" from its name in 1895 and concentrated on the manufacture of stationary engines. John Froelich's interest was primarily in tractors so he left the company at this time.

■ ABOVE ***A Volvo BM Valmet 405 tractor. Its maker's name carries the heritage of Volvo, Bolinder, Munktell and Valmet.***

The company took a renewed interest in tractors in 1911 and by 1914 had produced the forerunner of what became the Model R. It was powered by a horizontal two-cylinder engine and soon superseded by the Model N. This went on sale in 1916 and over its eight-year production run, around 20,000 were made. The Waterloo Boy Model N was sold in Britain as the Overtime by the Overtime Farm Tractor Company, based in London. The Model N had a massive chassis frame on which was mounted the fuel tank, radiator, twin-cylinder engine and driver's seat. The engine, which was started with petrol and then run on paraffin, produced 25hp. The use of roller bearings throughout the machine was considered innovative at the time of its manufacture.

This early tractor had differing but equally important influences on two other tractor companies. The Belfast agent for Overtime Tractors was Harry Ferguson: this was his first experience with tractors and started him thinking of better ways of attaching implements. It was also the Waterloo Boy that brought John Deere into the tractor business. In 1918 Deere and Company bought the Waterloo Gasoline Engine Company for $1 million and initially kept the Model N in production as a John Deere tractor.

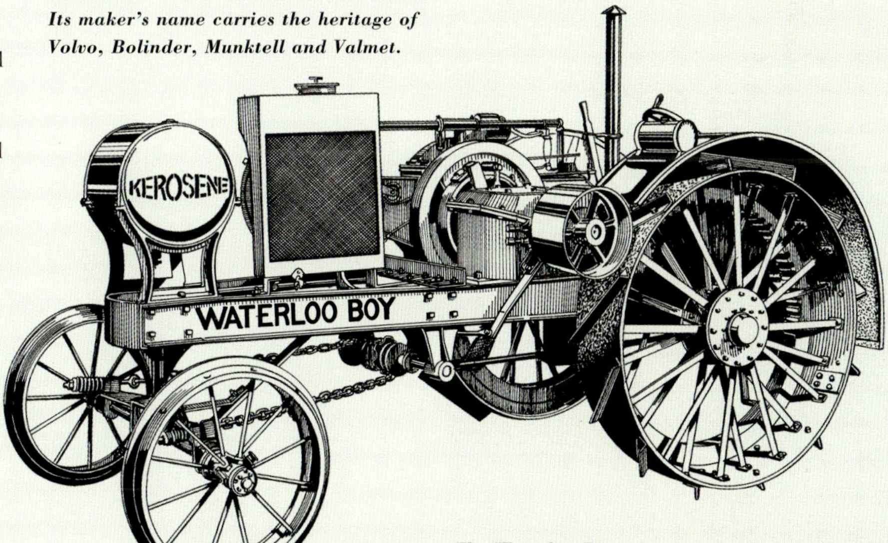

■ ABOVE ***The Waterloo Boy Model N kerosene tractor, the machine that brought John Deere into tractor manufacture.***

WHITE FARM EQUIPMENT

The White Motor Corporation of Cleveland, Ohio became established in the tractor manufacturing industry during the early 1960s, when the corporation bought up a number of relatively small tractor-producing companies. These companies were, in the main, established concerns with a long history of involvement in the tractor industry, often going back to its earliest days. In 1960 White bought Oliver but continued to produce the successful and popular Oliver 55 Models throughout the decade. Oliver had been in business since 1929 when it, too, had come about as a result of combining several small companies.

White purchased the Cockshutt Farm Equipment Company in 1962. This company's history stretched back to 1839. In more recent times Cockshutt manufactured tractors such as the Models 20 and 40. The 20 was introduced in 1952 and used a Continental L-head 2294cc/140cu in, four-cylinder engine and a four-speed transmission. The Model 40 was a six-cylinder, six-speed tractor. Following these acquisitions, White acquired

■ LEFT *Cockshutt was a long-established tractor maker and was acquired by the White Motor Corporation in 1962, after White had acquired Oliver and before it acquired Minneapolis-Moline.*

Minneapolis-Moline a year later. The brand names of all three companies were retained by White until as late as 1969, when the entire company was restructured as White Farm Equipment. During the 1970s White produced a tractor named the Plainsman. This was an eight-wheeler powered by an 8260cc/504cu in displacement engine that produced 169hp. Subsequently, White was itself acquired. A company based in Dallas, Texas, the TIC Investment Corporation, bought White Farm Equipment in 1981 and continued its business under the acronym WFE.

The Allied Products Corporation of Chicago bought parts of WFE including the Charles City, Iowa tractor plant and stock. In 1987 Allied combined White with the New Idea Farm Equipment Company, forming a new division known as White-New Idea. In 1993 the AGCO Corporation of Waycross, Georgia purchased the White-New Idea range of implements, and retained the White name for its brand of tractors until 2001. Models ranged from 45 to 215hp, and included proprietary systems, such as Synchro-Reverser, Powershift and Quadrashift transmissions. They were

■ ABOVE *The White 2-60 Field Boss was marketed as a White tractor during the latter part of the 1970s.*

■ LEFT *The 4-150 Field Boss was one of the large tractors made by White Farm Equipment.*

■ LEFT *This Model 60 White tractor was made in 1989 when the company was under the control of the Allied Products Corporation of Chicago.*

powered by Cummins direct-injected diesels. The range included the following models: 6045 and 6065 Mid-Size, 6090 Hi-Clearance, six Fieldmaster and three Powershift models.

■ **WHITE 6045**

The 45 PTO hp 6045 Mid-Size has a 50-degree turning angle, and there is a choice of two-wheel-drive or a model with a driven front axle. The Synchro-Reverser transmission has twelve gears in forward and reverse. The 6065 Mid-Size develops 63hp at the PTO and has a 12 speed Synchro-Reverser transmission and a four-cylinder engine. Both two- and four-wheel-drive models are available. The 6090 Hi-Clearance tractor is an 80 PTO hp tractor with generous ground clearance. It gives 69cm/27.2in of crop clearance and 59cm/23.2in of ground clearance under the front and rear axles, as well as 55cm/21.7in of ground clearance under the drawbar. The 6090 in this form has a synchromesh transmission with 20 forward and 20 reverse gears as standard. The 6175 and 6195 Powershift Series ranges from 124–200 PTO hp and offers an electronically controlled full power-shift transmission. It has 18 forward and nine reverse gears. The White 6215 Powershift has 215 PTO hp and a Powershift transmission with 18 forward and nine reverse gears.

Although White tractors are no longer produced by AGCO, the name lives on in the company's range of planters.

WHITE 8410 4WD TRACTOR	
Year	1998
Engine	Cummins B5.9 six cylinder
Power	145 PTO hp
Transmission	32 forward, 32 reverse
Weight	7303kg/16,110lbs

■ BELOW *The White A4T Plainsman of 1971 was a large articulated tractor with a 8260cc/504cu in displacement engine.*

OTHER MAKES

■ **WIKOV**

In the mid-1920s, in a Czechoslovakia recently independent from the Austro-Hungarian Empire, the two-cylinder Wikov 22 was made by Wichterie and Kovarik of Prostejov. Other noted Czechoslovakian motor manufacturers who offered tractors were Praga and Skoda, whose constituent companies had previously offered motor ploughs.

Praga offered the AT25, KT32 and U50 models while Skoda offered a four-cylinder powered, three-speed tractor designated the 30HT. It could be run on either kerosene or a mixture of alcohol and gasoline which was known as "Dynalkol".

ZETOR

The Zetor tractor company was established in 1946 in Brno, Czech Republic, and became one of the largest European tractor manufacturers. More than half a million Zetor tractors have been produced and have been sold in over 100 countries around the world. Zetor tractors are marketed and currently sold worldwide through two major distribution channels. The first of these is the companies of the Motokov Group, with offices around the world, while the second is the John Deere dealer network. This was made possible through long-term marketing agreements reached between the Motokov Group, John Deere and Zetor. Zetor tractors have been sold in the United States since 1982 and in 1984 American Jawa Ltd took over the distribution. Zetor tractors are distributed in America through two major service and distribution centres, one in Harrisburg, Pennsylvania and the other in La Porte, Texas. In 1993, under a distribution agreement reached with John Deere, Zetor was able to distribute a lower-priced line of 40–85hp tractors in what are considered to be emerging markets, starting with selected areas of Latin America and Asia.

Zetor designs and manufactures most of its own tractor components, including the engines that are designed to be fuel-efficient. Throughout its history Zetor has endeavoured to pioneer various innovations. It had one of the first hitch hydraulic systems, known as Zetormatic, which it introduced in 1960. Later, Zetor was the among the first tractor

■ ABOVE *A Zetor tractor exported to England and fitted with the Zetormatic hitch system, a hydraulic system for hitching implements such as this hay rake.*

■ LEFT *Zetor has always seen exports as an important part of its business. This 1970s model is in France but the company has exported to more than 100 countries worldwide.*

■ ABOVE *The Zetor 25 was a 25hp tractor with a two-cylinder diesel engine, introduced in 1945, and one of the earliest Zetor tractors to be exported from the Czech Republic.*

■ BOTTOM *The latest Zetor tractors such at these 6340 and 7340 models are becoming more popular with farmers across the world. The Proxima and Forterra models now range from 68 to 120hp with larger models becoming available soon.*

■ BELOW *For a time Zetor tractors, Polish Ursus tractors and ZT tractors from East Germany were almost identical, as the result of Soviet control.*

■ BELOW *This Zetor 3011 diesel tractor was manufactured in Zetor's Brno, Czechoslovakia, plant and exported to Britain, although others went to Ireland and as far as New Zealand in the 1950s.*

companies to manufacture fully integrated safety cabs with insulated, rubber-mounted suspension. The Zetor 8045 Crystal Model of 1986 had an engine of 4562cc/278cu in displacement and used diesel fuel. It produced power in the region of 85hp. It is a 4×4 tractor with 8 forward gears and two reverse. In 1997 the Zetor product line included ten different tractors. These ranged from the 46hp Models 3320 and 3340 to the 90hp Models 9640 and 10540. While Zetor is a Czech company, versions of its tractors are assembled in numerous countries around the world including Argentina, Myanmar, India, Iraq, Uruguay and Zaire.

ZETOR 8045 CRYSTAL

Year	1986
Engine	4562cc/278cu in in-line four cylinder diesel
Power	85hp
Transmission	Eight forward, two reverse gears
Weight	n/k

Farming Implements

The versatility of tractors is enhanced through the use of specialist implements designed for specific farming tasks, both for preparing the land and harvesting the crop. The implements are generally one of two types: those that are attached to the tractor and those that are towed behind it.

In some farming areas the soil can be too wet for the propagation of crops so machines that drain fields are used as well as machines capable of working in wet and heavy soils without becoming bogged down. Draining the fields can sometimes be achieved through the use of a mole plough which cuts narrow drainage channels into the surface of a field, allowing a network of such channels to carry away excess water. More recently machines have been developed that lay lengths of perforated plastic pipe that drains fields.

Maintenance of hedges is quickly achieved through the use of hedge trimmers while the quality of fields is upgraded through the application of

■ LEFT *Tractors such as this Farmall Row Crop model are designed for use in the cultivation of crops, and pass through fields with minimum damage to a growing crop.*

■ ABOVE *Four-wheel-drive tractors such as this Massey Ferguson offer sufficient traction to enable them to pull implements such as rippers and sub-soilers as here.*

■ LEFT *Modern tractors are often equipped with implements to the front and rear to maximize productivity by combining several sowing tasks into a single-pass operation.*

■ RIGHT *A four-wheel-drive John Deere tractor with a seed drill being towed by the tractor and pwered by its PTO. The drill delivers metered amounts of seed and fertilizer.*

■ BELOW RIGHT *Ploughing remains one of the timeless farming tasks for which tractors are essential.*

various chemical fertilizers in both powder and liquid form, and implements exist for the distribution of these fertilizers as well as the more traditional use of manure.

While ploughs are now more massive and complex than they have ever been, the concept of ploughing remains unchanged. The purpose of ploughing is to break up the top layer of soil in order to allow the roots of growing plants to penetrate the soil. Ploughs are designed to slice into the top layer and, through the curve of the mouldboard, invert it. John Deere's contribution to ploughing with the development of the self-scouring steel plough suitable for heavy

■ ABOVE *The hydraulic front loader is a versatile farming implement, especially when it can be fitted with a variety of tools as on this John Deere.*

■ RIGHT *A John Deere ploughing. The plough is attached to the tractor's three-point hitch and is adjustable to take into account soil conditions.*

■ ABOVE *John Deere is a manufacturer of a full line of tractors and implements incluidng tandem disc harrows such as this 235 model.*

■ BELOW *John Deere's air seeding system is a complex, efficient system of planting that makes sowing a one-pass operation, opening, seeding and closing as it goes.*

prairie soils cannot be overestimated. Ploughs are manufactured around the world by specialists such as Ransomes in the UK, Kverneland in Norway, both Niemeyer and Krone in Germany as well as the major full-line manufacturers such as John Deere, Massey-Ferguson and constituent parts of the AGCO Corporation. Cultivators are a vital part of preparing the land after ploughing and these are made by a similar range of companies. Rotary power harrows, soil packers, sub-tillers, tine cultivators and rollers are all specialized implements for dealing with a variety of field conditions.

Seeding is just as mechanized a process as ploughing and massive seed drills made by the likes of John Deere illustrate how far mechanization has come since Jethro Tull devised his seed drill. Despite this the machines still carry out the same task, namely that of depositing the seeds below the surface of the soil where they will germinate. Once the seeds are planted by means

■ RIGHT *A John Deere planter behind a John Deere tractor. To enable such large implements to be transported to fields they are designed to fold up behind the tractor.*

of a broadcaster or the increasingly popular seed drill, the farmer is likely to spray fertilizer and pesticides. The implements (and tractors) for this must pass through and over the crop with minimal damage, which has led to numerous high-clearance machines being devised and, of course, the row crop tractor. Drills and planters are made by the full-line manufacturers and specialists such as Smallford, Reekie and Hestair in the UK, and the likes of Vaderstad, Kuhn and Westmac in

■ LEFT *A John Deere rotary disk mower, designed for cutting grass and hay.*

■ BELOW *Planting is increasingly scientific, with tools controlling the depth at which the seed is planted and adding precise amounts of fertilizer.*

■ LEFT *The hay rake such as this, seen in England behind a Fergy TE2,0 was used to turn the mown grass to allow it to dry before being baled.*

■ BELOW *This vintage haymaking equipment indicates how the harvest is more precisely managed now.*

■ BOTTOM *A twin axle trailer, behind an International Harvester tractor, being used to carry away grain.*

Europe. Sprayers are produced by a considerable number of companies including Hardi, Vicon, ETS Matrot and Moteska.

Once the growing cycle is completed another array of specialist harvesting machinery is used. Apart from combine harvesters for grain and balers for hay there are specific harvesters for crops that include peas, beans, beet, cotton, sugar cane, root vegetables and tobacco. Geography and climate mean that some of these machines are specific to certain parts of the world. Massey-Ferguson, Claas, Deutz-Fahr, New Holland and John Deere are among the noted manufacturers of combines worldwide. In addition to self-propelled harvesting

machines there are a considerable variety designed to be towed behind tractors. One of the largest groups of these are mowers and rotary rakes, both of which are used for haymaking. In recent years balers have been developed considerably and towed balers are now capable of producing much larger hay bales than previously. Some of the new generation of balers produce large circular bales which pose their own problems of handling and storage, and specific loaders have been devised for this. Forage harvesters are also available in both self-propelled and towed implement forms for the harvesting of grass and for silage making.

The scientific approach to farming has led to the development of specialized loading and handling machinery including the rough-terrain fork lift and the loader. The hydraulic front loader was one of the first machines of this type, although the capabilities of even these have been increased in recent years. John Deere currently manufactures a range of tools for hydraulic loaders that include various sizes of bucket, a bale hugger, a pallet fork, a round bale fork and a bale and silage grapple.

■ ABOVE LEFT *The shift to round bales led to the development of a spike tool for handling the bales, to be fitted to hydraulic loaders.*

■ ABOVE RIGHT *This photograph from the late 1960s shows square bales being taken by trailer from the fields where they have been harvested to storage in a barn.*

■ RIGHT *A small Fendt Dieselross tractor equipped with a sidebar mower.*

■ RIGHT *Self-propelled aquatic harvesters are particularly specialized implements, designed for marine plants and weed beds.*

INDEX

MASSEY FERGUSON
HESSTON